THE
POST-HUMAN
CONDITION

Robert Pepperell

intellect™

OXFORD, ENGLAND

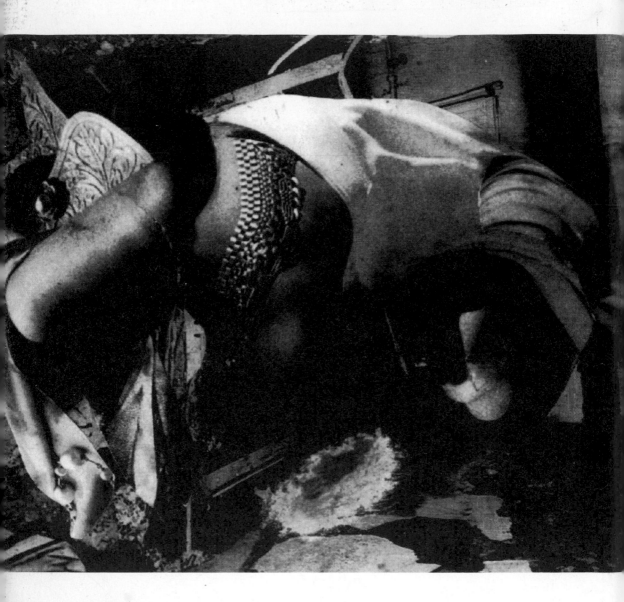

Graspings: wholes and not wholes, convergent divergent, consonant dissonant,

The fairest order in the world is a heap of random sweepings

Heraclitus, *Fragments*

THE POST-HUMAN CONDITION

Robert Pepperell

...om all things one and from one thing all.

First published in Great Britain (1995) in paperback by
Intellect™, Suite 2, 108/110 London Road, Oxford OX3 9AW.

Consulting editor: Masoud Yazdani
Copy editor: Wendi Momen
Cover image: Robert Pepperell
Layout design: Kevin Foakes (Open Mind)
Additional images: Rob Chapman

Thanks to:

Mum & Dad & family, Miles Visman, Janni Perton, Matt Black, Mike
Phillips, Masoud Yazdani, Rob Chapman, the Ninja crew, Kim and
Quinta Carmen, people who put good stuff on the Net and, most of all,
to Ruth. This book is dedicated to her.

British Library Cataloguing in Publication Data

Pepperell, R.C.
    Post-Human Condition
    I. Title
    006.3

    ISBN 1-871516-45-5

Printed and bound in Great Britain by Antony Rowe Ltd, Chippenham, Wiltshire

Contents

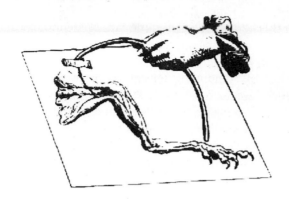

Foreword

I have employed the term Post-Human to mean a number of things at once. Firstly, it is used to mark the end of that period of social development known as Humanism; in this sense it means 'after Humanism'. Secondly, it is used to refer to the fact that our own view of what constitutes a human being is now undergoing a profound transformation. We no longer think about what it is to be a human in the same way that we used to. Thirdly, the term refers to the general convergence of organisms and technology to the point where they become indistinguishable. Taken collectively, these could be said to represent a new era in human development – the Post-Human era. The term is starting to gain wider currency and may be used in a number of different senses. However, the brief descriptions I have given above serve to outline its general meaning.

The 'Post-Human Condition' cannot be so easily defined. In simple terms we could say it is the condition of existence in which we find ourselves once the Post-Human era arrives. But that does not tell us very much and I believe a fuller sense can only emerge by working through the ideas presented in this book. In this respect I can't claim to have given a complete picture of the Post-Human condition; there are many topics and ideas that have been left out. In fact, there is very little that is not relevant to what I am trying to describe.

But, if I had to summarise my own feelings about the Post-Human condition, I would say we are approaching the *electrification of existence* – there is a tangible sense of a storm in the air.

Introduction

The background to this book is the incredible rate of technological change that we are now experiencing and which is affecting virtually every aspect of our lives. In medicine, at work, in leisure, in politics we are noticing more and more the encroaching influence of computers, telecommunications and miniaturisation. Our phone systems, which remained relatively static for 60 years, are now the means by which we can send and receive words, pictures and sound internationally. Television, which also grew at a fairly stable rate between the 1950s and the 1980s, has exploded in complexity within a few years such that we now have access to hundreds of services, with stereo sound and interactivity. The number of platforms on which we can listen to pre-recorded music has risen from a couple in the 1960s to something nearer 10, at the last count. Few people in the 1970s might have thought that they would ever own their own computer. Computers were huge boxes that took up whole floors and were attended to by men in white coats with clipboards. Now computers are almost as common in homes as fridges and, since the arrival of computer games, word-processors and spread sheets, people see them as sources of pleasure and convenience. We can get money out of walls, pay for goods with plastic cards, carry phones in our pockets, eat genetically modified tomatoes, carry computers in our hands. . .

These are the technologies of which most people are aware in their daily lives. Yet there is another strata of technological development about which most people are unaware. These more specialist developments may not have fed through into general consciousness, but their long term impact on human society will be no less dramatic than the changes we are currently experiencing. These are technologies such as neural networks, nanotechnology, genetic algorithms and artificial life which I shall shortly describe.

The intention of this book is not to analyse these technologies in detail since there are many other references which do this much more comprehensively than I could; it is not about the technologies in themselves, but about the impact that collectively they will have on our sense of human existence. I have labelled the effect of this collective impact the Post-Human condition, and I hope it will become clear why.

Post-Human technologies

We have imagined for a long time that our ability to develop and implement technology was one of the defining characteristics of humanity, something which assured us of our superiority over other animals and gave us our unique status in the world. Ironically, this sense of superiority and uniqueness is being challenged by the very technologies we are now seeking to create. Technologies are emerging which show that the balance of power between humans and machines is altering. It is a common fact of life that many workers are being replaced by machines since they can do many jobs more efficiently than humans can. Whilst there are no machines that can yet be said to be capable of taking over the world, the distinction between humans and machines is becoming less clear. The following is a summary of some contemporary developments that indicate this to be the case.

Virtual reality. Abbreviated as VR, virtual reality involves the use of high powered computers to build three dimensional environments in which a user can be immersed in real-time interaction with a mathematically generated world using stereoscopic headsets and spatially sensitive input devices. This means, in effect, that as one moves one's head, so the 3D representation moves, thus heightening the sense of an extended reality in which one is participating. Many users report that, after a few minutes immersion in high-resolution flight simulators, the 'reality' is just as convincing as if they were in a real cockpit. As graphics processors become increasingly powerful in the next few years, we can expect to see a dramatic increase in the levels of hyper-realism to be found in such systems. As a result, the separation between reality and virtual reality will seem to diminish in certain scenarios. VR development was originally sponsored by the military and used as a way of training pilots to cope with various combat situations. It has since been extended, both in military and civilian spheres, to include entertainment, general training and data visualisation. VR has also attracted pornographers, who offer simulated sex with computer generated partners and has, predictably, been labelled 'Virtual Sex'. In fact, the word 'virtual' has been corrupted to mean almost anything that happens on computers. The notion of virtuality has entered the popular imagination as a metaphor for the space inside computers. This implies that computer space is acknowledged as a place in itself, something that has its own dimensions and which accords to its own laws – its reality has been acknowledged! Steps are already being taken to introduce VR to the home market via games consoles and cable links. It is anticipated by many advocates of VR that the boundary between human reality and machine reality will soon become indistinct. This obviously has huge implications for those humans who are immersed in such worlds. Developments in VR that have been predicted include 'teledildonic' body suits for transmitting sensations to the body surface; 'eye-slave' control replacing head movement; direct neuronal induction that allows information to be 'written' directly onto the nervous system thus avoiding goggles and suits; and 'simulated worlds' which are self-contained realities such as cities or countries that exist only in a computer. With VR the implications for a transformed state of human existence are clear. For a compelling introduction to the world of VR see *Virtual Worlds* by Benjamin Woolley.

Global communications. The use of optical fibres, satellite and microwave distribution systems is transforming the rates at which data can be transmitted. In the digital world virtually any information can be encoded into a stream of 'bits' which can then be transmitted and stored in very high volume. In general, digital communications are preferred to analogue ones because they are less prone to noise and interference. Therefore, the potential amount of data that one can pass through any conduit with integrity is much greater. The immediate impact of global communications has been to transform the way we send information at home and at work. We now have long distance phone calls bounced off satellites, colour faxes, videophones, e-mail, cellular phones, domestic optical cabling with two–way information flow, as well as the Internet. The Internet changed from a virtually unheard of academic networking system to a global marketing phenomena within three years. It consists of a huge array of large computers, or servers, linked via 'big-pipe' lines and satellites that pump billions of bits of data across the world each day. The Net, as it is now known, was originally developed for military communications and academic research and was limited to carrying text messages and small files. It provided the original inspiration for the idea of 'cyberspace', that dimension of reality which consists in the pure flow of data. Like the word 'virtual', the prefix 'cyber' has been extended to mean anything vaguely connected with computers. With the advent of much faster servers and links, the Net now carries sound, images and movies that are knitted together in a global information complex known as the World Wide Web. The 'point-and-click' nature of the Web, giving simple access to inconceivable volumes of data, allows 'web-sites' to become natural extensions to the multimedia desktop, giving the impression that the world is a big hard disc that everyone shares. When virtual realities are combined with digital communications, we can easily imagine virtual meetings of thousands of people who are physically remote. Being bodily disabled will be less of a disadvantage as physical abilities will diminish in importance. In cyberspace, the concept of remote being is known as 'telepresence'. It is the notion that you can exist, work, interact at a distance using virtual reality and digital communications. In a telepresent environment it will be difficult to determine where a person actually 'is'. The classic vision of cyberspace is that described by William Gibson in *Neuromancer*.

'Surf o

control

can rid

Die. You can't

a wave, but you

it.'

[t.Post Human Cond]./ch+00./p.v

The Post Human Manifesto 1.11

Robotics and prosthetics. Because of the potential for expanding productivity and profits by automating skilled labour, intensive research continues into robot development. All modern car plants are highly automated, as are many other production processes. This is being accelerated by advances in computer control through parallel processing and learning systems that produce semi-intelligent robots, or 'knowbots'. The aim of much robotic research is to achieve autonomy for the machine, to free it from static sources of power and human support. Such mobile robots, or 'mobots', are intended for applications in space exploration, warfare and nuclear installations but may eventually find their way into the home as helpers or guards. Most robots in use today are blindly pre-programmed to do repetitive tasks, but research into machine vision, sound sensing and touch sensitivity will allow them to sense their environment and take 'real-time' decisions about how to operate. In recent years autonomous robotic research has not advanced dramatically owing to the overwhelming complexity that has been encountered in trying to make a machine do something as simple as walk. Rodney Brooks at the Massachusetts Institute of Technology (MIT) has suggested a simpler way that progress might be achieved. His concept of robots that are 'Fast, Cheap and Out of Control' consists of millions of tiny units, each programmed to do a simple task, but not subject to any overall control. In this sense they are a bit like an ant colony that can build large structures through the co-operation of lots of tiny workers. Brooks suggests that such creatures could be dropped on a planet surface and work together to clear an area of rocks for a landing pad. It would not matter that many of the minibots might die or stop working, because they can easily be replaced. This is an example of human engineering using models from nature to improve efficiency. An area where rapid progress is being made is in prosthetics or artificial body parts. There have been recent successful substitutions of tiny video cameras to replace lost eyes, artificial retinas are being prototyped, artificial hearts and pacemakers are in wide use. Also being developed are mechanical limbs that are controllable by nerve impulses. An area which has attracted considerable interest, especially amongst fiction writers, is brain implants which consist in attaching silicon chips to the nervous system to repair or enhance the brain processes. The idea is that such chips would be able to send electronic impulses to parts of the nervous system to trigger thoughts, memories or to 'download' new information. Using brain-wave analysers, it may be possible to control machines such as remote arms or eyes from a distance using thought.

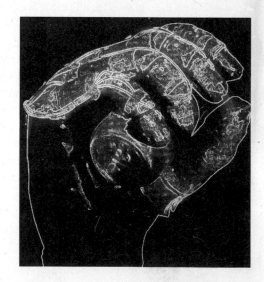

effectively integrating the body and the remote machine. With the increasing miniaturisation of technology, we can look forward to greater interaction between machines and organic tissue. With such developments it is apparent that the practical distinction between machine and organism is diminishing.

Neural networks. By arranging individual 'neurons' in complex networks, researchers are able to construct computer systems which have the ability to learn from experience. Such techniques are supposed to emulate, in a modest way, the operation of the human brain – which is currently viewed as a huge matrix of interconnected neurons – thus the term 'neural networking'. A network of numerical arrays is set up inside the memory of a computer, each of which has a link to the other. Some arrays, or neurons, are given the job of receiving input data, some are told to calculate the data and others give the output of the calculation. This is a fairly basic mathematical model of the human neuron, although there are some important differences. Initially the arrays are set at random values, but as regular input is given the system starts to stabilise and give regular output – it has learned something. It is hoped that by this approach it will eventually be possible to develop intelligent computers that can think, feel, reason and learn from experience (this is the view, for example, of people like Marvin Minsky of the Artificial Intelligence department at MIT). Whilst this research is in its infancy, it indicates the trajectory of future developments. Currently, neural nets have been used in market research where huge volumes of customer data is analysed for trends, in the Japanese stock market where programs learn about economic data and suggest investment routes, in handwriting recognition which has allowed the automation of form processing and postal work, and in industrial quality control where production lines can be monitored and modified if necessary. Possible future applications have been suggested, such as face and voice re-cognition for security access, automatic transport systems, on-line intelligence databases, virtual teachers and even artificial consciousness itself. Neural networks of today do have severe limitations if they are to be seen as models of the human brain (they are usually digital serial rather that analogue parallel, as the brain is) but they do show how machines can have the ability to adapt and learn, qualities that are so essential to human being.

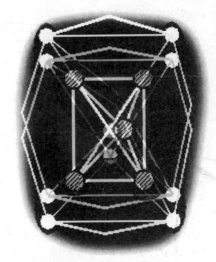

Nanotechnology. Nanotechnology represents the technique of designing or evolving tiny machines that can be programmed to operate in environments such as the human body. Such machines might fight diseases, increase physical performance or prevent ageing. In his influential book *Engines of Creation*, Eric Drexler describes some of the means by which little machines could be created and what they could be used for. Nanotechnology is creating machines out of molecules. It consists in arranging molecules into certain shapes that will perform given tasks in certain environments. In

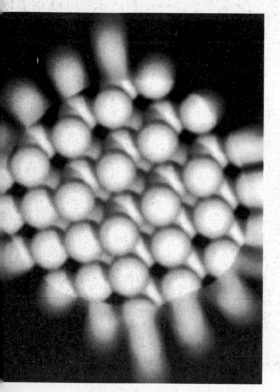

this sense, nanotechnology is trying to create artificial proteins, the building blocks of organic matter; it is creating organic machines. According to Drexler, nanomachines will be able to design and assemble other nanomachines. Such 'universal assemblers' will operate at an atomic level building molecular compounds to order.

'Because assemblers will let us place atoms in almost any reasonable arrangement, they will let us build almost anything that the laws of nature will allow to exist. In particular they will let us build almost anything we can design – including more assemblers. The consequences of this will be profound, because our crude tools have let us explore only a small part of the range of possibilities that natural law permits. Assemblers will open a world of new technologies.'

Drexler p. 14

Some of the applications of nanotechnology seem fantastical yet, according to Drexler, are based on proven scientific principles – spacesuits like living skin, as strong as steel, that are programmed to adapt to your body as you move around so that you hardly feel them. The skin, whilst protecting you, also passes on the sensory data you need to feel your way around with your hands and feet. We could produce molecular engines to be inserted into the blood to seek out and kill malignant cells and viruses, or mend damaged DNA. Dying cells could be revitalised to re-grow lost tissue. Large machines, such as rocket engines, could be built by billions of tiny molecular workers 'growing' complete structures from programmed 'seeds'. Whilst many of these remain highly speculative, the notion of molecular machines has attracted considerable interest. There seems no essential reason why this approach could not be adopted as the relevant technology advances. Yet again, such organic machines would blur the distinction between organic and mechanical.

Genetic manipulation. It has been known since the 1950s that the chemical basis of life is DNA. This complex molecule contains all the information about how organisms develop, how they behave and, to some extent, how they die. Human DNA today holds traces of heredity that date back to the beginning of life. Shortly after it was identified, the hope arose that life itself could be controlled if we could gain control over DNA. In fact, it turns out that DNA is an extraordinarily complex molecule that controls

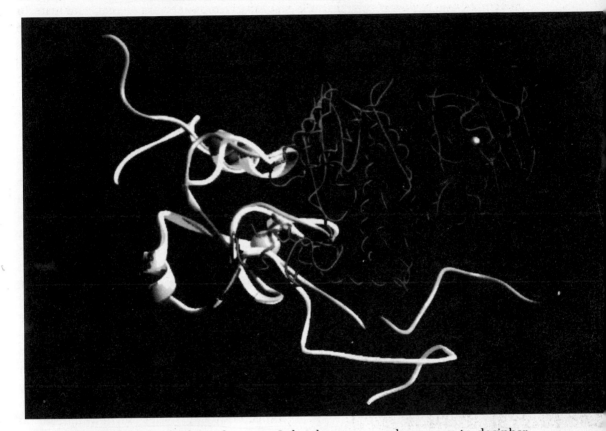

extraordinarily complex biological events. It has by no means been easy to decipher the way DNA reacts with other chemicals, or to determine what each part of the DNA chain does. Since the 1980s genetic synthesis has become highly advanced and various techniques have been developed that allow the structure of DNA to be modified for various reasons. Gene therapy attempts to treat certain diseases that are caused by faults in DNA by replacing the faulty strand with a working one. Genetically engineered livestock and produce have been marketed that display beneficial features. As a result of the Human Genome Project, which aims to decode the genetic structure of humans, it is apparent that there is great potential for genetic manipulation of the human species. The obvious implication is that, once the human has been reduced to a series of codes, such codes can be 're-mixed' in a number of ways to produce a variety of mutant offspring having varying degrees of humanness.

It is likely that genetic codes, being huge in volume, will be stored and manipulated with computer systems. This implies that computers will be able to design new organisms from a database of genetic codes. The development of gene manipulation, combined with in vitro fertilisation techniques, suggests that we might be able to change the traditional notion of what a human is. Some geneticists, notably Richard Dawkins, have claimed that DNA is actually a machine for making life. What's more, this machine is digital, in the same way that computers are digital, and its sole purpose is to ensure its own reproduction. As he states in *River Out of Eden*, 'We – and that means all living things – are survival machines programmed to propagate the digital database that did the programming.' Viewed in this way, there is no distinction between the mechanical and the organic when it comes to considering DNA.

Artificial life. Artificial Life was defined in 1987 as 'the study of man-made systems which exhibit behaviours characteristics of natural living systems.' A typical A-life project would consist of creating a virtual space in the computer in which digital organisms, sometimes called 'critters', can live, breed, feed, fight and die. These creatures might not look like much more than strings of numbers, or specks on a screen, but they are living out complex, interdependent existences which have much in common with real colonies of cells or ants. The behaviour displayed by artificial communities is often called 'complex' or 'emergent' in that it is often difficult for the programmer to determine in advance what the colony will do. This is true even though each individual critter has very limited and predictable functions. Research into complex systems, such as bird flocks, has been revolutionised by recent advances in computer modelling techniques. It has been shown that by attributing individually simple behavioural rules to a large number of interacting units extremely diverse and complex behaviour emerges. Such computer models suggest both ways in which actual

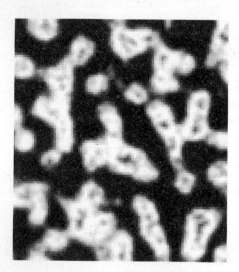

life may have begun and ways in which life might be simulated. In some ways computer viruses can be considered a form of artificial life. They are a type of parasite that relies on humans passing the virus from machine to machine. Their sole purpose is to replicate, although they often have the effect of destroying their host – the computer operating system. Some biologists consider organic viruses to be self-replicating machines, and not a form of animate life at all. Artificial life forms are often able to breed and in doing so can pass characteristics to their offspring just as organic species can. If the critters are set some task, for example to be good at getting through small holes, then those offspring that can get through holes better are rewarded with survival. This can be expressed in a *genetic algorithm* which is a piece of computer code that creates random solutions to problems. The ones that work are kept and the ones that don't are discarded. Genetic algorithms will be discussed later in this book. An example of A-life that has received wide attention is the Cellular Automata or CA. These are computer organisms, or cells, which work on very simple rules determined by the condition of each neighbouring cell. Even though the rules by which they run are very simple, the behaviour they display can be alarmingly complicated and unpredictable. The best known example is a game called 'Life' which is available as freeware for almost any computer platform. The potential for artificial life forms to combine with robotics, neural networks and human genetic manipulation suggests that we are heading towards a time when the distinction between actual life and artificial life will be less valid. An introduction to A-life is the book *Artificial Life* by Stephen Levy.

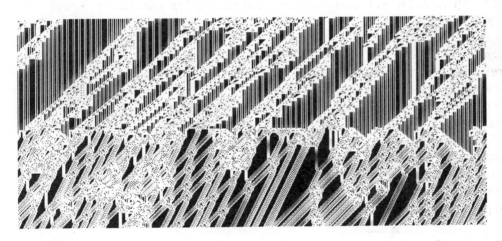

This is by no means an exhaustive survey of Post-Human technologies. But I hope that, from this sample, it is evident that many living functions will be machine replicable and many machines will acquire life-like qualities. Given current developments we can imagine a scenario in which the digital DNA code for an intelligent robotic organism is networked to multiple nodes via an optical fibre matrix, using a virtual reality communications environment, to be reconstructed from source molecules by nanotechnology devices. The net effect of these developments is what we call Post-Humanism and it leads us to ask how will we distinguish between the artificial and the real, the real and the simulated, the organic and the mechanical. For practical purposes, it will be a mere diversion to argue about such terminological distinctions – unless you are an academic philosopher.

Disclaimer
I do not claim that anything stated in this book is the truth. I only claim that the ideas which I put forward could be useful.

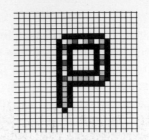

'The Post-Human
era begins in
full when the
output of
computers is
unpredictable'

The Post Human Manifesto 8.1

CONSCIOUSNESS, HUMAN EXISTENCE AND PHILOSOPHY

Consciousness,
Human Existence
and Philosophy

No finite
division can
be drawn
between the
environment,
the body
and the
brain. The
human is
identifiable
– but not
definable.

1. Consciousness, Human Existence and Philosophy

For centuries we have struggled to understand our own existence. We have tried to make sense of what we are and how we relate to the world around us. In early human history it seemed that forces of nature, controlled by gods, determined human existence. By enhancing our technological capabilities, we have gained increasing confidence in our ability to exert control over those forces and impose our will on nature. In the humanist era, this has led to the view that we, with our highly developed intelligence and technologies, are superior to everything else in nature, and indeed, that the purpose of the universe itself is to produce human existence – a theory known as the Strong Anthropic Principle supported by eminent physicists like John Wheeler (see Barrow and Tipler, *The Anthropic Cosmological Principle*).

Today the possibilities suggested by synthetic intelligence, organic computers and genetic modification are deeply challenging to our sense of superiority. Such developments awaken deep rooted anxieties about the threat to human existence from technology we cannot control or do not understand (a fear articulated by Mary Shelley's *Frankenstein* creature). We are aware that we are capable of creating entities that may surpass, and even dominate, us and are now seriously facing up to the possibility that attributes such as human-like thought may be created in non-human forms. Whilst this is one of our deepest fears, it is also one of the holiest grails of computer science. Despite the enormous problems involved, the development of artificial consciousness may happen sooner than we imagine. Would such an entity have human-like thoughts, would it have a sense of existence? Such questions are difficult to answer given the redundant concepts of human existence that we have inherited from the humanist era. As will be shown shortly, many widely accepted humanist ideas about consciousness can no longer be sustained. In addition, new theories of science based on computer modelling are starting to demonstrate the profound interconnections between all things in nature. This has implications for traditional views of the human condition and for some of the oldest problems in philosophy.

Consciousness

'Mental phenomena, all mental phenomena whether conscious or unconscious, visual or auditory, pains, tickles, itches, thoughts, indeed all our mental life, are caused by processes going on in the brain.'

John Searle, *Minds, Brains and Science, p. 18*

It is a commonly held belief that the brain determines consciousness. In this discussion I shall use the word consciousness to refer to all those attributes we usually associate with a sentient human, such as thought, emotion, memory, awareness, intelligence, self-consciousness and so on. The unique part of a person, their mind, is thought to exist within the substance of the brain. Roland Barthes, in his book *Mythologies*, speaks of 'The Brain of Einstein' which had been bequeathed by the great physicist to two hospitals upon his death.

'A photograph shows him lying down, his head bristling with electric wires: the waves of his brain are being recorded, while he is requested to "think of relativity". (But for that matter, what does "to think of" mean exactly?) What this is meant to convey is probably that the seismograms will be all the more violent since "relativity" is an arduous subject.'

Joseph Guillotin, who developed the comparatively rational and humane execution machine, collected severed heads and tried to revive them in order to communicate with the after-life in the belief that the head contained the essence of a person. People now invest in having their frozen heads preserved in a cryogenic state, hoping that future science will be able to revive them from this portion of the body. Computer scientists trying to develop intelligent computer systems through the technique of neural networking devote their energies to the modelling of the human brain by digital means. Consciousness, thought and mind are generally regarded as being exclusively functions of the brain, despite the fact that their exact location within the brain is yet to be established. Post-Humans believe that this view of consciousness being located in the brain cannot any longer be sustained.

If by consciousness we mean a compound of feelings, emotions, memories that are exhibited by the living being and not by the dead, then these are as much a function of the whole body as of the brain. When I *feel* unhappiness it is in my chest and arms. When I am frightened, it is in my bowels and legs that the sensation is strongest. If I am amused it is my mouth and cheeks that are significantly altered. When I am alert it is my muscles that are tense. When I am moved by music it is my whole body which tingles or dances. If I am bored my body starts to fidget. All these apparently 'mental' states seem more easily identified by their

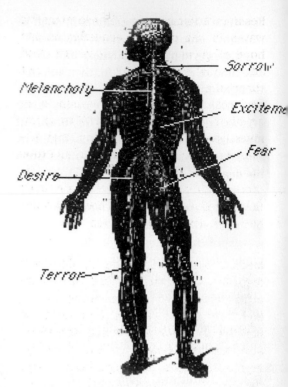

'Consciousness is the function of an organism, not an organ.'

The Post-Human Manifesto 2.2

'Consciousness is not exclusively restricted to the brain.'

The Post-Human Manifesto 2.1

'physical' attributes. Is it possible, or useful, to distinguish mental and physical things?

The Post-Human view of consciousness (the human ability to think, feel and know) is that it is a phenomenon that is distributed throughout the whole body with no one organ being solely responsible.

One does not understand consciousness by studying the brain alone. For example, researchers now use scanners (devices such as the Superconducting Quantum Interference Device and Fast Magnetic

Resonance Imaging) to observe magnetic waves in the brain, presumably in the hope of eventually locating where mind and consciousness are. It is not surprising that, given certain tasks to perform, the subjects display activity in certain regions of the brain. What is not investigated is the possibility that the same stimulus (a flashing light, an erotic image, thinking about relativity) may produce an effect elsewhere in the body that is of equal importance in contributing to activity in the brain.

Medical science, in general, does not dispute that brain functions are intimately linked to functions of the body. The motor system, the central and peripheral nervous systems, the regulatory and homeostatic systems, the sense organs, all work *with* the brain rather than *for* it. This is particularly true if we study responses such as sexual arousal, stress, depression, fear and hunger which all have physiological components. The effect of neurological feedback between the brain and other parts of the body cannot be ignored.

'For better or for worse, in reality we are not centred in our head. We are not centered in our mind. Even if we were, our mind has no centre, no "I". Our bodies have no centrality either. Bodies and minds blur across each other's supposed boundaries. Bodies and minds are not that different from one another. They are both composed of swarms of sub-level things.'

Kevin Kelly, *Out of Control, p. 64*

Surpassing the mental/physical divide

Descartes is often cited as being responsible for framing the dualism between mind and body, between the non-physical act of thinking and the physical material of which we are made. He was, however, convinced that the brain was the organ through which immaterial thought arose and that the pineal gland, located in the brain, played the central role in this.

The Cartesian dualism, between 'thinking stuff' and 'material stuff', is now largely discredited and the contemporary neurologist is more likely to believe that the mind is somehow contained within the material of the brain rather than being an immaterial 'ghost in the machine'.

'The prevailing wisdom, variously expressed and argued for, is *materialism:* there is only one sort of stuff, namely matter – the physical stuff of chemistry, physics and physiology – and the mind is somehow nothing but a physical phenomenon. In short, the mind is the brain.'

Daniel Dennett, *Explaining Consciousness, p. 33*

In fact, virtually every serious contemporary study of consciousness I have come across assumes that the mind is in the brain. Yet even though the Cartesian dualism is discredited by the materialists, a new dualism is emerging from their approach – that of the division between the brain and the body – the Brain/Body dualism. The materialist dualism says that the brain is responsible for the processes of thought, consciousness, emotion (in other words, the mind) and other parts of the body are not. This view is supported by disciplines such as psychology, neurophysiology and cognitive science which, in general, adopt a 'brain-centred' methodology of the mind, virtually ignoring the role of the body's contribution.

But, despite these approaches, it is becoming clear that the apparently obvious distinctions between brain and body are inadequate. Recent developments in the two 'hard' sciences of medicine and physics suggest that the implicit opposition of mind, body and reality is questionable, if not a severe impediment to progress. For example, in medicine it is increasingly accepted that physical illness can have psychological causes and cures, with symptoms like stress having neither an exclusively mental nor physical location. The fact that alternative therapies that take a holistic approach to diagnosis and cure are being provided by the National Health Service in Britain shows that this complementary approach to the patient is gaining acceptance amongst a traditionally sceptical medical profession (complementary therapies such as visualisation and massage are now available on the NHS for cancer patients at the Hammersmith Hospital, London). Recent theories of quantum physics have suggested that the traditional division between mind and reality is in doubt. In the Copenhagen interpretation of quantum reality the conventional boundary between the observer and the observed is brought into question, as is the boundary between mind and reality. The Copenhagen interpretation is a way of interpreting the results of sub-atomic research that holistically binds the observer and the observed in such a way as to make the outcome of an event dependent on the researcher. As David Peat says in *Einstein's Moon:*

'This holistic nature of the atomic world was the key to Bohr's Copehagen interpretation. It was something totally new to physics, although similar ideas had long been taught in the East. For more than two thousand years, Eastern philosophers had talked about the unity between the observer and that which is observed. They had pointed to the illusion of breaking apart a thought from the mind that thinks the thought. Now a similar holism was entering physics.'   Peat *p. 62*

Extensive research has been carried out into the effect upon human consciousness of sensory deprivation. In cases where the person is denied sensory stimuli for long periods of time, the normal functioning of the mind breaks down. Without the continuous flow of varied information that the mind is used to receiving from the body, the mind turns in on itself. Kevin Kelly, in *Out of Control*, cites examples of the detrimental effect of denying visual stimulation to sighted patients and has this suggestion:

'"Black patch psychosis" is something ophthalmologists watch for on the wards. I think the universities should keep an eye out for it too. Every philosophy department should hang a pair of black eye patches in a red firealarm-like box that says, "In case of argument about mind/body, break glass, put on."'   Kelly *p. 68*

If we accept that the long-held separation between mind and body, between the mental and the physical, is being undermined, and that the tide of ideas is running against it, then we must accept that our mind and our body might be continuous. Many materialists would say that they have no trouble in accepting the continuity between mind and body. They would say that since the mind is made of matter in the same way that the body is made of matter then consciousness is simply one expression of matter and the body is another. The mistake they make is to confine consciousness to one portion of matter, namely the brain.

Consciousness as a non-linear process

Many people will still insist that conscious thought occurs in only in the brain. It is an assumption, but can it be proved? The problem arises of what thought is, how do we detect it and measure it? Where is it happening? The only usual evidence we have that another person is thinking is from their outward physical actions such as gesture, speech and expression (this is true even in the case of a brain scanner since it can only monitor a certain effect of thinking and not the complete thought itself). Given that these expressions are present in a conscious person we are observing, where could we specify that thought is actually happening? Is it, as is generally supposed, happening in the brain with the consequential reactions filtering outwards to the limbs and lips? This is the orthodox view in which activity in the body is seen as either contributing to, or responding to, the activity of the brain but not in itself part of the conscious process. The body either contributes to thoughts via input from the sensory system, or responds to thoughts via the motor system. This could be considered a linear model of thought, a sequence of steps each separate from the other, each determining the next and all being controlled by the brain. Something like this is proposed by computational psychologists (those who believe the brain is like a computer) with their modes of 'input', 'output' and 'processing' in humans being analogous to those of a serial computer. In their view, thoughts can be broken down into a series of logical statements that run in sequence much like a piece of computer code. In this linear model a central controlling device is assumed, and it is natural to follow the analogy and regard the brain as the Central Processing Unit (CPU). If the brain is like a giant computer (albeit a very complex one) then the body is relegated to the status of a peripheral device supplying input data and energy and responding to output data and commands. The outward expressions of thought, or the bodily sensations that accompany thought, are seen as products of thought rather than constituents of the thought itself in the same way that a computer monitor displays the output of the CPU.

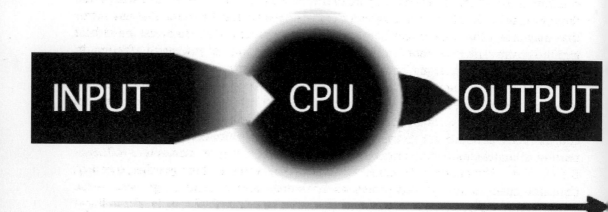

But how much longer can this model be useful? Even the most enthusiastic proponents of the computational model acknowledge the huge complexity involved in replicating actual human thought processes. This model has inherent limitations one of which is the very mind-boggling complexity of the processes it is trying to simulate. Humans have a severe problem in understanding the intricacies of their own make-up and the degree to which we know anything about our mental processes is still very limited. Might we have to accept the possibility that the human mind is just too complex to be modelled along the lines described above? It is possible that the attempts to understand conscious activity by dividing the thinking system into component parts and then trying to piece together the parts in a logical and linear way will flounder in the face of overwhelming complexity. Some theorists, such as Roland Penrose in *The Emperor's New Mind* and John Searle in *The Rediscovery of the Mind*, believe that many processes of human thought are inherently impervious to algorithmic modelling – that is, they cannot be reduced to logical programs. Might we have to adopt another approach?

Following recent developments in the field of Chaos theory, could we not say that thought is more like a process of dynamic, interrelated events, with multiple stimuli and responses occurring simultaneously throughout the nervous system? Rather than following a sequential model in which inputs and outputs are peripheral to a central processor, could we not think of a model in which inputs and outputs are part of the central processor – to the extent that there is no *central* processor? In other words, the processes we are discussing (thought, consciousness and the mind) could be distributed throughout the system that gives rise to them rather than being confined to any one part. After all, we have already said that the only way we can determine whether or not someone else is thinking is from their physical expressions. Why should such physical expressions, or their associated sensations, be any less a constituent of a thought than that part that occurs in the brain? If we can accept that thought may be distributed throughout the body then we must assume that any factor that may affect the body might have a bearing on thought. Consciousness must be a highly sensitive process that is influenced by a huge range of interacting factors. In Chaos theory such complex and sensitive systems are described as exhibiting non-linear behaviour. A non-linear model of consciousness would view complex events occurring alongside each other, and acting upon each other, so that no one event can be isolated as a cause or origin. A general pattern of behaviour would emerge that could not be described in a linear, predictable way (see below). Such a model demands that we acknowledge all the potential forces that might act upon a person to influence the state of consciousness. To name but a few, these would include weather, memory, chemical changes in the body such as hormones and enzymes, age, sex, social conditioning, personality, skills, reflexes, general health and so on. In a non-linear model we cannot rule out the influence of any factor that may affect consciousness, however minutely – even if that influence is non-local. That is to say, the complex processes we know as 'thought' cannot be explained by reference to the material of the brain alone. There are many other factors that have a direct influence on the processes of thought and to exclude these is to create an arbitrary barrier between parts of the system that may affect each other. In the context of the Post-Human condition, the non-linear model is preferable to the linear since a dynamic conception of thought allows for an integrated mind and body which a functioning being represents.

A note on non-linear systems

In simple terms, non-linear systems are those which cannot be described by linear equations. Such systems are often called 'complex dynamical' or 'turbulent' in that they represent activity that is chaotic and unpredictable. An example of a non-linear system would be a cloud of gas or a turbulent river. In recent times the concept of non-linearity has been used to describe many phenomena from the weather to the price of oil. Linear equations are seen to be useful in describing 'ideal' situations whereas non-linear equations are often used to try and describe 'real' situations – things that are messy and complex. One of the major features of non-linear systems is that their behaviour is seen to be sensitive to many simultaneous conditions. To describe fully such a system we cannot rule out the effect of even very small perturbations since they may become magnified and cause global changes in the system – the so-called 'butterfly effect'. For a more detailed description of non-linearity, see one of the many books on Chaos, such as that by James Gleick.

Consciousness as a complex process

For many years researchers and philosophers have postulated the existence of a 'seat of consciousness' or some physical centre in the brain that coordinates all other mental activity. For Descartes this was the pineal gland or *epiphysis,* but more contemporary researchers have suggested other areas of the brain that may be responsible. Penrose summarises several such suggestions in *The Emperor's New Mind,* chapter 9. Still the idea persists that there must be some cells or structures within the brain that could ultimately be said to be the 'conscious' centre of the mind. The fact that, after intensive work, no such centre has yet been identified gives support to the view that it may not exist, at least in the form in which it is expected.

Such expectations highlight the difference between the mechanistic approach characteristic of the humanists and the 'complexified' approach adopted by the Post-Humanists. In Post-Human terms, consciousness can only be considered as an emergent property that arises from the coincidence of a number of complex events. In this sense it is like boiling. Given sufficient heat, gravity and air pressure the water in a kettle will start to boil. We can see what boiling is, we can recognise it as something to which we give a name. We do not consider it mysterious, yet we cannot isolate it from the conditions that produced it. We cannot isolate consciousness from the conditions that produce it any more than we can isolate boiling. Consciousness is a property that emerges from a given set of conditions.

Given the right amounts of heat, gravity, water and air pressure water will boil. The 'boiling' is a property that emerges from a given set of conditions and cannot be reduced to any one part of the system.

A note on complexity

Complexity theory holds that in a complex system the whole is more than the sum of the parts. This means that even though we may be able to break up a system into its constituent parts, we will not be able to learn about the global behaviour of the system by studying them individually. The global behaviour is something that emerges when all the constituent parts are exerting their influence on each other. Without the mutual effect of the constituents on each other the critical state of complexity is not reached and the global behaviour does not appear. As clearly described by Stephen Levy in *Artificial Life*:

'A complex system is one whose component parts interact with sufficient intricacy that they cannot be predicted by standard linear equations; so many variables are at work in the system that its overall behaviour can only be understood as an emergent consequence of the holistic sum of all the myriad behaviours embedded within. Reductionism does not work with complex systems, and it is now clear that a purely reductionist approach cannot be applied when studying life [and, I would add, consciousness]: in living systems, the whole is more than the sum of its parts. . . this is the result not of a mysterious dram of vital life-giving fluid but rather the benefits of complexity, which allows certain behaviours and characteristics to emerge unbidden. The mechanics of this may have been hammered out by evolution, but the engine of evolution cannot begin to fire until a certain degree of complexity is present. Living systems epitomise complexity, so much so that some scientists now see complexity as the defining characteristic of life.'

Levy, p. 7 (my comments in box parentheses)

An example that is often given to illustrate complexity is that of a flock of birds. Taken collectively, the behaviour of a flock of birds seems well choreographed and purposeful. The flock avoids obstacles, circles over food and prey, travels halfway around the world whilst performing all sorts of loops and whorls in the sky. Yet there is no central control to this behaviour. The birds are not just mimicking one 'leader' bird. Circular flocks can have no leader. Complexity theory explains this phenomena by saying that the global behaviour we see exhibited by the flock emerges from the interaction among the individual birds. In *Artificial Life*, Stephen Levy quotes the person who first modelled such behaviour on a computer, Craig Reynolds:

'The motion of a flock of birds is. . .simple in concept yet is so visually complex it seems randomly arrayed and yet is magnificently synchronous. Perhaps most puzzling is the strong impression of intentional centralised control. Yet all evidence suggests that flock motion must be merely the aggregate result of the actions of individual animals, each acting solely on the basis of its local perception of the world.' *ibid. p. 76*

Complexity theory has been incredibly useful in modelling life-like phenomena on computers that are analogous to those seen in nature. Stephen Levy's book gives an extensive account of these experiments. What is striking about such simulations, and what is most useful to our account of consciousness, is the purposeful, almost 'mystical' properties that even fairly simple systems exhibit. Cellular Automata, little cell-like creatures that live, grow and mate in a computer's memory, quickly seem to take on those attributes of 'animism' we normally associate with other living things. They are born, they die, they struggle, they reproduce, they try, they fail. This is not because any such animistic properties have been programmed in. Such a programming task would be awesomely difficult. It is simply that these properties emerge when relatively simple things are allowed to interact with each other in a system. Biologists and philosophers such as Henri Bergson have postulated that the phenomena we know as life rests on some essential 'spark', the *élan vital*, which is the thing that distinguishes animate and inanimate matter. The exact location of such a spark has never been determined, even though many have sought it. Yet complexity theory provides us with just such a spark, the appearance of animation and purpose that arises in a complex system. It is not 'located' in any one part of the system and it does not emerge until the system is up and running. The 'immaterial spark of life' is nothing but the appearance of complexity.

Opposite page. Pictures can be seen as a type of complex system in which a recognisable image emerges from a number of smaller, distributed events. In this case the printed dots that make up the ink screen on the page are the individual components which, collectively, give rise to the appearance of a face. The appearance of a face does not consist in any of the parts or dots, but we are able to recognise it as we simultaneously perceive their united effect. In this case, the emergent property is the illusion of a coherent picture. Such a description can be true of any material (silver based film emulsion, video screens, laser printers, faxes) that has an informational content that is greater that the sum of its parts. That is, to take the case of a graphic on a computer screen, the mere addition of all the pixel values would produce a number, but that number would have very little informational content. However, a specific arrangement of pixel values on a screen can give rise to an image (informational content) which the numerical values of the pixels alone does not convey.

In the same way that a 'spark of life' was postulated but never located, an 'immaterial mind' has often been proposed as a way of accounting for the sensation of consciousness. This immaterial mind, which is also synonymous with the 'spirit' or 'soul', has never been successfully located in any part of the body, but is assumed to have something to do with the brain. But we know that the brain and the body are *extremely* complex processes consisting of many interacting and interdependent things. It is not at all surprising then that, given a system of such complexity that has evolved over so many years, something as animated and purposeful as human consciousness should emerge.

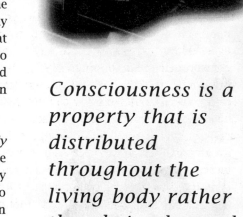

Therefore, in considering consciousness as a complex process it becomes apparent that the conception of an mind that is separate from the body is not needed and the search for any one cause or 'seat' is misdirected. Some parts of the system may be more significant than others and these may be the areas of the brain in which the search for a 'seat' has been historically concentrated. But unless the brain, or those parts, can be shown to produce the mind *on their own*, without the need for any other tissue, then it is mistaken to assume that the brain is the mind. As far as I know, no researcher has suggested that a dismembered brain, or any dismembered part of a brain, can be conscious.

To say that conscious thought is not *exclusively* a function of the brain, does not deny that the brain has a significant part to play. It is merely to state that the brain contributes to consciousness but does not determine it. In other words, the brain may be responsible for a large proportion of consciousness but this does not mean that it *is* consciousness.

Consciousness is a property that is distributed throughout the living body rather than being located in any one part

The Post-Human conception of consciousness

In terms of the Post-Human condition it is beneficial to consider thought and consciousness as functions of the whole being. When we come to look at synthesising creativity and recreating mental activity with computers, it will be useful to consider a model of the conscious mind that is continually receiving complex and unpredictable data through and from its sensory apparatus, and responding to that data in unpredictable ways. Since the human being is so complex, and is being stimulated in such a variety of ways, we must accept that we cannot precisely predict behaviour but must, as with the weather, allow for chance and randomness. When thinking in general about human thought processes, we must be aware that they are not brain determined. Since thought occurs in the whole body, it is sensitive to both external environmental and internal chemical forces. I believe this has huge implications for researches such as cognitive psychology, psychoanalysis and neurology as well as artificial intelligence and neural networking. Some of these will be discussed in later chapters.

Human existence

Like the separation between mind and body, the separation between the body and the environment has deep philosophical roots in our understanding of the universe. I wish to argue that the generally accepted division between the human and its environment is inadequate in the Post-Human era and, therefore, redundant. *no you can't just say that ucocking bollox*

Fuzzy entities

Our bodies represent a continuous field of sensory apparatus that is perpetually responding to stimulation from the environment. So long as we are alive activity does not cease anywhere in our bodies, there is no point that is static or unchanging. The eyes, skin, ears and nose are continually responding to fluctuations in the environment, and to some extent, changing the environment in return by sweating, breathing, sneezing, giving off odours, releasing pheromones and so on. Even when asleep we are still sensitive to light, heat, movement and sound. Since a human cannot be separated from an environment we must accept that the human is a fuzzy edged entity that is profoundly integrated into its surroundings. There is a perpetual exchange of liquids, chemicals and energies with the environment in the form of urine, faeces, menstrual fluid, hair, air, sperm, food, water, skin, sound, light and heat. There is no fixed state of a human, nor can we measure any absolute edge. We can only know the human entity as an approximation – a contingent description of a bunch of substances and events. We are in continual mutation from egg to decaying corpse, never separate or isolated from an environment which we are woven into and woven of. It is impossible to think of a living human being *not* in an environment, for without one we soon die. Therefore, *it is a condition of a being's existence that it exists within a suitable environment*, just as it is a condition of thought that the body is functioning. *anyedi*

As a practical illustration of the fact that humans are not confined to the boundary of their skin I shall describe a remarkable facility displayed by my cat. My cat knows that the person I live with is more likely to feed it than I am. In the flat where I live the main

'No finite division can be drawn between the environment, the body and the brain. The human is identifiable, but not definable.'

The Post-Human Manifesto 2.8

'There is nothing external to a human
because the extent of a human cannot be
fixed.'

The Post-Human Manifesto 2.10

front door is shared by the flat upstairs. A number of people from that flat go in and out at all times of the day. Despite the fact that I don't often feed it, the cat likes to sleep on my lap. From the position where I sit with the cat in my lap it is just possible, through our own door and corridor, to hear the sound of a key being inserted into the front door. The facility in the cat I have noticed is this: even though people use the front door many times in a day, the cat will never wake up *unless* it is the person I live with who puts her key in the door. As soon as she does so, the cat jumps up and runs towards the door in anticipation of being fed. I have observed this on many occasions, and only very rarely does the cat not behave in this way. Short of endowing my cat with some supernatural sense, the most obvious explanation is that it is responding to the smell of that person whom it associates with food. The remarkable thing is the speed and distance at which this recognition occurs – instantaneously and through two doors and two corridors. It is clear from this that there is a field of 'odour' that extends beyond the skin boundary of a person, but which is in a real sense part of that person, a part of what constitutes that person, at least as far as the cat is concerned. This is a fact well recognised by those who use dogs to track human scent.

The Post-Human conception of human existence

If we accept that the mind and body cannot be absolutely separated and that the body and the environment cannot be absolutely separated, then we are left with the apparently absurd, yet logically consistent conclusion that *consciousness and the environment cannot be absolutely separated*. A continuum exists throughout consciousness, body and environment which means that any break in that continuum, for example between a lung and the air that it breathes, is contingent and arbitrary.

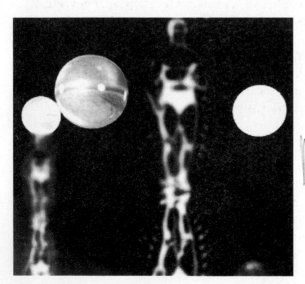

The general implication, which cannot be ignored, is that we can never determine the absolute boundary of the human. The consequences as far as the Post-Human condition is concerned are profound. It means that human beings do not exist in the sense in which we ordinarily think of them, that is as separate entities in perpetual conflict with a nature that is *external* to them.

Some might argue that if a bullet that was external to me became internal (i.e. I was shot), I would soon know the difference and promptly reassess my opinions. That is, the impact of material reality proves the existence of the external world. However, whilst a bullet might cause severe problems to my continued viability as a conscious being, it would not negate the fact that my body has no fixed boundaries. It would simply mean that those indefinite boundaries had undergone a transformation, probably increasing the surface area over which I am distributed, making the job of fixing my boundaries even less precise.

An alternative model of the mind, body, reality problem

The traditionally accepted models of human existence are now starting to seem inadequate. The advent of the Post-Human era demands a more flexible model of the relationship between the environment, body and consciousness than we currently have.

I propose a model of human existence based on four interconnected media. Each of these covers several of the traditional disciplines of study but is based on continuity rather than separation. I have used the idea of the medium to suggest a fluid, multi-dimensional arrangement of things and events, an arrangement that is dynamically inter-connected so that changes which occur in one place will have consequences over the whole. The distinctions between each of the four media are arbitrary and contingent; they are only relatively separate. As will be seen, each medium is part of all of the others.

The environmental medium – Consisting of the 'universe', 'reality', 'nature', 'the physical world', mineral, chemical, meteorological. This is usually the domain of the hard physical sciences such as chemistry, physics, astronomy, ecology, geology, etc. It describes the totality of interacting chemicals, forces and energies throughout all space and time, and particularly those of our own planet which affect us. In traditional terms the environmental medium would have been regarded as 'external reality'. *Realistically now coming* Particularly crucial to the Post-Human thesis is the inclusion of technology as part of the environmental medium although, as we have seen from the introduction, it is increasingly becoming part of the other media as well.

The organic medium – Consisting of the organic structures that support life, such as cells, bones, flesh, metabolic reactions, organs, etc. This is traditionally the domain of the life sciences such as biology, bio-chemistry, genetics, medicine, zoology, anatomy, etc. The organic medium describes all manner of chemical and energetic processes that are regarded as being alive. Differentiating between the inanimate and animate is not a precise science, and there are several accepted and contested definitions of what constitutes life. However, this need not worry us, since an event can equally well be a part of the environmental medium as well as the organic without getting distracted by the need to produce absolute distinctions.

The sensory medium – Consisting of the nervous system, sense organs, reflexes, involuntary behaviours. In traditional discipline terms we are moving into the area of neuro-psychology, neurology, neuro-chemistry, neuro-physiology, etc. The sensory medium describes the ways in which an organism and its environment respond to each other – how changes in one can produce changes in the other. What is vital about looking at sensory systems in this way is that they are seen as processes that are profoundly linked to the environment, and not regarded as self-contained, isolated systems. There is a subtle, but important, difference between regarding the eye as a organic window onto an external world and regarding it as a device whose structure is dynamically linked to fluctuations in light intensity around it. The first sees the eye as a thing that is separate from, but responsive to the environment. The second sees the eye, and the way it changes, as a part of the environment as much as the environment is part of it.

The conscious medium – Consisting of the brain, motor system, neural feedback, learning, intelligence, memory, characteristics and behaviour, relationships. Normally covered by the studies of psychoanalysis, psychiatry, psychology, para-psychology, neuro-psychology, and the social and soft sciences such as sociology, politics, semiotics, philosophy, etc. The conscious medium is used to refer to the multiple processes occurring within an organism that are generally regarded as constituting consciousness. It is not separate from the sensory medium, but a part of it. It is more useful to consider things like thought, self-consciousness and awareness as functions of something wider than just the brain – they are functions of a whole organism. By using the model of a conscious medium we are not restricted to locating consciousness in one particular organ.

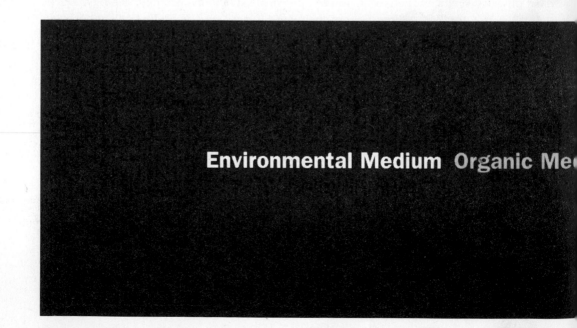

Environmental Medium Organic Med

It is true that the brain is the most viable centre for the processing and coordination of neural impulses since it contains the highest concentration of neural cells, or neurons, in the body. It does not follow from this that the brain is solely responsible for conscious activity. These four media are not independent of each other. They are all totally integrated, interdependent and inseparable. Each includes the other. To draw a distinction between them is arbitrary and it is only because the weight of tradition, and in the interests of comprehension, that they are distinguished at all. To see how aspects of a particuar event might be distributed through the media let us look at the story of Sir Isaac Newton's falling apple which led to his consideration of gravity. To Sir Isaac the apple, the tree from which it fell and the garden in which he sat, were a part of the environmental medium. When the apple landed, there was direct contact with a portion of his organic medium (his hair and head) which led to a response by his sensory medium to the effect that something had hit him. On becoming aware of the motion of the apple his conscious medium was compelled to consider the problem of gravitational forces. Of course, were he to have eaten the apple it would then have become part of his organic medium and the nutrition derived from it may have contributed to the energy required by his conscious medium to think about gravity. In later chapters of this book I shall be referring mainly to the *cognitive* medium when discussing the Post-Human conception of thought. As I shall explain, I will use this term as a shorthand reference to the combined sensory and conscious media. I will also try to remind the reader that the cognitive medium is, in fact, continuous with the environmental and organic media. If this seems a little awkward now, it will become clearer with familiarity. Remember, we are trying to overcome two thousand years of accumulated beliefs.

ognitive Medium

ensory Medium   Conscious Medium

Philosophy or how we think about ourselves

All philosophy is inevitably a product of the times in which it is conceived rather than a depository of eternal, timeless truths. Throughout the pre-humanist and humanist eras philosophers struggled with problems concerning the relationship between God, nature and the human being. Whilst these struggles have been infinitely complex, it is fair for the purposes of this argument to say that there have been two broadly opposing views about the human condition that have divided philosophers since the early Greek times. Essentially there have been those who hold an *idealistic* view of the world and those who hold a *materialistic* view of the world. These two views come into particular conflict when the problem of the relationship between *mind* and *reality* is discussed. To summarise the conflicting views:

Idealism

The idealist holds that the only things that exist are ideas. In idealist terms the whole structure of reality is to be understood through consciousness. All attempts to know the world in itself are futile since all data about the world must inevitably be processed by the body's senses (which are selective) and passed to the mind for interpretation. Therefore, there is no value free, or objective knowledge of reality. The existence of reality is subject to the existence of a conscious being.

It is easy to reconcile this view with the existence of a God since it perpetuates a mind/reality split. This means that whilst there might not be much hard evidence of God in the real world, he can justifiably be said to exist in the form of an idea in which people believe. Nearly all religious belief is idealistic in the sense that it accepts a reality or existence that is outside of, and separate from, earthly reality.

Idealism has gained a reputation for developing absurd propositions such as the claim that nothing existed before human consciousness, and that the thinker is the only thing that actually exists, since nothing else can satisfactorily be proved to exist – a black hole known as solipsism.

Materialism

The materialist view (sometimes known today as physicalism) denies that the mind obeys different laws from physical reality. For the materialist nothing exists except matter, or reality as defined by the 'hard' laws of physics. Thought is a product of matter, being merely a special example of material organisation. Far from the mind determining how the world is viewed, the mind is a product of real events in the world, the world determines the mind. The mind is just as much of an objective reality as the world. Matter has an objective existence, independent of thought.

For nineteenth-century thinkers, materialism was very important, since it seemed to conform with the new discoveries of science that promised an ever more precise grasp of natural phenomena. Dinosaur bones were collected and studied, giving credence to the idea that the world existed long before humans, at the same time alarming the creationists. Many scientists believed in the concept of 'ether' which was thought to be a fundamental material of the universe which accounted for the behaviour of light. Diseases like cholera were starting to be controlled by the application of scientific principles such as hygienic waste disposal. In a political sense, materialism seemed to prove what was obvious to many: that humans were responsible for their own conduct and conditions without reference to a mysterious outside agency such as God.

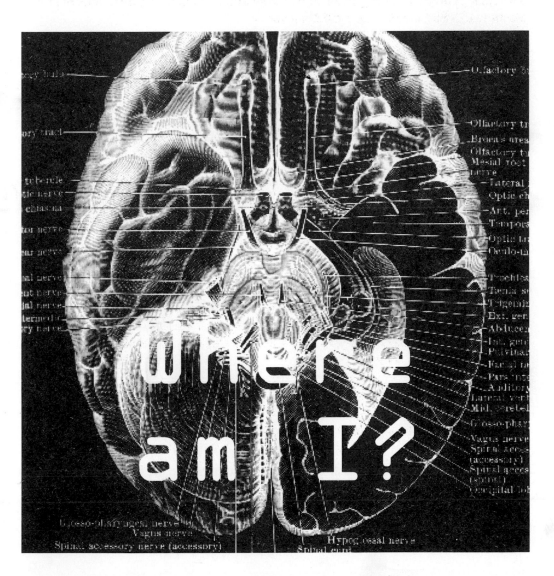

The end of the affair

What is absorbing about the debate between idealists and materialists is that it has endured for so long without ever having been resolved. The reason that it has not and never will be resolved is that both idealism and materialism are right and wrong at the same time. They are right in the sense that as models of the universe they fulfilled the requirements of the times in which they flourished, and they are wrong because they both make the same mistaken assumption. They both assume a division between the mind and reality, between the human mind and an external reality when, in fact, there

is none. Since both arguments contain this basic misconception they can never be resolved. In traditional philosophy *there is an assumed separation between the thing that thinks and the thing that is thought about.* In idealism the conscious mind (the thing that thinks) can only have partial knowledge of reality (the thing that is thought about). It can never be proved that the sensory data that is received gives an accurate representation of what it purports to describe, since we have no independent means of verification. In materialism, the mind (the thing that thinks) is made of the same stuff as the real world (the thing that is thought about) yet is unique in that it is conscious of its existence in a way that most other matter is not. As Post-Humans we know that it is a mistake to separate 'the thing that thinks and the thing that is thought about'. However, we should not be too conceited about this revelation, since it is only with the benefit of the Post-Human point of view that we can conceive of a universe in which humans and nature are not separated. For most of Western history this distinction has been taken as given. I have already described above why I believe the distinction to be invalid and I shall show why, in later chapters, it is *necessary* that we hold this view. If one removes the concept of the separation between human and nature, then many traditional philosophical questions become futile. For example, the question 'How do the mind and reality interact?' has been answered – they do not 'interact' because they are not separate. It is we who draw an artificial distinction between them.

These old battlegrounds of philosophy can now be left to cultural historians, since they no longer bear any relevance to our Post-Human era. Developments in scientific thought have dispelled many of the assumptions on which such philosophy was based. Idealists can no longer claim that nothing existed prior to human consciousness without denying the whole weight of empirical evidence that shows the existence of a pre-human universe. Nor can they make a very convincing case that reality only exists in the mind, that reality is an 'illusion'. To say something is an illusion is to imply that there must be some 'truer' state that is being masked. Yet the possibility of knowing this 'truer' state is ruled out by idealists on the grounds that it cannot be independently verified. Therefore, the 'illusion' might as well accord with the 'truth'. And not only is materialism mistaken in assuming a division between mind and reality, it is also flawed on the question of whether there is actually any matter 'out there' which can be pinned down as constituting reality. Relativity theory showed that there is no finite substance of matter, since matter, time, gravity and space are all defined interdependently. Quantum theory, whilst not questioning the existence of reality, gives strong support to the view that mind and matter cannot be separated and that the existence of matter is not a simple fact. For a view on the overturning of the traditional concept of matter see *The Matter Myth* by Paul Davies and John Gribbin:

'. . .matter as such has been demoted from its central role, to be replaced by concepts such as organisation, complexity and information.' Davies and Gribbin, *p. 9*

They quote Heisenberg:

'In the experiments about atomic events we have to do with things and facts, with phenomena which are just as real as any phenomena in daily life. But the atoms or the elementary particles themselves are not real; they form a world of potentialities or possibilities rather than one of things or facts.' *ibid. p. 21*

The end of philosophy

The Post-Human sees no dichotomy between mind and matter. It is only a 'problem' to those who maintain the distinction. Post-Humans deny the existence of any distinctions other than those that arise in the mind. Distinctions can no longer be thought of as existing independently of our thought. This applies equally to the distinctions that are drawn between aspects of reality for the purposes of study and investigation – such as the distinction between philosophy and science. Philosophy can no longer be held as a separate branch of investigation as distinct from biology, chemistry or physics (nor, for that matter, can anyone ignore the biological and chemical implications of physics, nor the physical and chemical implications of biology and so on). All science has philosophical implications and all philosophy has scientific implications. Consequently, what is left that is unique for philosophy to study, other than the work of other philosophers? The traditional enmity between philosophers and scientists serves only to secure the position of those who perpetuate it: it is nothing short of a survival tactic.

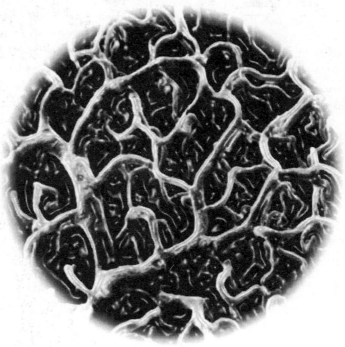

'The idealists think that the only things that exist are ideas, the materialists think that the only thing that exists is matter. It must be remembered that ideas are not independent of matter and that matter is just an idea.'

Post-Human Manifesto 2.14

THE ULTIMATE NATURE OF THE UNIVERSE

ULTIMATE NATURE OF THE UNIVERSE

chapter

2

LEVELS OF RESOLUTION

THE APPEARANCE OF ORDER

Science, Nature
and the Universe

MODELLING REALITY

nervous system

ORIGINS CAUSES

2. Science, Nature and the Universe

Computational technology has profoundly changed our view of science and how we look at the universe. Certain types of calculations involving high levels of recursion, impossible to carry out with pencil and paper, are ideally suited to the large number-crunching machines available to scientists and mathematicians since the 1960s. Experiments on such machines gave rise to new ways of thinking about phenomena which, until then, had defied computational analysis. Chaos theory, which is a gift to us from computers, has shown that many phenomena that seemed random can now be considered chaotic (that is, their behaviour can be modelled with non-linear algorithms), that outcome depends much on initial states and that most measurements are relative rather that absolute. Catastrophe theory has demonstrated that all complex systems give rise to discontinuous features that evade analysis in terms of smooth, continuous formulae. Complexity theory has shown that locally predictable events in a computer, when influenced by any other such events, produce unpredictable global behaviour; the outcome is beyond our control. When considering phenomena such as artificial life (life-like 'organisms' generated by computers) and self-regulating robots, we have to acknowledge the limits of our capacity to understand complexity and hand over some responsibility for outcome to the machine.

'Properly programmed, computers could become entire, self-contained worlds, which scientists could explore in ways that vastly enriched their understanding of the real world. In fact, computer simulation had become so powerful by the 1980s that some people were beginning to talk about it as a "third form of science", standing halfway between theory and experiment. A computer simulation of a thunderstorm, for example, would be like a theory because nothing would exist inside the computer but the equations describing sunlight, wind, and water vapour. But the simulation would also be like an experiment, because those equations are far too complicated to solve by hand. So the scientists watching the simulated thunderstorm on their computer screens would see their equations unfold in patterns they might never have predicted.'

Waldrop, *Complexity*, p. 63

We are coming to rely on the computer as a means of modelling more and more complex natural phenomena. These recent developments have thrown into question some of the very principles upon which traditional (humanist materialist) scientific methods are based and have undermined many long held beliefs about the nature of the universe. The humanist materialist conception of the universe can be described as that view which predominated prior to the existence of computers. The compound effect of those changes brought about since the advent of the computer is now starting to be widely felt and it is vital to understanding the Post-Human condition that we appreciate the shift away from a humanist materialist conception of the universe that is now occurring.

Where philosophy and science meet

Science and philosophy meet when the fundamental nature of the universe and human existence are considered. The question that is so often asked, but never convincingly answered by science or philosophy, is 'Why are we here?' In posing this question several assumptions are made. Among them are:

1. That there will be an answer.
2. That, if there were an answer, it would be satisfactory.
3. That if the answer were satisfactory it would be because it provided a final cause for human existence. This final cause would not be open to any further analysis of the kind that might ask, 'What is the cause of the final cause of human existence?'

Since none of these assumptions are valid, the question of why we are here becomes even more baffling.

What is the resolution of reality?

In trying to answer such questions we come up against the problem of resolution. How far are we able to *resolve* the question of why we are here? Are we here because God put us here; if so, why? Are we here because we evolved from jellyfish? If so, why did jellyfish evolve? We can only resolve any question insofar as our knowledge about the universe extends, and the extent to which we know about the universe is determined by the resolution at which we are able to view it.

In everyday life we operate at a normal human scale based on the size of our bodies relative to the objects and forces around them. For example, doors are usually six feet six inches high, things that get knocked over fall to the ground, we can't see things in the dark, we can't fly unaided – all things that are thought of, especially in philosophical conversations, as constituting commonsense reality. The level of resolution with which we view the world, the amount of detail we see in it, is dependent on the human scale of existence. If we start to observe phenomena that are invisible at the normal human scale by using microscopes, telescopes, particle accelerators, x-rays, computer models, etc., then we are changing the resolution of our viewing position. We are extending our knowledge of the universe by increasing the level of resolution at which we observe things. Having gained the ability to alter the level of resolution with which we observe the world, the question must arise as to how far one can go in magnifying, particle accelerating, deep-space probing before no more levels of resolution can be found. In other words, what are the limits of the universe and of our knowledge about it?

New information, new truth

Since all human existence is conducted at the normal human scale to which certain physical laws apply *before any investigations outside of that scale are made*, then it is natural for researchers to assume that such laws will extend to all scales that are now, or ever will be, observable. This was very much Newton's view (or at least the view of his followers), when he extended laws governing motion on earth to cosmic motion, on the assumption that the same logic would apply at any scale since the laws of motion must be universal. Early in the twentieth century it was shown that whilst laws of motion may be accurate and useful at the human scale, they are not so on an cosmic scale. Einstein showed that minute variations in gravitational pull have significant impact on the trajectory of large masses, and that the cosmos is by no means a reliable machine that obeys regular, fixed laws.

In Post-Human terms, there are no limits to knowledge about the universe. It can be extended indefinitely.

Through using improved measuring equipment and mathematical modelling, Einstein exceeded the level of resolution of observation that was available to Newton. Consequently, a different logic, relativity theory, was need to explain the new data. Yet, relativity theory immediately seemed at odds with human experience at the normal scale: time is shaped like a banana, people can travel in spaceships and come back to earth years younger than their twin, my watch is slower on a moving train than the clock on the platform. With the advent of sub-atomic research and quantum mechanics things got even stranger: one particle can be in several places simultaneously, experiments seem to know what outcome the experimenter expected and so on. Scientists even found it necessary to institute a maxim, Heisenberg's Uncertainty Principle, which states that it is experimentally impossible to measure the position of a sub-atomic particle and its velocity at the same time. Sub-atomic events can only be regarded as probabilities rather than the certainties implied by classical mechanics (for a fuller description, see Chapter 7). From the current findings of particle and astro-physics it seems that however deeply we probe into space or sub-atomic particles, at whatever resolution we view the universe, we get no closer to grasping its ultimate nature. In fact, we only discover that the universe is more complex and mysterious than we could have imagined. Yet we continue to explore it largely on the assumption that since things seem to obey laws at a human scale they must inevitably do so at all scales, whether we have yet observed them or not. Such an assumption is at the root of Einstein's objection to the Copenhagen interpretation of quantum reality which sees sub-atomic events as essentially probabilistic. He believed that in the same way human-scale phenomena seemed to have a cause, all other phenomena should abide by the same logic – that is, they should not be entirely random and 'causeless'. He could not accept that God played dice with the universe.

The universe will always be more complex than we will ever understand and it is dishonest of scientists who dream of final theories not to admit this

Ultimate theories

Science will never achieve its aim of comprehending the ultimate nature of reality. It is a futile quest, although many scientists do not acknowledge this yet. The universe will always be more complex than we will ever understand and it is dishonest of scientists who dream of final theories not to admit this. It might be said, in the defence of scientists, that comprehending the ultimate nature of reality is not their aim. I would argue that even though it may not be the aim of all scientists, there is a powerful and significant body of theory that has an implied trajectory towards ultimate comprehension.

'However, if we do discover a complete theory, it should in time be understandable in broad principle by everyone, not just a few scientists. Then we shall all, philosophers, scientists, and just ordinary people, be able to take part in the discussion of the question of why it is that we and the universe exist. If we find the answer to that, it would be the ultimate triumph of human reason – for then we would know the mind of God.'

Stephen Hawking, *A Brief History of Time*, p. 175

The possibility, however remote it might be in the mind of any cosmologist or physicist, that there is an ultimate and unifying explanation of all nature, I would argue, has not been forsaken. The justification often given for investment in huge particle accelerators is that the knowledge gained will lead us closer to understanding the origins of the universe, and possibly the 'secret of the universe'.

'The question of the existence of a 'Secret of the Universe' amounts to discovering whether there is some deep principle from which all other knowledge of the physical world follows.'

John Barrow, *Theories of Everything*, p. 201

Whatever the validity of such a goal, there are those in the scientific community who believe in the dream. The dream is that the materialist scientific project has within its methodology the capacity to understand all aspects of natural phenomena. That is, given enough time and enough resources, all aspects of nature will succumb to scientific understanding.

'The dream of a final theory inspires much of today's work in high energy physics, and though we do not know what the final laws might be or how many years will pass before they are discovered, already in today's theories we think we are beginning to catch glimpses of the outlines of a final theory.'

Steven Weinberg, *Dreams of a Final Theory*, ix

This hope is not new. Barrow cites a theory of everything proposed by Bernhard Riemann in the nineteenth century and Laplace, with his concept of the *Mécanique céleste*, is often noted for his over enthusiastic response to Newtonian mechanics in the eighteenth century. The theory of everything is rooted in the humanist project. The basic optimism that humans, through the tool of science, will be able to rationalise the totality of natural phenomena is an inevitable corollary to the belief that humans are the most important things in the universe. The humanists see no reason, ultimately, why human knowledge should be limited and science is the means through which their knowledge can be expanded – without limit.

To know the ultimate nature of the universe (or, if you prefer, the 'Theory of Everything' or the 'Final Theory') would require knowing everything about the universe, everything that has happened and everything that will happen. One cannot restrict a theory of everything to an arbitrarily disjointed branch of study, e.g. physics. One cannot propose a theory of everything and then say that it might leave some things out. If *one* thing were not known it would imply that all knowledge of the universe is partial, incomplete and, therefore, not ultimate. Since it is impossible even accurately to measure the coastline of Britain because there is no defined point where the coast stops and the sea starts, then how can we ever be confident that we will be able to isolate and measure *any* finite entity in the universe?

'All measurement methods ultimately lead to the conclusion that the typical coastline's length is very large and so ill determined that it is best considered infinite. Hence, if one wishes to compare different coastlines from the viewpoint of "extent", length is an inadequate concept.'

Benoit Mandelbrot, *The Fractal Geometry of Nature*, p. 25

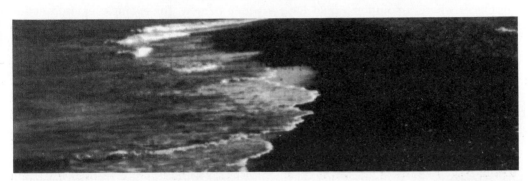

All measurement must be relative and contingent and all knowledge must be relative and contingent. We can know more, or less, but not everything. The notion of an ultimate explanation of the universe implies *absolute* knowledge of the universe. Even if there were a brain large enough to store all this information it would not only have to be as big as the universe it knew about, but bigger in order to contain all the information it knew about itself. We are starting now to think of the universe as an integrated and complex whole rather than a clockwork machine made up of discrete parts that obey fixed laws. Yet we are left, inevitably, with traces of the humanist dream in the completion of science.

I do not argue that we should abandon science in general, or even high-energy physics in particular. What I argue against is the allocation of limited resources, both intellectual and financial, to a project that has no hope of being fulfilled. To hold out the hope of a final solution in return for securing huge funding (as in the case of CERN or the Superconducting Super Collider) can only be done in ignorance or with dishonesty. I would argue that such resources would be better targeted at other problems where a solution would have a wider benefit, for example environmental pollution, the crumbling former-Soviet nuclear reactors and weapons systems, and global resource management.

The illusion of cause and effect

Many fundamentalist beliefs of science, such as the assumption of a final theory and the belief that all things must have causes, arise from the problem of resolution that we described earlier. As we have said, the difficulty in answering certain questions lies in the fact that we assume the laws that sustain predictability on a human scale must be extendable to all scales. That is, because most questions we ask are answered largely to our satisfaction, we assume that all other questions can be answered in a similar way. For example, if the question 'Why have you brought an umbrella?' is answered with the statement, 'Because it is going to rain,' enough information has been provided to satisfy the demands implied by the question. However, the conversation could continue, 'How do you know it's going to rain?' Reply, 'Because the sky is full of black clouds.' 'Why is the sky full of black clouds?' 'Because there's a

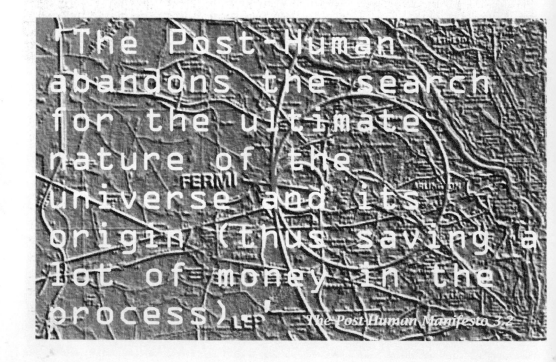

'The Post-Human abandons the search for the ultimate nature of the universe and its origin (thus saving a lot of money in the process).' *The Post-Human Manifesto 3.2*

> 'The Post-Human
> realises that the
> ultimate questions
> about existence and
> being do not
> require answers.
> The answer to the
> question "Why are
> we here?" is that
> there is no
> answer.'

The Post-Human Manifesto 3.3

trough of low pressure over the area.' 'Why is there a trough of low pressure over the area?' and so on until we travel through the bounds of known science into cosmic speculation. In other words, no question starting with 'why' can ever receive a complete answer. This is because no phenomena has any original cause or single determinate beginning. We can only make relatively precise judgements as to the causes or origins of an event.

To take another example, chaos theory or the theory of sensitive initial states if often *chaos* illustrated with reference to the 'butterfly effect'. Briefly, this states that the relatively insignificant flap of a butterfly wing in, say, Africa can ultimately *cause* a storm in Canada since the insect's movement will be magnified from a tiny gust, to a breeze, to a wind and finally to a storm. Initially this seems seductive, and yet we must ask, what caused the butterfly to flap its wings? A gust of wind perhaps? The search for origins is as futile as the search for the ultimate explanation of the universe since, finally, they are the same thing.

All who claim to seek causes for phenomena should remember that all causes have causes. Likewise, it is futile to seek the origin of the universe, since all origins have origins.

All origins are ends and all ends are origins.

Ordering the universe

'Whatever is the ultimate nature of reality (assuming that this expression has meaning), it is indisputable that our universe is not chaos. We perceive beings, objects, things to which we give names. These beings or things are forms or structures endowed with a degree of stability; they take up some part of space and last for some period of time.'

René Thom, *Structural Stability and Morphogenesis, p.1*

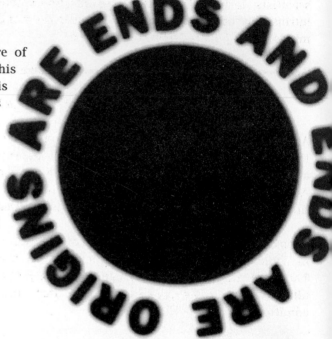

If we accept that the universe has no origins and no ultimate explanation then we must at least be able to say that it does follow some patterns and rules – there are forms and structures. If this were not the case, everything would be totally random and nothing would be predictable. The sun always rises, things always fall downwards, computers always crash just before you've saved your work. These facts would imply that the universe is intrinsically ordered in some way, even if we do not understand all the ways in which this might be so. We will shortly come to the question of why we perceive order in the universe, but first we should consider the scientific attitude to disorder.

Scientists traditionally give privilege to order over disorder in the assumption that they are gradually discovering the essential laws of nature. Until recently the whole point of classical scientific method was that understanding arose through establishing what was predictable, certain and repeatable in anything under investigation. James Gleick quotes mathematician James Yorke in *Chaos*:

'The first message is that there is disorder. Physicists and mathematicians want to discover regularities. People say, what use is disorder. But people have to know about disorder if they are going to deal with it . . . They're running a physical experiment, and the experiment behaves in an erratic manner. They try to fix it or give up. They explain the erratic behaviour by saying there's noise, or just that the experiment is bad.'

Gleick p. 68

Speculation stimulated by the surreal results of particle accelerator research has led scientists such as David Bohm to question whether there is such a thing as an intrinsically ordered universe or whether the notion of order merely exists in our minds and is *imposed* upon the universe?

'Is order simply within the mind? or does it have an objective reality of its own?'

David Bohm, *Science, Order and Creativity, p. 120*

As well as perpetuating the mind/reality separation, this notion still has at its heart the implication that true understanding only arises when we can distil the order out of a system, thereby dispelling the disorder that is synonymous with non-understanding. According to such science, whether order is in the mind or in reality, the fact that a final order for everything is being sought is the predominant concern.

'This book, however, proposes that the notion that everything that happens takes place in some order (which, however, depends on broader contexts for its meaning). Therefore, while there is ambiguity within particular contexts, the notion of an ultimate limit to the meaning of order that holds in all possible contexts is not admitted.'

ibid. p. 135

The search for order and regularity at the expense of disorder and irregularity is a fundamental error. Nature is neither essentially ordered nor disordered. What we perceive as regular, patterned information we classify as order; what we perceive as irregular, unpatterned information we classify as disorder. This tells us more about the way in which we process information than it does about the intrinsic presence of order or disorder in nature. Humanist science assumes that all phenomena are subject to physical laws and that some of those laws are well understood, some partially understood, and some unknown.

The humanist contempt of disorder

'The myth of science as a purely logical process, constantly reaffirmed in every textbook, article and lecture, has an overwhelming influence on scientists' perceptions of what they do. Even though scientists are aware of the non-logical elements of their work, they tend to suppress or at least dismiss them as being of little consequence. A major element of the scientific process is thus denied existence or significance.'

William Broad and Nicholas Wade, *Betrayers of the Truth, p. 126*

Such a view could equally well be expressed in relation to the scientific view of order and disorder. When considering the concept of order we must lay equal emphasis on the notion of disorder that is displaced in general by our culture and in particular by humanist science. In this regard it is interesting to note that, historically, science has often operated under a paradigm of conquest not dissimilar to the imperial mentality that engulfed Europe in the nineteenth century. The attempts to define 'disorder' and 'order' according to social values were intimately connected with what purported to be *discovery* of natural law but in fact turned out merely to be *construction* determined by prejudice and the promotion of self interest. Scientists 'discovered' things in the same way that people 'discovered' African tribes (the implication being that they did not exist prior to discovery).

The overall aim was the conquest of chaotic nature and disorderly heathens in the name of civilisation and progress – progress being the desire to increase the rate of material consumption. Central to this is the imposition of a set of ideas, often supported by scientific theories, that constructed a universe in accordance with the desires and aspirations of certain interest groups. For example, 'discoveries' were made that women were mentally inferior to men ('illogical women'), or that blacks were 'natural slaves', or that people with certain facial characteristics were criminals. Particular behaviours were classified as 'disorders', such as homosexuality and masturbation, as though the act of classification itself were a discovery. In fact, we now accept that these were pure constructions masquerading as discoveries, which does not mean they were any less potent at the time they were in force. Many of Freud's theories concerning children and women's sexuality have now been discredited, as have many of the 'cures' he claimed to have effected. Was Freud discovering things about women and children in his researches, or was he constructing a theory which conformed to the prejudices that he, as a Victorian doctor, would have held? Was he attempting to impose a logical structure on that most illogical of things, the human mind, by imposing order on messy and disorderly phenomena? He would not have been the first, or the last, to do so.

What is clear is that scientists' attempts to construct an ordered universe do not occur in isolation from the dominant values of the times in which they live. Those dominant values tend to perpetuate the 'order of society' against those disorders that are deemed threatening. Throughout history there are many examples of science, or the name of science, being used to try and assert order in the face of the untidy complexity of the real world. From the 'scientific socialism' of Marx and Engels to the gruesome eugenics underpinning the 'new order' of the Third Reich, the concept of scientific infallibility has held out the prospect of 'cleaning-up' the irregularities of society. The historical role of science as the means by which order may ultimately be conferred on humanity and the universe is now rapidly being abandoned. It is no longer fashionable to believe that society can be ordered in any absolute way, any more than a large company or a local community can. We are rejecting the belief that any complex system can be ordered or understood in an orderly manner. We are starting to accept that those facts that we find difficult to formulate into tidy equations are not just pockets of transient ignorance that have yet to succumb to the rigours of scientific enquiry. Facts like stock market crashes, tornadoes, human eccentricities, riots, wars and quantum probabilities cannot be understood in terms of orderliness or linear functions. They cannot even be understood as 'disorders'. They are features of the essential complexity of the universe in which we live – a universe so complex that full understanding, in the commonly accepted sense, is beyond our grasp.

Belief and partial models

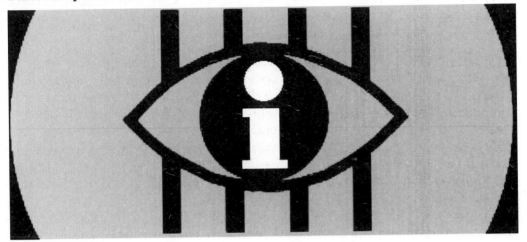

It is often the case that the less one knows the more one can believe.

All this speculation and research into the nature of life and the universe is often justified as a search for truth, as though the universe were concealing the truth about itself. What is clear is that all theories and explanations of all phenomena are simply *models* or descriptions that are more or less accurate, more or less useful. The model of the universe that was accurate, in that it was useful, to ancient societies was that the earth was flat and supported by an elephant. To other societies the truth consisted of the fact that all planets revolved around the earth. Later this truth was replaced by another which claimed that planetary motion could be defined according to fixed and universal laws. All these truths were models based on partial information, even though claims were often made that the models were complete, and in this respect are no different from the truths or models that we use in contemporary science. The problem with claiming any model is complete, or any absolute truth is knowable, is that to know anything *absolutely* requires that all factors that affect it can be accounted for. This means that all dimensions of a thing must be considered, which is impossible.

'The fundamental reasons for the stability of matter are still unknown and the stability of the proton remains unexplained . . . Furthermore, even when a system is controlled by explicit laws of evolution, it often happens that its qualitative behaviour is still not computable and predictable; as soon as the numbers of parameters of the system increase, the possibility of close calculation decreases – what Bellman has called the curse of dimensionality.'   Rene Thom, *Structural Stability and Morphogenesis, p. 322*

Dimensions are qualities of a thing that are used to describe it. For example, if we look at a snooker ball with a view to knowing everything about it, the complete truth about the ball, we could use the spatial dimensions x, y and z to plot its position relative to some arbitrary point, v to plot its velocity relative to some other speed and t to indicate the time in which it exists relative to some other arbitrary time. We would need to know its mass which is relative to gravity, volume which is relative to the sensitivity of our ruler, colour which is dependant on the lighting conditions and our viewing apparatus. In addition to these we would have to account for its reflectivity which will be uneven, its smell which is difficult to quantify, it greasiness, number and dimension of dents and chips, age, history, level of radioactivity, chemical composition, sentimental or financial value, social and economic conditions that brought about its manufacture . . . *ad infinitum.* Just because we choose not to consider most of these factors when we discuss a thing does not mean that they are irrelevant. They all contribute in some way to the phenomena of the snooker ball, but it would be impossible and impractical to take them all into account. So any model or description of any thing must of necessity exclude some relevant information about it, since nothing can be isolated from the context that allows it to exist in the first place.

Thus all models, or descriptions are partial although this does not mean they are not useful.

' . . . the dimension of the space and the number of degrees of freedom of a local system are quite arbitrary – in fact, the universal model of a process is embedded in an infinite-dimensional space. This is obviously necessary: there is no doubt that the closer the study approaches the infinitesimal, the more degrees of freedom are needed, so that all qualitative representation of microscopic phenomena will require the use of an infinite-dimensional function space.'   *ibid. p.6*

The scientific search for truth, therefore, can only be realistically considered as the search for *better models.* Models improve as we increase the resolution at which we are able to view things. If, then, we can abandon the dichotomy between 'truth' and 'falsity', with their implications of absoluteness, we must accept that belief must be contingent and arbitrary – contingent because we acknowledge the possibility of future investigations leading to different models and arbitrary because we can only model parts of the universe and never the whole. There is nothing wrong with producing models; there is little else we can do. The problem arises when *we equate the model to the reality that is being modelled.*

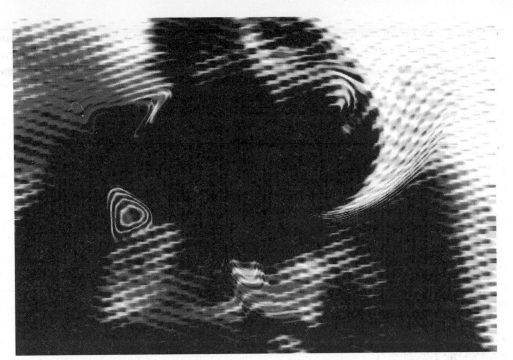

'The Post-Human is entirely at ease with the ideas
of "paranormality", "transcendence", the "supernatural", and the "occult". The Post-Human does not
accept that faith in scientific methods is superior
to faith in other belief systems.' *The Post-Human Manifesto 3.15*

The Post-Human conception of the universe

'To each partial system, relatively independent of the environment, we assign a local model that accounts qualitatively and, in the best cases, quantitatively for it's behaviour. But we cannot hope, a priori, to integrate all these local models into a global system. If it were possible to make such a synthesis, man could justifiably say that he knew the ultimate nature of reality, for there could exist no better global model.'

ibid. p. 7

As has been stated, there are no origins, ends, complete answers or final reasons for the existence of anything. There is no bottom or top to the universe. Our models about how the universe works are always going to be partial and incomplete, so we will never be able to produce a complete model of how everything works. The only global model of the universe is the universe itself. In addition, there are no absolute separations or divisions between any 'things', or between ourselves and the environment and, in fact, the self and the environment are more accurately conceived as one unified whole rather than as being disconnected.

However, this continuous view of the world does not seem to comply with our every-day experience in which things *do* seem separate and self-contained. Why is it that the world seems to be made up of lots of separate things interacting with each other and which cause things to happen to each other, if everything is a unified whole – if there are no absolute divisions between things? To help with an understanding of this problem, Post-Humans propose that:

Everything **that exists** *anywhere* **is** *energy.*

Energy has four properties:
1. It is everything and everywhere
2. It is manifested in an infinite variety of ways
3. It is perpetually transforming
4. It always has been and always will be the above

If anything is ultimate about the universe, this is it. Nothing can exist that is not energy. Even an abstraction, such as memory or emotion, needs energy to be thought or stored.

Energy and matter

For thousands of years scientists and thinkers have assumed that the universe must be 'made' of some fundamental stuff that would account for the solid matter we see all around us. The ancient Greeks thought that atoms were the irreducible particles from which all other matter was formed. The common wisdom amongst nineteenth century scientists and philosophers was that *ether* was the most basic material in the universe. In the early twentieth century Einstein called into question the distinction between matter and energy. Subsequent research posited the existence of a complex sub-atomic universe that included quarks, gluons and positrons amongst others. In investigating such phenomena it proved impossible to maintain the traditional distinction between particles and waves since both displayed qualities of the other. As we suggested in Chapter 1, it has become more practical to consider such sub-atomic particles as forces or energy transformations rather than actual stuff, i.e. solid matter. What appears as solid matter on one level, for example a piece of metal, turns into a web of volatile energy packets when investigated at a quantum level. A planet may appear as a large mass in the sky, but on closer inspection may turn out to be a ball of vapour, which in turn will be made of tiny packets of energy. Sub-atomic researchers are continually proposing the building of huge particle accelerators to see if there are any more fundamental particles than those already known. In the light of all this we might question whether the traditional concept of matter being made of anything other than interacting forces is still viable. Is there an ultimate matter that cannot be reduced to anything else? So far it has not been found. The results of scientific research would seem to support the idea that matter, as a final and fundamental substance, is not a reality but only seems like solid 'stuff' at the human scale. It is more useful to think of the universe manifested as energy packets, energy waves, energy transformations.

To then ask the question 'What is energy?' is to make the same mistake as asking 'Why are we here?' – it assumes there is an answer.

Everything is energy

If we can accept that everything is energy, devoid of any final stuff or substance but only solid when viewed from a certain position, it profoundly affects the way we consider the universe. It means that all we can talk about or describe, at any level of enquiry, is the process of transformation of energy. In one way, this greatly simplifies the universe since it means that all scientific and philosophical end-eavour has a common base – that is describing the way in which energy is transformed. However, merely by saying everything is energy does not reduce the universe to a undifferentiated whole. What makes the universe seem so complex is the variety of ways in which energy is manifested and the diversity of the transformations it undergoes. Clearly the energy in a fire is not the same as energy contained in a block of ice. This does not negate the fact that all we talk about, and talk with, is energy, and all *things* are representations of energy in varying states.

Consider any object or process. Any information we have about it is energetic, for example, its colour, the noise it makes, its weight. Humans are masses of energy. Living humans, operating in societies, represent complex energy flows of production and consumption. Humans represent energy in electrical, chemical, kinetic and magnetic forms. The galaxies are vast and uncharted fields of energetic forces such as light, radiation, gravity and mass. Even time itself cannot be measured or comprehended in any terms other than changes of energies, a clock hand moving, a candle burning, an atom oscillating.

There is no final stuff in the universe, not even on a sub-atomic scale. When we put our hand on a table and the hand is resisted, the 'stuff' that is resisting, that we call matter, is a particular form of energy exerting an equal and opposite force to our hand. The fact that the table and hand are composed of smaller, identifiable packets of energy merely proves the same point on a different scale.

The universe is a process of energies
The environment is a process of energies
The body is a process of energies
Consciousness is a process of energies

Whilst we have many theories and much knowledge about all the different forms energy takes, all we can really say about it is that it changes from one form to another.

If a light is turned on, energy has changed
If a bomb explodes, energy has changed
If the grass grows, energy has changed
If the sun sets, the body sweats,
the mice eat and the wings beat – energy has changed.

In this sense we can see that humans and the environment are different expressions of energy. The only difference between them is the form that energy takes. Moreover, as stated in the previous chapter, they are totally integrated.

Energy and order

There is a law of physics, known as the Second Law of Thermodynamics, that states that in any conversion of energy from one form to another some is lost to the system. This law, also known as entropy, describes the tendency of ordered systems to gradually decay into disorder through energy loss. For example, in a steam engine (for which the second law was originally developed) the conversion of heat to mechanical energy is only efficient to a degree of 50 to 80 percent. The rest of the energy is lost through noise, heat escape and friction. More heat energy, therefore, is put into the system than is reclaimed as mechanical energy. To be able to maintain a particular state of order (in this case a working steam engine) requires constant input of energy. Steam engines will not spontaneously start working on their own. Left to themselves, steam engines will remain in a virtually static state, although some very slow decay will occur due to oxidisation of the metal, etc. The implication of entropy is that any structured system can only exist by virtue of the energy that is consumed in creating it and maintaining it. Without such energetic input the system would decay into a 'disordered' state; it would lose its form and structure and become a shapeless, formless noise. The notion of entropy has since been extended to refer to many systems other than steam engines. It has been used, for example, to state that the whole universe is inevitably decaying into a formless void on the basis that energy seeks a state of equilibrium (the 'heat death of the universe'). It is suggested that all the forms we know in the universe represent energy in a state of non-equilibrium and that, owing to entropy, this condition will be resolved into equilibrium. In simple terms, 'everything goes downhill'.

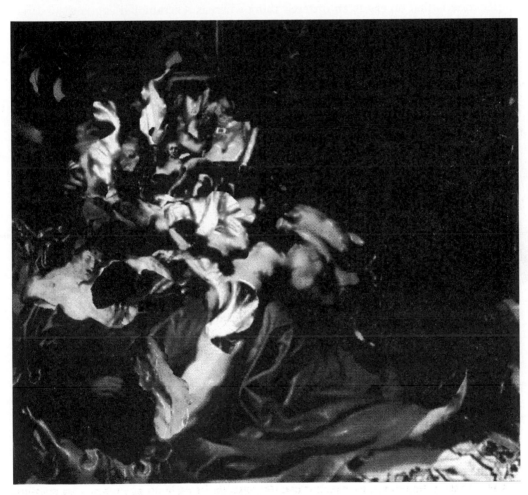

Nothing is permanent

My argument against this is that such a scenario might be true if there were a finite amount of energy in the universe. In a closed system, energy can be used up and a state of equilibrium reached. But as far as the universe is concerned, there is no reason to believe that there is a limited supply of energy. The universe, so far as we can tell, is infinite in size. Why, therefore, should it not contain an infinite amount of energy? With an infinite supply of energy there is no reason to suppose that an infinite number of forms cannot be created and maintained. In addition to this, I dispute the objective use of the terms 'order' and 'disorder' as though they were some sort of absolute states. Entropy is often summarised in the phrase 'you can't unscramble an egg'. The implication is that an egg is an ordered thing whereas a scrambled egg is disordered and the process of disordering is irreversible. As will be made clear in Chapter 3, order and disorder are not absolute, objective states, but products, jointly, of the condition of things in the environment and our subjective perception of them.

In Post-Human terms we take order to mean those things that display *more* perceptible form or structure and disorder to mean those things that display *less*. Any form or structure is something that embodies energy in a state of non-equilibrium. Any act of creation requires the consumption of energy and the thing created embodies the energy expended in its creation. In order to maintain its form, that thing must resist the tendency of the energy it embodies to decay into a state of equilibrium. Creation involves the transformation of energy from one state to another. It does not matter that, in the process of creation, some energy may be lost since there is always enough spare energy in the universe to create all the forms we know and more. Some scientists have claimed that life violates the second law on the grounds that energy should be decaying into formless disorder rather than forming ever richer organic and chemical structures.

'A living organism could be defined as a system that maintains and even expands its ordered structures by constantly taking up external energy. This does not contradict the second law. A steam engine also runs for a very long time if it is continually stoked. The supply of energy is thus employed for maintaining and expanding structures. On earth, this energy comes mostly from the sun . . . The survival of life is understandable in principle, then, as long as the necessary transformations and material flows are financed by a large energy supply. In this sense life is very expensive.'

F. Cramer, *Chaos and Order*, p. 16

Cramer makes the case that order *(more* perceptible form) emerges spontaneously in certain media given the appropriate influx of energy. He cites the case of Bérnard instability, a phenomenon whereby visual patterns emerge in a heated liquid when there is a critical temperature difference in plates below and above the liquid. What this and many other examples demonstrate is the fundamental role energy plays in the formation of structures in the universe. The deduction is that everything that has perceptible form, from DNA to distant galaxies, relies for that form on the state of energy which it embodies.

Differences in energy

The infinite way in which energy is expressed allows us to understand the apparent separateness of things in the world. Humans, being manifestations of energy with a certain level of stability, are sensitive to particular intensities of energy such as x frequency of light, x amount of heat, x exposure to radiation and so on. If the intensities of energy to which the human is exposed fall outside those which are able to induce change in the sensory medium then they will have little or no effect on the person. If they fall within the sensitivity range of the sensory medium, then exposure to them will cause change in the person, a shift in their energy state. For example, sudden exposure to a red light will induce a shift in the energy state of the optical apparatus that is sensitive to that frequency and may have consequential effects such as a driver stopping their car at a traffic light.

Because energy is manifested in so many different ways, and in ways that seem to us either very permanent or very fleeting because of our particular time scale as humans, it seems that there are separate things in the universe, things that are divided from us. We see rocks, trees, stars, lights, gases, animals which to us all look like separate things. They seem to have boundaries and self-contained behaviour patterns. We know they are made of different substances and display different characteristics. But, because things display differing characteristics we are unable to think of their common attribute – the fact that they are all manifestations of energy. Because of the different manifestations of energy in a diamond and us, it does not seem like there can be a very profound link, but there is. Both are largely composed of carbon.

'The appearance of matter is an illusion generated by interactions among things at the human level of resolution.'

The Post-Human Manifesto 3.13

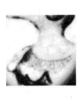

chapter

3

Order and Disorder, Continuity and Discontinuity

3. Order and Disorder, Continuity and Discontinuity

Recent scientific ideas have forced us to reassess how we perceive order and disorder. These new scientific ideas of chaos, catastrophe and complexity challenge the old humanist ideas of mechanism, reductionism and determinism and, as such, can be considered as the Post-Human sciences, or at least, as having Post-Human implications. In Post-Human terms, order and disorder are not irreconcilable opposites but properties that arise from the way in which we view the universe. 'Strange attractors' are products of the advances made in mathematical research since the introduction of computers. They represent something that is both ordered and disordered at the same time. In *Chaos*, James Gleick describes the early work of meteorologist Edward Lorenz. In the 1960s Lorenz was carrying out work on weather prediction using a computer to help with the large amount of calculations involved. He found that, during the long process of recursive calculation, a tiny difference between two input numbers would, over time, produce a huge difference in outcome. This phenomenon, known as 'sensitivity to initial conditions' is at the heart of what came to be known as chaos theory. In further work, Lorenz modelled systems such as water wheels which, given a constant supply of water, should have displayed predictable behaviour. Using three non-linear equations to model the system, he plotted the resulting output in graphic form as maps. Deterministic science would suggest that any system should, given a constant input of energy, settle into a regular pattern of behaviour – that order should arise:

'Instead, the map displayed a kind of infinite complexity. It always stayed within certain bounds, never running off the page but never repeating itself either. It traced a strange, distinctive shape, a kind of double spiral in three dimensions, like a butterfly with two wings. The shape signalled pure disorder, since no point or pattern of points ever recurred. Yet it also signalled a new kind of order.'

Gleick, *Chaos, p. 30*

The Lorenz attractor

There are many other examples in mathematics, topology and the study of dynamical systems that illustrate the surprising unity of order and disorder. In the study of bifurcations, fractals and non-linear systems it has become apparent that seemingly ordered procedures can give rise to seemingly disordered results. Ivar Ekeland describes the well-known example of the 'Bernoulli shift' in his book *Mathematics and the Unexpected*. The Bernoulli shift (known as the Baker transformation) consists in taking a regular object, such as a square shaped piece of dough, and applying a simple transformation. The dough is stretched to twice its width and half its height. Then it is cut in half and one half put on top of the other.

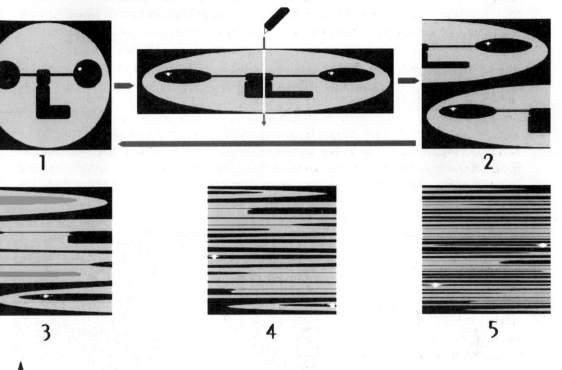

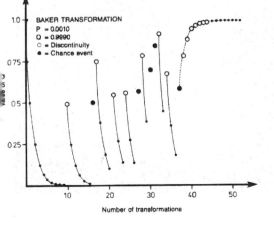

Left: A graph showing the effect of repeated Baker's transformations. After the tenth transformation a large discontinuity occurs, represented by the value Q. From then on the process becomes seemingly erratic and unpredictable, with no apparent continuity in the value of Q despite the orderliness of the transformation.

The transformation is repeated many times, a process known as iteration. Although this seems on the surface a very deterministic, orderly procedure it soon leads to the appearance of chaos. If two close points in the dough are followed around through the iterations it is soon apparent they start to diverge from each other in a dramatic way. In fact, after a critical number of iterations the position of the points becomes unpredictable. As Ekeland says,

Illustration of bifurcation

' . . . this process leads quickly to chaos – apparently to total disorder. Any small piece of the square is spread more and more evenly throughout the whole . . . until there is an equal likelihood of meeting it anywhere in the square.'   Ekeland, *op.cit. p. 52*

Ekeland concludes (and he is not the only one) that apparently predictable, ordered phenomena can give rise to unpredictable, disordered phenomena. At a certain critical point in the iteration a discontinuity occurs. The smooth, continuous graph that plots the point's position up to a certain number of transformations suddenly jumps and a split, or *bifurcation*, occurs that leads the process in two directions at once. Each branch can then split in the same way leading, within a short time, to a hugely complex and chaotic state.

These ideas are discussed at length with great clarity in a number of books on the subject of chaos (see Bibliography). For a fuller understanding of the concepts, I recommend that you refer to these since it is not within the scope of this book to reiterate their mathematical proofs. The point I wish to make clear is this: it is now widely accepted that the traditional dichotomy between order and disorder is no longer valid.

'Order and chaos, regularity and unpredictability, are woven together like land and sea on the beach when the tide is drawing out, leaving behind a maze of puddles and wet sand, so that it is impossible to tell where the water ends and where the dry land begins.'   *ibid., p. 47*

As a result, the belief that ordered things are intrinsically different from disordered things can no longer be sustained. A new understanding of the relationship between order and disorder is emerging in the Post-Human era.

To illustrate how randomness can arise in an apparently deterministic system try the following experiment. Take a coin and place it on a vertical surface about 30 centimetres from the floor. Draw a circle around the coin. Now try letting the coin drop a number of times. Each time you should try to position the coin in the circle in the same way. No matter how many times you let it drop, or how accurately you try to position the coin, its landing position will always vary. The initial positioning of the coin is apparently fixed and determined yet it falls in a chaotic way.

4 heads

3 tails

5 tails

1 heads

2 heads

Relative order

The proof that order and disorder are relative qualities lies in the fact that one defines the other just as in language words do not have absolute meaning but acquire meaning in relation to each other (see Chapter 4). The amount of order or disorder in something can only be measured relatively. A thought experiment can demonstrate this. Imagine a box of matches. All the matches in the box are lined up in rows pointing the same way. There is a certain amount of order in the way the matches are arranged. Now imagine the matches are tipped out onto a table from a height of 30 centimetres. We would say that this pile of matches is disordered compared to how they were arranged in the box. Imagine that the matches in the pile were laid out end to end to form a rough line; we could say that we have restored a certain degree of order in that the matches in the line are more ordered that they were in the pile. If the same matches were then lined up on a totally flat surface using the most accurate laser measuring devices to ensure complete linearity so that we could say they were arranged in a perfectly straight line, all exactly the same distance apart, we would have attained a new degree of orderliness over that represented by our original, hand-made, line. Even in this case, there will not be absolute uniformity, since all the matches will vary slightly in length, width and curvature from each other. Therefore, this arrangement still contains a certain degree of disorder.

Anything we *perceive* can be considered to contain different degrees of order and disorder, regularity and chaos. Even the most seemingly orderly things we see are subject to very slight variations and irregularities if observation is carried out at a sufficiently high resolution. In other words, if you're looking for order it depends where you start.

'This distinction between regular and catastrophic points is obviously somewhat arbitrary because it depends on the fineness of the observation used.'   Thom, *op. cit. p.38*

'Order and
disorder
are
relative,
not
absolute
qualities.'

The Post-Human Manifesto 4.1

The appearance of order and disorder is subject to the level of resolution at which something is observed. Order and disorder are not intrinsic, objective facts that exist independently of their observation, although many scientists dispute this.

A scientific definition of disorder and complexity

What we perceive as ordered and disordered is often culturally determined and scientific authority is a strong force in determining cultural beliefs. Logicians will assert that there are mathematically 'objective' ways of defining disorder and complexity – ways that are independent of human subjectivity. Whilst these definitions may be useful in certain applications, they remain open to relativistic interpretation. One of the main ways in which disorder is measured is by determining the amount of entropy in a system. We have already encountered entropy in the previous chapter as the Second Law of Thermodynamics. We know that energy is required for the maintenance of form and structure and that during the process of converting energy from one form to another some is lost – normally in the form of heat. In the example that is often given of a box of gas, it is theoretically possible for the gas molecules to be distributed within the box in an infinite number of ways. For example, it is possible that all the molecules may decide to move into one corner of the box, although it is much more likely that they will be distributed roughly evenly throughout. The state in which the molecules are all collected in one corner of the box is described as low entropy, and the state where they are distributed evenly is called high entropy. Low entropy is usually associated with order (lack of randomness) and high entropy with disorder (a lot of randomness). This distinction is based on the law that the natural tendency of systems is to lose energy, the energy which is embodied in the order of the system. The natural tendency of systems is to energetic equilibrium. Without the intervention of some other energy source, the highly improbable states (which we know as order) turn into the more probable states of disorder – formless noise. Therefore, the gas collected in one corner is seen as ordered because it is a highly improbable state whereas the gas distributed evenly is called disordered because it is the most probable state – the closest to equilibrium.

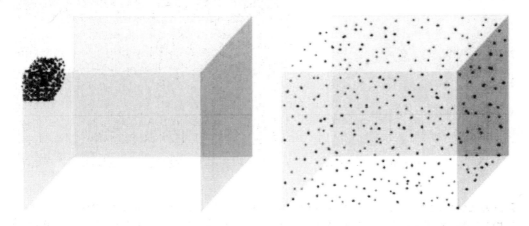

For an authoritative scientific account of this process I have turned to Roger Penrose and his book *The Emperor's New Mind*. Whilst this book is mainly concerned with refuting the claims made on behalf of the artificial intelligence community it also offers a valuable overview of the current thinking in many areas of contemporary scientific opinion. For, to give Penrose credit, the possibility is acknowledged in this account that not all people may agree on what order is. Speaking of a glass of water that has fallen from a table, only to be shattered on the floor, he ponders:

'It seems, also, that the various observers' aesthetic judgements might well get involved in what they deem to be 'order' rather that 'disorder'. We could imagine some artist taking the view that the collection of shattered glass fragments was far more beautifully ordered than was the hideously ugly glass that once stood on the edge of the table!'   Penrose, *op. cit. p. 401*

Penrose raises the question, is order a subjective quality imposed by an observer (admittedly one who, he thinks, has eccentric tastes) or is it a quantifiable attribute that can be objectively measured in scientific terms? Penrose, being a scientist, argues the latter although, in my view, he does so unconvincingly. He clearly admits that the shattered glass of water might be viewed as an orderly object if only it were practical to keep track of all the motions of particles dispersed by the crash.

'For, in a more subtle sense, the higher entropy state [disordered] in these situations [the broken glass] *is* just as "specially ordered" as the lower entropy state [ordered], owing to the very precise coordination of motions of the individual particles.'

ibid. p.399 (my insertions in box parentheses)

What he admits is just what I was about to say. That is, the molecules of glass and water dispersed across the floor are no less *intrinsically* ordered than those perched, however precariously, on the table. To return to our box of gas, that we find it harder to *perceive* the order in a random gas cloud as opposed to a structured gas cloud says as much about the way we perceive order as it does about any intrinsic order in the gas. For given the right viewing apparatus, the order in the 'random' cloud may display regularities of a subtle kind that would normally be invisible to us. The toss of a coin is normally taken as an emblem of randomness. One would not expect to find any order in a list of outcomes. Yet the tossing of a coin can also be seen as a totally deterministic process if all the factors of the toss are taken into account. Just because it is *impractical* to take all these factors into account does not mean the tossing of a coin is either purely random or purely deterministic. Randomness and determinism are qualities we ascribe to a process depending on the amount of factors we are able to control and observe.

Having given us an extensive mathematical definition of the objective measure of disorder, Penrose is obviously aware that it may still be vulnerable to subjective interpretation. He tries to rescue the validity of his 'objective' measure of disorder by claiming that 'Entropy refers to *manifest* disorder'. He does not provide evidence that the *manifest* nature of any ordered/disordered system is anything other than a subjective interpretation of that which appears to be manifest. It is merely based on the fact that the probable location of molecules in the un-smashed glass is more easily determined than their location once the glass has been broken. In other words, that which looks like order to us is manifest order and that which looks like disorder is manifest disorder. Again, we cannot refer to the intrinsic orderliness or disorderliness of any system but only what is within our power, as humans, to compute as orderliness or disorderliness.

I do not deny that humans perceive differing levels of order and disorder. I shall explain why we do. The mistake, however, that many scientists make is to assume that because we, as humans, perceive varying levels of order and disorder then these qualities must be essential properties of the universe that exist independently of our perception. The temptation then is to try to objectify them, to define them. As far as I can tell, such objectifications cannot proceed without introducing some element of subjective interpretation. Let us briefly consider whether complexity can be objectified.

'Complexity in the universe is an objective element, not a subjective chimera. A bacterium is objectively more complex than an atom, just as a mouse is objectively more complex than a bacterium.'

Ervin Laszlo, *The Creative Cosmos, p. 48*

On a commonsense level this seems perfectly reasonable – things that have more parts are more complex. However, we are reminded that 'commonsense is what makes the world seem flat' and that it is not necessarily the best guide. The truth is that no one knows how complex an atom is. Nor do we know how complex a mouse is. The results of sub-atomic research suggest that the atom may be infinitely complex in itself whilst also being subject to influences from other atoms at infinitely large distances. There is certainly no sense it which it can be claimed that we are close to a total understanding of an atom nor what non-local forces may influence its properties. To say that a mouse is more complex than an atom is merely to state that ∞^{10} is a greater sum than ∞^2, in other words, that one infinite thing is more complex than another. Does the universe care if we consider things to be complex or not? No, complexity is in the eye of the beholder.

As if to give concrete foundations to his argument, Ervin Laszlo (who, according to the sleeve notes, is 'considered the world's foremost exponent of systems philosophy and general evolution theory') refers us to an appendix in his book designed to remove any doubt we might have as to the objectivity of complexity (ibid. p. 233). He only succeeds in giving his argument concrete boots. Opening confidently by saying, 'There are ways of measuring complexity in real world phenomena that are independent of the subjective complexity experienced by observers', he goes on to offer three levels of proof, which I shall summarise. Firstly, we are told of a method of defining complexity that relies on the number of 'yes/no' choices needed to construct a system from its elements. Without explaining very clearly the operation of this method he immediately dismisses it as only being useful in 'comparatively simple' cases. Secondly, we are offered the Seth-Pagels method which, we are told, is a 'more sophisticated measure of complexity'. Seth-Pagels' 'thermodynamic depth' method states that complexity is greatest when a state is farthest away from total order and total randomness (as exemplified by atoms in a crystal lattice on the one hand and the molecules in a cloud of gas on the other). As has been made clear elsewhere, notions of *total* order and disorder are, at best, contingent. A crystal may be highly regular when viewed at one level but it is not totally ordered. At a quantum level its components are unpredictable. The simple act of observing it introduces some perturbations, however slight. A cloud of gas may seem very irregular when viewed at a certain level but it is not totally random. We have already stated that apparently random phenomena can have deterministic (that is, 'orderly') features if viewed with sufficient precision. Randomness and order remain partially subjective properties despite the assumptions of the 'thermodynamic depth' method. The final proof offered by Ervin Laszlo is the

'still more sophisticated measure of complexity' known as the Kolgomorov-Chaitin-Solomonoff definition, which turns out to be the weakest. After being offered a description of this precise algorithmic method we are immediately informed that, 'This program has been subsequently shown to be impossible to compute: the very concept of a general algorithm for finding the shortest program for computing a given entity involves a logical contradiction.' Surely this limits the usefulness of this method. Possibly realising the fragility of his case, Laszlo then concedes that 'no fully satisfactory measure of complexity has yet been devised' and goes on to generalise about complexity being somewhere in between order and chaos.

The end of objectivity and quantification

Whilst it might be in the interests of humanist scientific method to propose that we can objectify disorder and complexity, it is certainly a task fraught with subjective assumptions and severe limitations. Humanist science (as opposed to sciences with Post-Human implications such as chaos, catastrophe and complexity) has traditionally sought to objectify and quantify, to reduce the subjectivity and qualitative nature of human experience.

'Newton based his theoretical work on the belief that the project of natural philosophy was to explain all there was in heaven and earth through the fundamental measurables, the quantifiable qualities of matter and motion – size, shape, distance and hardness. This metaphysical commitment to sticking numbers on things and then explaining their behaviour by reducing the numbers to abstract law-forms written in algebra, has become a dominant aesthetic in modern science – an ethic, even – and a dominant process in the management of social affairs.'

Mike Hales, *Science or Society?, p. 122*

The Post-Human view of science does not deny the validity of the use of algebraic methods in modelling the universe, since that is what computers (which have given rise to Post-Humanism) use to do their calculations. But the thing that has become clear from the use of computers to model reality in an algebraic way is that natural phenomena are essentially unquantifiable. That is, reality is so complex, so sensitive to initial conditions that no computation, however complex, will be able to account for all the phenomena we see around us. Speaking of the early Lorenz experiments with computer-based weather forecasting and their unpredictable results, James Gleick writes:

'It was only a wobble from a clumsy computer. Lorenz could have assumed something was wrong with his particular machine or his particular model – probably *should* have assumed. It was not as though he had mixed sodium and chlorine and got gold. But for reasons of mathematical intuition that his colleagues would begin to understand only later, Lorenz felt a jolt: something was philosophically out of joint. The practical import could be staggering. Although his equations were gross parodies of the earth's weather, he had faith that they captured the essence of the real atmosphere. That first day, he decided long-range weather forecasting must be doomed."

Gleick, op. cit. p. 17

Reality is essentially non-computable, although this does not mean that we cannot produce sophisticated models of systems with a limited number of parameters. Computers allow us to produce such models to a degree of sophistication never before possible. What we should be wary of, however, is confusing the model of reality with reality itself. Ironically, whilst those sciences with Post-Human implications may be seeking to achieve the same ends as humanist science, namely to complete modelling of the universe by computational means, the resulting computer-based calculations that ought to have made the job easier have pointed to the very impossibility of achieving this end. Computers have revealed the futility of *complete* computational modelling. We can create a computer model that displays *qualitatively* similar behaviour to real world phenomena, but it can never be *quantitatively* precise.

Therefore, the attempts outlined above to quantify notions of order and disorder in anything other than an abstract sense are flawed on the grounds that the quantification is only valid for an idealised, isolated system. Since in nature there do not exist any real isolated systems, we are forced to deal with the qualitative aspects of real phenomena, and qualitative properties are, by definition, subjective. Our discussion of consciousness in Chapter 1 is a case in point. Scientists have tried to quantify consciousness by treating it as an isolated system, something that is restricted to the brain. This is the materialist view that consciousness is an objective property of a certain type of matter. In the Post-Human view, consciousness is a quality that emerges from the co-presence of a number of complex factors, of which the brain is only one. Since the number of factors is so enormous (the billions of active neurons being only a part) the complexity involved is of such a high order that we are excluded from quantifying the process – it cannot be isolated. We are forced to accept that our knowledge of consciousness will remain subjective, although this does not rule out the possibility that we might be able to produce a qualitatively analogous form of consciousness in a non-human medium.

Difference, order and energy

We have stated that order and disorder, like complexity and simplicity, cannot be quantified in an objective sense, but must remain open to some subjective, relativistic interpretation. This is not to say that qualities of order and complexity have no meaning; we will often refer to them in subsequent chapters. What it means is that certain things will appear as more complex or behave in a more orderly way when viewed at a certain level of resolution. The normal level of resolution is the human scale of observation and at this scale certain things seem ordered and disordered, complex and simple. But just because we view them in this way at the human scale does not mean they are *intrinsically* ordered or complex, since they may look different when viewed at other resolutions.

Given that we are not denying that humans perceive order and disorder, how do such perceptions arise? As discussed in the previous chapter, the universe can be considered as a flux of energy states in continual transformation. There is no finite substance to which all matter will finally be reducible. Although this might seem theoretically acceptable at the sub-atomic scale, it seems less relevant at the normal human level of perception where there does seem to be difference, contrast and conflict between solid, separate things. As a result of viewing such things on a daily basis, we believe that such forms and structures around us display more or less order. For example, looking in a garden we see leaves, flowers, branches which are all more or less static. They all seem to be separate from each other. The grass seems to have no discernible effect on the leaves of the tree. All the shapes seem consistent and stable, which would indicate that there is a natural order. Even if we acknowledge that no two blades of grass are exactly the same, there must be some essential regularity in the way it grows each spring, year after year. How is it, then, that we can claim that in this garden nothing is separate and there is no intrinsic order?

In Post-Human terms, the apparent distinctions between 'things' and their perceived qualities of order and disorder are not the result of innate divisions within the structure of the universe. Nor are they a product of any intrinsic, objective order that the universe contains. They are *jointly* a product of:

a. the variety of ways in which energy is manifested in the universe
b. the way in which the sensual processes in living entities operate

Energy in the universe is manifested in an infinite variety of ways. Even within the standard energy demarcations of light, heat, sound, potential, electrical, chemical, etc. there are unlimited variations of intensity and temporality. In fact, no two occurrences of any event are exactly the same. They must occur at either a different time or different place or else they cannot be distinguished from each other.

'One cannot step twice into the same river, nor can one grasp any mortal substance in a stable condition, but it scatters and again gathers; it forms and dissolves, and approaches and departs.'
Heraclitus, Fragment LI

Organisms respond to varying quantities, and to different qualities, of energetic stimuli – between levels of light, noise and smell for example. The organic structure of a living thing will adapt chemically, electrically, metabolically when changes of a significant degree occur in its environment. For example, a sudden drop in atmospheric temperature might lead to goosebumps and shivering. Energy shifts in the environment of a certain level will be reflected through changes in the organism and metabolic changes result. In simple terms, the organism will be aware that some 'thing' has happened. If such stimuli are perceived to occur with some regularity, then this may be counted as order. For example, the sun has risen every day on earth for many billions of years, and may continue to do so for many billions more, so the stimulus it provides generates a certain sense of order on earth. The fact that the sun did not always rise on earth (prior to the existence of earth) and that it will not always do so (when the sun dies) suggests that the sense of order it gives rise to is not eternal. From this we can see that difference and order need not be considered as objective, eternal properties that humans can observe in an impartial way. It is perfectly consistent with current scientific thinking (although not all would agree) to suggest that difference and order in the universe are qualities that *appear* to an observer. No doubt the force of this appearance leads us to believe that they are facts independent of our observing them, hence the belief that the universe must be, in some way, intrinsically differentiated and ordered. This belief, historically, has given rise to

the assumption of eternal and universal 'laws of nature', and the attempt by humanist science to uncover them.

Continuity and discontinuity

Whilst the ways in which energy might mutate and transform are infinite and often unpredictable, the ways in which energy manifestations are perceived by an observer can always be described with two simple qualities – continuity and discontinuity. Continuity is non-interruption of space-time. Discontinuity is a rupture in space-time. Both qualities can be discerned in all events depending upon how they are viewed. In other words, one phenomenon can be said to display a certain amount of continuity but may be relatively less continuous than another phenomenon. It may display relative amounts of stability and instability or relative amounts of similarity and difference.

Qualities as perceived by an observer

It is crucial is to note that energy manifestations should not be thought of as *intrinsically* continuous or discontinuous, that is there are no absolute qualities of energy. Energetic states will appear as either continuous or discontinuous to an observer depending upon their viewing position, that is, the quality of (dis)continuity is *context sensitive*. To take an apparently simple example, look at the arrangement of dots in this diagram.

To an observer there are several expressions of continuity and discontinuity in this diagram.

1. The dots are the same size and shape as each other (continuity)
2. The edges of the dots are distinct from the paper, which is white (discontinuity)
3. The dots form a row (continuity)
4. One dot deviates from the row (discontinuity)
5. The space between the dots is even (continuity)
6. The white paper has been disrupted by the dots (discontinuity)
7. The ink of the black dots is solid within their boundaries (continuity)
8. The dots are stable and do not move in relation to the page (continuity)

These qualities only apply when you are holding this book a few feet away from your eyes. Decreasing the level of resolution (moving far away) would see the dots merging into a single line as with newspaper photographs which, when magnified, are made of discrete dots that merge to give the impression of a continuous image when viewed from a short distance (see pages 12 and 13). Increasing the level of resolution shows that the dots are a broken and irregular stain on a web of paper fibres and a detailed comparison reveals that each of the dots is unique in that the paper fibres and ink distribution is complex. Therefore, what can be considered as continuous or discontinuous is subject to the resolution of the viewing position. There are no absolute continuities or discontinuities. They are defined in relation to each other.

Consider the next diagram.

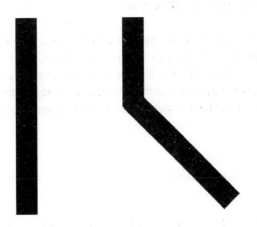

Whilst the line on the left displays discontinuity inasmuch as the black ink is separate from the white paper, the shape itself can be considered a continuous line. The line on the right has the distinction of having a further discontinuity by way of an angular bend at its centre.

One line is straight, one is bent.

Consider some phrases common in the English language:

Bent as a ten bob note
Bent as a banana
Straight and narrow
Crook (as in villain)
I put them straight
A straight person
Bent cop
Kinky and straight sex

Implied in these phrases is the notion that continuity (straightness) is synonymous with order, the rule of law and honesty whereas discontinuity (bentness) represents disorder, dishonesty and deviation (as in kinky, twisted, warped, etc.).

The extent to which continuity and discontinuity are fundamental to our ability to perceive order and disorder cannot be over-stressed. All difference and order in the universe appear as a result of our ability to discern continuous and discontinuous properties. There is nothing we do, feel, hear, say or think that is anything other than a continuous or discontinuous transformation of energy.

Some things that can be said about (dis)continuity:

· Discontinuities are things: things are discontinuities
Nothing can be a 'thing' if it is not differentiated from some other 'thing' by displaying discontinuity, by having an boundary. A 'thing' is a difference. When describing the human body names are given to the areas that display discontinuity, change and difference. For example, the face is most densely mapped by names in proportion to the amount of surface area it covers since it has the most differentiation of features. The torso is very lightly mapped in relation to the large amount of surface area that it accounts for since it is a comparatively featureless terrain.

· Nothings are continuities
'I felt nothing', 'Nothing happened' – meaning that a certain continuous state was not punctuated by a discontinuity or significant change.

· Regular (dis)continuities are order
Any (dis)continuity that is perceived to occur with regularity might be construed as ordered, stable and determined; for example menstruation, night and day, periodic cycles, shapes and patterns.

· Irregular (dis)continuities are disorder
For example, dripping water, cloud formations, scribbles – things often labelled unpredictable or complex.

· Continuity is an absence of discontinuity
This is not necessarily order. For example the continuance of ink within a printed character. An area of space or time that is not perceptibly punctuated by any discontinuity. Also, in language, the continuation of associations, the absence of breaks or stops in the flow of ideas.

· Continuity is regular discontinuities
Such as a rhythm, a stripy pattern, regular differences in space and time.

· Discontinuity is change

Change being transformation of 'something' relative to 'something' else, either another thing or state. Some difference must be perceptible for change to have occurred, that is some discontinuity must be present.

Things

What distinguishes 'things' from each other is the perceived discontinuity that they display to an observer. The different manifestations of energy between a philosopher and a chair allows them to appear distinguished. The distinguished male philosopher might debate whether the chair 'actually' exists or whether he 'actually' exists. Such debates are best left to philosophers. What cannot be disputed is that, prior to doubting the existence of the chair, he is only able to refer to it as a 'thing' by virtue of the fact that it displays discontinuities that distinguish it from the fireplace, the sherry glass and the large philosophy book on the table. The chair itself may be of that

comfortable kind familiar to philosophers in which the leather upholstery is restrained by buttons. Taking the chair as a whole, the buttons now form a discontinuity that punctuates the surface of the leather. Yet, since they are probably arranged in a regular, diamond shaped manner, their relation to each other forms a level of continuity.

In Post-Human terms we can see that whilst there may be no intrinsic divisions among things (since all things are expressions of energy) an organism will perceive differences because energy is manifested in different ways and an organism is sensitive to different levels of energy. These varying manifestations of energy can be perceived as either continuous or discontinuous, these qualities being entirely relative to each other. Things only appear to be distinct from each other insofar as they display discontinuity. The existence of order or disorder is, therefore, a function of both the perceptual apparatus and the energetic expression of that which is perceived. Order does not exist separately from its perception.

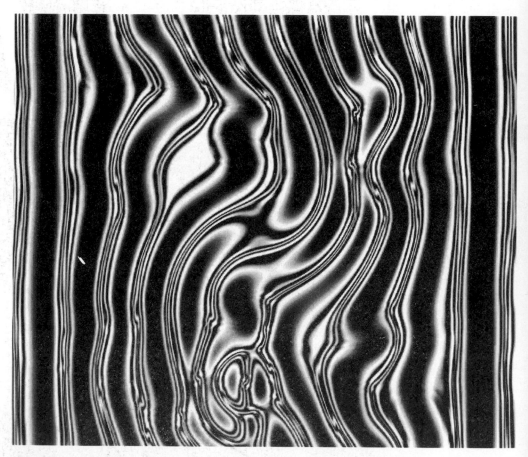

'The characteristic of all form, all morphogenesis, is to display itself through discontinuities of the environment.'
Thom, *op. cit. p. 9*

Topology of
the Post
Human

*Continuity
and
Discontinuity
in Language*

*How we hate
uncertain
signs. How
we are
seduced by
ambiguity.*

4

Being, Language and
Thought

4. Being, Language and Thought

The human organism is sensitised by virtue of its sensory system to energetic changes in the environment within certain frequencies. These energetic fluctuations induce modifications in the sense organs and the nervous system. The sensory information which humans receive is both unpredictable and predictable. In order to function, a human must be able to cope with both. In addition, the human is subject to energetic fluctuations from within the body (its metabolism, etc.) that are liable to have behavioural consequences which affect the environment arising from the need to consume food, water, heat and materials. In Post-Human terms the procession of energy transformations between the environment and the organism represents a continuum. This leads us to a view of human existence in which humans are essentially submerged in the environment. This is in contrast to the humanist view, which sees humans as essentially distinct from, in opposition to and superior to nature. This continuous view of human existence not only rejects the long held belief that humans are in opposition to nature, it also rejects the long-cherished belief that human consciousness is a unique case amongst natural phenomena – to the extent that it can never be replicated in any other medium. In Post-Human terms, consciousness is a process of energy transformations like any other.

Being

'Noam Chomsky said that animals and small children live in a world of "states" and not in a world of "objects", in a world, that is, without order or coherence. Language alone allows the order of the world to be instituted, and then allows acts of reflexion and of consciousness upon the world and upon sense impressions to be carried out. Language serves above all as an organ of thought, consciousness and reflection. It thus provides the mind with an autonomy from the lived experience, allowing it to maintain a distance between itself and the lived experience.'

Anika Lemaire, *Jacques Lacan, p. 51*

It has often been argued by child psychologists and psycho-analysts that self consciousness emerges in a child when they become aware of *differences.* In developmental theory it is argued that the newly born child is unaware of divisions. To it, the world and itself are a continuous, existential reality. Later however, when the nervous system is more fully developed and more experience is gained in the world, the child is able to differentiate more clearly. The child is distressed when the mother leaves and is comforted when she returns, implying that the child can distinguish between itself and its mother (see Freud's much quoted account of a child's response to the absence of its mother in *Beyond the Pleasure Principle*). The notion of separateness is later reinforced when the process of language acquisition starts. The difference between things is continually pointed out (literally, didactically, deictically) and marked by an oral signal such as 'mama', 'dada' then later 'horsey', 'table', 'house' and even later 'semiology', 'gluon', and so on. This process, sometimes called 'splitting of subject, acquisition of language' in psychoanalytic jargon, leads to an experience of the world in which all things are separated from each other and from oneself by naming. Whilst things will appear to be separate owing to the response of the nervous system to stimuli (that is, stimuli vary, so response varies) these separations are, in the human, reinforced by language to an extent that is not true of other species. In humans the emergence of full consciousness coincides with the full acquisition of language. It may be argued that a small, pre-linguistic baby is still conscious and it is certainly true that it is aware, although not in the reflexive, *self*-conscious sense that normally applies.

If it can be accepted that reinforcing the appearance of divisions among things with language creates something we know as human consciousness (as distinct from the conscious-ness of other species) then it could follow that the repetition and reinforcement of the divisions over time creates a sense of being. If one has learnt to distinguish between a thing and its environment and that distinction holds up one minute later, or a day later, then a certain stability has been established. By compounding this process *over time* a sense of being emerges. Being arises from the recog-nition that different things have a certain amount of stability and recurrence. Of course, nothing is entirely stable at all times, and one will soon learn that even apparently stable things can change. As one learns to depend on stability, whilst remaining aware that apparently stable things can change, the human becomes locked into a permanent conflict between

All divisions are functions of being rather than divisions intrinsic to the universe.

reliance on stability and awareness of its potential loss. *I* only exist in the presence of stability. Only later in life, when stability is tediously persistent, will we disturb it with chemicals, art and dangerous sports. Humans are attracted towards stability, but intrigued by instability. How anxious we are to order everything, how willing to submit to orders given by others. We are prone to reject the unstable, unless we have been granted permission to enjoy it!

Being is the sum of all continuous thoughts that are stable over time. Having built up a stable pattern of thought, which is dependent on the relative stability of the environment, then we count on a certain continuity of existence – a sense of being.

Language

Language is a self-referential system in which no identifiable elements (phonemes, nouns, utterances, etc.) have absolute or pre-given authority in themselves. Instead there exists an arbitrary arrangement of signals, forged by consensus over time, whose mutual opposition within a structure ensures that we are able to refer to distinctive concepts with some predictability. For example, a branch is a branch because it is neither a leaf nor a trunk. The words or sounds may be interchangeable but they must remain distinguishable from each other in order to be able to refer to different concepts (with some exceptions). There is no natural or pre-given relationship between the word 'branch' and the concept of branch. These units of linguistic discourse are commonly called 'signs'. For the classic text on the 'structuralist' description of language see F. de Saussure, *Course in General Linguistics*.

Semiology is the 'science of signs' and was developed to formalise the study of meaning in society. One of its more useful consequences has been to extend the notion of language from being merely that which is spoken to include all the images, symbols, conventions and gestures that are 'meaningful' from road signs to hem lines. This extension is justified on the basis that meaning is articulated through non-spoken information (such as shapes of furniture, car designs) just as much as is it articulated through the spoken or written word. For a discussion of this theory see Roland Barthes, *Elements of Semiology*. Despite the fact that semiology has been discredited in a number of ways, I believe this enlarged description of language is valid. In this discussion I shall use the word language to mean not just what is spoken, or even written, but the whole structure of articulated meaning that pervades our culture – the general *discourse* of society.

Language and order

The question is sometimes asked, 'Does order exist in the real world or in the brain?' The answer is neither and both. The brain is not an instrument transplanted onto nature in order to observe it but a product of it. We cannot stand outside of the world (real or imagined) so as to analyse it in an objective way.

How would humans be if we did not perceive order – that is, if we did not construct a view of the world as being, at least partially, stable? On a biological level, we would be ineffective since all stimuli would be chaotic – nothing would be learnt. We become desensitised with familiarity, otherwise every night train that went past would wake us up – this avoids us being in a state of perpetual confusion and shock – a process known as *habituation*.

'Animals respond to a novel stimulus or event. If the stimulus or event occurs repeatedly and has no interesting consequences, the animal stops responding to it. In this sense habituation is a very adaptive aspect of behaviour. Without it, animals would spend most of their time responding to all kinds of irrelevant stimuli.'

Richard F. Thompson, The Brain, p. 350

In this way, the repetition of stimuli, and the resulting sense of stability, helps to produce a sense of order in us. It can be seen from this that a sense of order does not arise spontaneously and independently in the 'brain'. It arises in parallel with those regular environmental stimuli to which we become habituated.

A sense of order is generated which, through repetition and association, confirms our being and has the effect of making things *seem* intrinsically ordered (not forgetting that this is reinforced by our habit of denying that which is disordered). As stated above, language and consciousness depend for their complexity on the degree to which we divide and fragment everything. The process of fragmentation inevitably gives rise to associative links among the fragments (we divide a branch from a leaf, but branches and leaves are obviously associated). Language encodes these fragments, and links among fragments, in a formal structure of signs, words and syntax. Insofar as this linguistic structure is stable, predictable and regular, it represents a type of order.

Order is an affirmation of being. 'I order, therefore I am.' The process of ordering, which we know as being, is continually threatened by a potential loss – loss of being, *death*. It is the ever present threat of discontinuity, the state of not knowing, fear of disorientation and the drift into a meaningless vortex that draws us to the continuum and compels us to grope for order. Here is the motive for seeking the continuous and rejecting the discontinuous. Discontinuity in perception threatens discontinuity of being.

'We and other mammals appear to be driven by nature towards certainty. This may in fact be the basis for the existence of various belief systems. A person firmly committed to a belief system does in fact "understand" the world and the nature of the controls that operate, even though this understanding may be quite wrong.'

Thompson, op. cit. p. 202

Linguistic meaning is grasped through negotiations with the world in the desire to affirm certainty. To make this process less abstract, we must refer to the real forces that are exerted upon us and which contribute to the formation of regular structures within language; for example, the need to acquire a consistent supply of food, the desire to influence or react to other people as well as social structures to which we are subjected. These forces have a tendency to promote certainty and eliminate unpredictability in a more or less deliberate way.

Language is a system which is, to a large extent, ordered. For it to be useful it must display coherence and regularity. In this way, language relays the stability of the world. We perceive trees and houses in the environment that display relative stability. The words 'tree' and 'house' are relatively stable referents to those objects we perceive.

It must be remembered that we are only using the notion of 'ordered' in a contingent sense. As we saw in the last chapter, things that seem ordered on one level can seem chaotic on another. Order arises from the way we look at the world and does not exist independently from the way we look at it. Language is just as prone to chaos as the world which it represents.

Language and continuity

However chaotic or ordered we know language to be, we can discern within it differing amounts of continuity and discontinuity. Consider a relatively continuous flow of linguistic signs:

. . . watch > look > see > vision > sight > view > vista > scene > spectacle . . .

This sequence, or any like it, can be seen as a *continuum* since it does not require much diversion to pass from one word concept to the next.

Language ordinarily moves in a continuum – through the path of least resistance. Just as energy is conserved in nature (things do not jump up hills of their own accord), given the choice between two alternatives, language will take the easiest path. As a result, one normally assumes the most obvious meaning in any communication. This assumption is the basis of much comedy, which requires that the audience infers the most obvious meaning first, only to be surprised when a non-obvious meaning is revealed. For example,

> 'Is anything worn under the kilt?'
> 'Nae, it's all in perfect working order.'

. . . where the most obvious meaning of 'worn' refers to garments.

Linguistic continua are the fabric of cognition, reason and meaning. They are bobbing floats strung out in chains on dark seas of meaninglessness.

Consider a relatively discontinuous flow of linguistic signs:

. . . bite > chunk > meaty > sample > simple > offal > shed > gentle > picnic. . .

This sequence, or any like it, can be seen as *discontinuous* since it requires a greater diversion to pass from one word concept to the next. You will notice, however, that even in the process of reading the list you are forced to assert conceptual links between the words that I did not intend to be present (especially if it is read several times). The construction of links in the face of apparent 'linklessness' betrays our involuntary desire to construct meaning. Even in the case of an apparently non-sensical sequence we still attempt to draw out some thread of continuity:

''Twas brillig, and the slithy toves Did gyre and gimble in the wabe:'

Lewis Carroll 'Jabberwocky', *Through the Looking Glass*

My construction of meaning: 'It was a brilliant, cold day and slippery frog-like creatures danced and frolicked in the fast flowing river.'

Language, philosophy and the logic of definition

What is the relationship between the perception of a thing and the naming of it? Does one perceive things that don't have names? Does something's name alter our perception of it? The answer in both cases is 'sometimes'.

Many philosophical problems lie in that fact that because we *name* something in order to distinguish it, we therefore assume that it is *actually* distinct. Because we have named something called the brain it allows us to forget that the brain is actually part of the feet!

Most philosophical problems are debates about language. They arise because of the mistaken assumptions *a.)* that language is consistent, *b.)* that because a word exists there must exist a 'thing' that it represents and *c.)* that the things which are represented should, in themselves, be consistent. I am sure a debate could be constructed around, for example, the difference between 'consciousness' and 'thought' which would demand considerable academic resources, such as sherry and pipe tobacco, and possibly even a full scale conference. However, it would be not much more than a debate about the difference between a 'motor car' and an 'automobile' since both disputes would be based on the mistaken assumption that because two *words* exist it must necessarily follow that two separate *things* exist for each of the words to refer to.

We must remember that when we use a word to refer to a thing, we do not refer to an isolated thing, since nothing can be isolated. This arises from an interesting property of language which reminds us that nothing can be defined in an absolute sense – *nouns are both exclusive and inclusive simultaneously*. In other words, they refer to an object exclusively in order to differentiate it from all other objects, but at the same time imply the inclusion of the functional context of the object that makes it whatever it is.

When I refer to the human heart it is not to an isolated piece of meat floating in a perspex box but to a functioning organ that is part of a dynamic organic system. A heart is relatively separate from the lungs, but to absolutely separate it would mean the heart would die and no longer be a heart in the same sense but a lump of meat. This reinforces the fact that words do not have absolute definitions; we can only be relatively precise. Thinking about language in this way can be seen as a type of *holistic* linguistics in which the *inclusive* function of language is given privilege over its *exclusive* operation.

Many of the philosophical problems with language arise from the conflict between the imprecise nature of language on the one hand, and the desire to impose a logical structure on the other. Logic, by definition, is the precise analysis of defined terms that relate in a rational way. Logic deals with boundaries, defined limits and fixed quantities. Words, sentences and meanings do not have boundaries, defined limits and fixed quantities. Language is slippery. In the *Philosophical Investigations*, Wittgenstein considers the requirement that investigation of language should be resolved logically:

'The more narrowly we examine actual language, the sharper becomes the conflict between it and our requirement. (For the crystalline purity of logic was, of course, not a result of investigation: it was a requirement.) The conflict becomes intolerable; the requirement is now in danger of becoming empty. We have got on to slippery ice where there is no friction and so in a certain sense the conditions are ideal, but also, just because of that, we are unable to walk. We want to walk: so we need *friction*. Back to the rough ground!'   Wittgenstein, *Philosophical Investigations, remark 107*

If it can be accepted that the meaning generated by a word is relatively and not absolutely stable then it will greatly relieve the pressure on philosophers of language to try and *quantify* what is meant by meaning. Wittgenstein, as an eminent logician, struggles with the barrier that logic imposes on an understanding of *real,* as opposed to ideal, language:

'The ideal, as we think of it, is unshakable. You can never get outside it; you must always turn back. There is no outside; outside you cannot breathe. - Where does this idea come from? It is like a pair of glasses on your nose through which we see whatever we look at. It never occurs to us to take them off.'   *ibid. remark 103*

If there is something to be learnt from all the linguists and linguistic philosophers who have pre-seeded us it is that language is exasperatingly complex. We should take heed of this and accept, as many tenured scholars will be unable to do, that language will always be more grotesque than the sum of any logic we may construct to describe it.

Language is a stranger, even to us.

Deconstructing language and the language of deconstruction

There is a philosophy of language that has been extremely influential in European and American academies since the 1970s. Deconstructionism arose from the French schools of structuralism and post-structuralism and has been important in showing how meaning is socially 'constructed' rather than being natural or pre-given. It operates around the principle of linguistic signs developed by Ferdinand de Saussure outlined above. In stressing the socially constructed nature of language it attempts to reveal how words and ideas are not neutral, impartial symbols that we freely choose to express ideas. Rather, it exposes how words and the meanings they embody have a rich ecology of interconnections and evolutionary history that defies linear interpretation. The methodology it adopts is the literal deconstruction of texts, usually passages of writings of other philosophers, in order to show that the text does not represent a finite, fixed truth. All texts are open to interpretation and no single meaning can be assumed: all texts are, to some extent, volatile when they are read. A key figure in deconstructionism is Jacques Derrida, whose work is highly controversial (in the academic community at least). Some critics have taken the upshot of his work to imply that there can be *no* meaning in a text, that everyone can read something different, that interpretation can go too far. Whatever view one takes on this, Derrida is pointing to something that has long been denied by those who see language as something more fixed and linear. When one is reading (or for that matter listening) *one is not solely concerned with that which is being read*. The possible meaning to be derived from a text is greater than the sum of the words on the page:

'Derrida entertains the curious hypothesis of a 'programming machine', one that would at least set certain limits to the play of aberrant interpretations. It is a notion related to his metaphor of "multiple reading heads", intended to suggest (by analogy to the record, playback and erasing heads in a tape machine) the way we read simultaneously what is there in front of us and also, in the process, a potentially infinite range of intertextual meanings and allusions, some of which may very well obscure or efface the immediate sense of "the words on the page".'

Christopher Norris, *Derrida, p. 201*

To say that the meaning of a text is not fixed is not say that it is meaning*less*. It is merely to state that no two readings of a text can be identical. The result of two people reading the same text might be that they both have almost identical interpretations. Yet the possibility must exist that the same text could be interpreted in vastly different ways. The case of Nietzsche and his appropriation by the Nazis is often cited in this regard. This is because all texts are read in some context and the context may vary drastically. The context in which something is read (or spoken) contributes as much to the meaning as do the actual printed, or spoken, words. Even two occurrences of the *same* person reading the *same* text do not produce identical results. A love poem read when you're in love does not have the same meaning as one read when you're not. This view of language operation is sympathetic with the view of other complex phenomena we have discussed in previous chapters – that all non-linear, complex systems (and the operation of human language is certainly a complex system) are highly sensitive to small perturbations. They are context sensitive and their boundaries cannot be fixed with precision. Total predictability and stability are ruled out; language defies reduction.

However, the name 'deconstruction' seems to imply that something else is being attempted. Given that a text is a social construction riddled with ideological assumptions and prone to aberrant interpretations, the task deconstruction seems to have set itself is, literally, to 'de-construct' that which is constructed, thus revealing some *other* truth in the text that was concealed in its construction. The process of deconstruction is often taken to mean 'pulling apart' by exegesis some text, film or speech in order to get at some truth that otherwise would have remained concealed. In practice this can often mean examining the frames of a film in minute detail or scrutinising a text through the etymology of each word in it – the process of 'textual analysis'. The hope that such methods will lead to a revelation of truth is just as hopeless as thinking we might understand the behaviour of a flock of birds by examining each bird individually. For it is merely another form of reductionism, another construction. If we try to isolate a sign or a unit of meaning in an effort to 'deconstruct' it we are removing it from the context that supported its meaning and thus we distort that which we wish to analyse. This process carries us into an analytic mode of discourse that is specifically different from apprehending *in situ* the sign which we originally intended to deconstruct. It is impossible to isolate a sign in order to analyse it objectively, because in doing so we change it. This might be called the 'uncertainty principle' of semiotic analysis after the principle of particle physics that excludes us from knowing the location and velocity of a particle simultaneously since analysis disturbs both. For a description of the uncertainty principle see Chapter 7.

Language as a non-linear process

In Chapter 1 we suggested that consciousness could be thought of in terms of a non-linear process. In the same way that many cognitive scientists have sought to describe consciousness in terms of ordered, linear functions, many linguists have sought to apply the same logic to human language. This is understandable in light of the fact that linguistics sees itself as a 'science' and the traditional methodology of science is to investigate subjects in a linear way – to prise out what is orderly and consistent, and to disregard what is disorderly or incalculable. Linguists tend to idealise language in order to make it quantifiable. Real language can be likened to a turbulent fluid. The catastrophic ruptures between continuous flows, the flips and reversals of meaning, are instantaneous and unpredictable. Whilst there is a certain amount of stability the fluid is never the same twice, it has recognisable form but is not fixed. In this model no element of language can be autonomous just as in a fluid there are no autonomous components. The part affects the whole and the whole affects the parts. Just as a turbulent fluid is non-periodic, language can never repeat itself – we can never say the same thing twice. A repeated message has a different meaning from one that is sent once.

This non-linear model asks us to reject the standard conception of language, which is one of an abstracted linear operation of signs. Real, messy, language can be considered instead as a field, a matrix of infinite-dimensional events, any apparent order being dependent on the context in which it is articulated.

Language function and the proximity of concepts

If we can say that ordinarily we strive to maintain our view of the world as being ordered, and that is something we do to preserve our sense of being, then language is one thing among many that we are likely to interpret in an orderly way. Language, *insofar as it is stable*, is one of the things that contributes to a view of a world that is consistent and regular. Words and signs are conventions that gain their stability through repeated use. In any human group a consensus will form about the significance of certain discernible signs. This being so, language develops a consistency that is no different to the consistency of any stable stimuli to which we are exposed. They always do roughly the same thing and we come to rely on them. In this way a continuum develops within language that is the sum of its stable occurrences.

When we think we recognise meaning (whether it is the 'correct' meaning or not) we are benefitting from our investment in the stability of a common language bond. This bond consists in a set of conventions whereby any sentence we understand arises from the precipitation of a chain of association leading from one concept to another in a relatively continuous way. I would say that the degree of continuity is determined by the amount energy required to pass from one concept to another through the chain of association. The greater the amount of energy required, the less continuous the chain. Having precipitated the activation of one concept, further concepts may be activated – whether we like it or not! Someone may not wish to be reminded of an idea. However, the appearance of a certain cue may precipitate the unwanted idea in spite of a conscious wish to forget it. From this we can deduce that the extent to which we can control our own thoughts is limited. To some degree we are at the mercy of the probability of one idea leading to another – the procession of thoughts is partially independent of our will. This is something that advertisers take great advantage of by creating associations in our minds between certain ideas and certain products. When we see a certain chocolate bar we think of a tropical island, when we see a certain brand of cigarettes we think of cowboys, when we see a certain soft drink we start humming a jingle.

What determines which other concepts are activated? Many things, such as the semantic proximity of the concepts to one another, personal experience, cultural convention, the immediate context, the physiological state of the individual, the inflection of expression – many of the factors, in fact, that the traditional study of language discounts for practical reasons. Ideas that can proceed from one to another with relatively little effort (energy) can be considered continuous. Ideas that require great effort (energy) to travel between can be considered discontinuous (see below 'An energetic model of human thought').

The presence or absence of 'meaning' in language is determined by the amount of energy required to pass from one concept to another. Difficult meaning arises from the co-existence of concepts that are semantically distant, that is, when there is not a well established connection between them. However, the path between concepts that have little or no connection may be too difficult to travel. For example the phrase 'The yesterday of refractive stepshine', whilst not meaningless, is certainly awkward to assemble by the standard of most phrases.

Memory

Imagine having to learn two columns of numbers that correlate as in the case of the stopping distances of cars laid out in the Highway Code:

> 20 mph>12 metres
> 30 mph>23 metres
> 40 mph>36 metres
> 50 mph>53 metres
> 60 mph>73 metres
> 70 mph>96 metres

It is your task to learn that 20 goes with 12, 30 with 23 and so on. The usual way to achieve this is through repetitive chanting in the manner that multiplication tables are sometimes learnt at school. Having chanted the list only two or three times, it would take a great deal of mental effort (energy) for most people to recollect the pairs of numbers correctly. Having chanted the numbers 20 or 30 times, the amount of effort (energy) required to recollect a pair of numbers would be significantly less.

When we have learnt something thoroughly, because we have invested a lot of effort (energy) in bonding certain pairs of concepts (e.g. the numbers) we are able to recall them at a later time with very little energetic cost. This is especially so if we re-stoke them with energy by continually using them. We can imagine that such well learned memories are stored at a higher priority than other memories about which we are much less concerned.

It is debated in the fields that study such matters as to whether humans retain all memories throughout their lives, or whether some memories are lost, repressed or misplaced. While this is a question that will be very hard to answer in an absolute sense, it is clear that some things are more memorable than others and that we certainly give priority to particular recollections. Many would accept that a memory that was brought into existence at a great cost in terms of energy should take longer to fade than its weaker counterpart. A memory brought about through particularly traumatic circumstances may stay with us all our lives, although it may be repressed. In most cases a memory will fade unless it is recharged by regular use, which implies it relies on some energetic capacity for its storage.

In nature, stored energy is likely to disperse unless restored by the application of additional energy. This tendency is referred to as entropy, the natural inclination of ordered systems to decay into disorder (see the discussion of entropy in Chapter 2). Immense portions of the mental experiences of our daily lives seem to be forgotten quite quickly, at least in our conscious mind. However, there are many occurrences of sudden memory recollection that are surprising when memories we thought we had lost return. Events or people may remind us of things about which we may not have thought for years. Such memories can return as vividly as though they were from the previous day. The evidence from hypnosis suggests that deep rooted memories can be revived under certain conditions, often revealing things about which the subject had no conscious knowledge at all.

From this we can speculate that the energetic charge that represents a specific memory may be retained for many decades without ever being consciously referred to. To recall it we might have to be specifically reminded of it, or we may come across it during some random wandering through our mind. This points to the amazing capacity our mind has to retain apparently insignificant thoughts and to make seemingly random connections between them. Yet we have very little knowledge about how such memories might be stored or retrieved. Those who follow the computational model and think of the brain as a big computer, tend to regard memories as discrete blocks of data stored on some huge hard disc. As such they will be stored in specific locations that are accessed by the 'program' of our mind.

Bearing such things in mind, let us consider the following: Our memories should not be thought of as 'blocks of data', that is, as discrete units of memory which are 'filed' away in the brain and turned on or off. The particulate view of memory follows from a particulate view, which posits the brain as made up of different parts each of which are responsible for different functions. Such a view is supported by those neurologists and psychologists who see the brain in terms of *localised* functions that are located in particular parts of the brain. Rather, can we imagine the memory as a *transformed potentiality*.

Transformed potentialities

The predominant biological processes that give rise to thought can be spoken of as a 'cognitive medium' (a conjunction of the sensory and conscious media described in Chapter 1 which I shall call the cognitive medium for sake of brevity). At our current state of knowledge this includes neurons, the nervous system, the brain, sense organs, various hormones, neuro-transmitters, bio-feedback mechanisms as well as others as yet unknown. Speaking of the cognitive medium allows us to locate thought in the biological processes of the human body (i.e. thought is not independent of the body) without falling into the old trap of locating it exclusively in the brain. We must be immediately reminded that the cognitive medium is not a discrete system but is part of and continuous with the organic and environmental media.

Note: The following discussion assumes some basic knowledge of the behaviour of neurons and the human sensory system. Since there are many excellent introductions to the subject I shall not attempt to provide one here. In particular, I recommend *The Brain, A Neurological Primer* by Richard Thompson which is referred to elsewhere in this book and which I have used to clarify, in my own mind, many of the ideas below.

Let us try to describe some of the processes by which memories may be created and thoughts may be activated. Imagine that a scene is presented to a viewer with which they are about to become familiar. Some energy emitted from the scene will be absorbed by the viewer (light, sound, smell, etc.) and distributed around the cognitive medium. The cognitive medium, following standard laws of physics, will try to distribute the incoming energy by the path of least resistance. That is, familiar types of input will travel through familiar paths– a process sometimes known as *canalisation*.

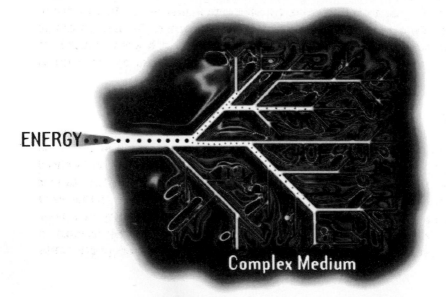

ENERGY

Complex Medium

A diagrammatic representation of the process of canalisation

The principle of least resistance allows us to maintain comprehension because we are not having to set up new cases for each input, thus stability is maintained. If the scene is completely new or overwhelming (by analogy with rivers, a flood), then the energy input into the body will not be able to follow pre-established paths and new ones will have to be created. When an unfamiliar stimulus enters the body it will try to create a new path; the more powerful the stimulus the more significant the path. In physiological terms, such paths would most likely consist of neural webs – strings of neurons with synapses firing, creating paths of higher potential. Such paths of neurons, stimulated and triggered to form a new shape, might be called *transformed potentialities*. This follows the well documented fact that neurons are able to adapt by changing their *potential* to fire or not fire. Each specific memory may consist of a pathway of neural connections. Each path may be discrete inasmuch as it relates to a particular memory, but not isolated insofar as it will be connected to many other paths through which it might be activated. The transformed potentiality represents the sum of all such paths that contribute to a thought even though they may occur in widely differing areas of the mind at once. In this sense, we regard thoughts as being *distributed* rather than localised, a distinction that will be made clear shortly.

However, when talking about neurons we must remember that they alone cannot be responsible for thoughts and memories. Even though neurons are the cells in which thought is generally supposed to occur they do not act alone. Each neuron is embedded in a rich culture of blood vessels, neuro-transmitters, peptides, hormones and other neurons. Many chemicals in the brain remain unidentified and many that have been identified are not understood. No one who studies the brain denies that these 'extra-neuronal' compounds have a decisive influence on the functioning of each neuron, even if it is not clear how. Given that we also have to take the effect of the body into account when studying brain activity, we are left with a system of such immense complexity that to reduce thought to the study of neurons alone is going to give us, at best, a very incomplete picture. I wish to emphasise that when I refer to neurons in further discussions I do so only in a contingent sense. The neuron can be spoken of contingently as a mechanism of the body but must imply a whole matrix of chemicals and events that are just as much a part of the process as the neurons themselves are.

Models of thought

In order to contrast the localised view of thought with the distributed one I am proposing, let us use a model. Imagine the London Underground map. The localised view of the mind construes the brain as being something like this map. The stations represent the ideas, thoughts and memories and the tracks represent the pathways or links between them. Cockfosters could be the memory of my first day at school, Elephant and Castle my knowledge of where I live, Shepherd's Bush my memory of where I used to live. I can get to any memory by taking the appropriate route.

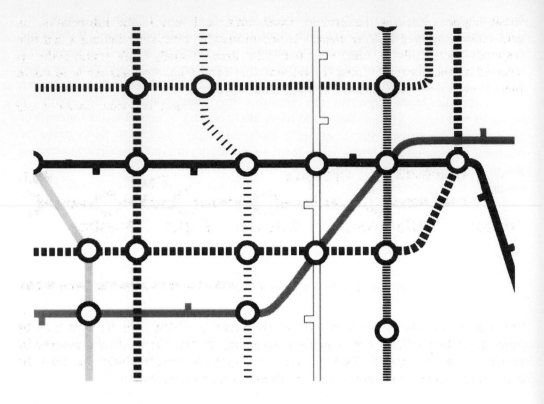

An imaginary Underground map (for copyright reasons, I am not allowed to show the real one). It is tempting to draw an analogy between the layout of the stations and lines and thoughts in the mind. Are thoughts stored as discrete units connected by lines, or are they distributed over the entire network?

Contiguous stations could be contiguous thoughts, and so on. In this model, the brain contains clumps of data (the stations) that are connected via links (the tracks) to form a network of memories, thoughts, ideas, etc. Of course this is idealised and simplified, as is the tube map, but we must face the fact that any model of the brain will have to be very simplified. Multiplied in complexity many billions of times, one could build up a working model of the brain from this analogy. This view fits well with the current model of the brain - that it is made up of different parts that handle different functions.

This view of the brain, in which particular areas of the brain do particular things, is exemplified in the study of perception by the "Grandmother cell" hypothesis. Briefly stated, theorists have suggested that a particular perception may be represented in the tissue of the brain by a cell. In *The Brain*, Richard Thompson quotes Nobel prize winning neurologists Hubel and Weisel:

'What happens beyond the primary visual area, and how is the information on orientation exploited at later stages? Is one to imagine ultimately finding a cell that responds specifically to some very particular item? (Usually one's grandmother is selected as the particular item, for reasons that escape us.) Our answer is to doubt there is such a cell, but we have no good alternative to offer.'

in Thompson, op. cit. p. 243

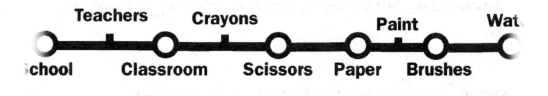

This correlates with a localised view of the brain in which each thought may be represented by a cell, as is each memory, each concept. Most brain studies proceed by seeking to identify specific locations that correspond to specific things we think the brain does – where is memory, where is arousal, where is redness, etc.?

The reason I am suspicious of this description is that most people accept it as valid. Its origins lie in the reductionist model bequeathed to us by humanist science. Our knowledge of human consciousness is so slight at this stage that any widely-held view about how it might operate is bound to be wrong.

'No neuron is just a receiver or ultimate destination of information. It only serves to pass it on. Therefore we should not consider individual neurons as *knowing* or *understanding* anything . . . Similarly, we must assume that even those neurons whose activity has been shown to represent the detection of specific sensory pattern . . . cannot be said to have anything like a knowledge that the feature is present. They function merely as links in the chain that leads to cognition.'

Erich Harth, The Creative Loop, p. 48

Look again at our Underground map. Imagine that a thought or memory is a *route* rather than a station. In other words, the station is not the depository of a whole idea but part of a journey through which the idea is expressed. A memory does not consist of any one part of the network but only appears when it is travelled. *The thought is the journey rather than the destination.*

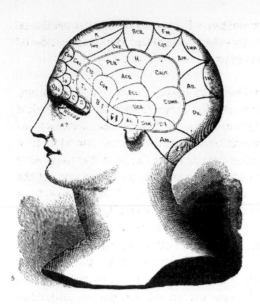

The now discredited science of phrenology attempted to map specific areas of the brain to specific mental attributes

On the Underground a line connects a series of *junctions* as well as stations. Junctions allow travel in many directions as well as straight through lines. When I commit something to memory, a new idea or piece of information, I define a new route through the network. The new route may contain branches of previous routes, as would be the case if I learnt more about a particular thing. It may join together old branches that have until now been separate, as would be the case if I suddenly realised the connection between two ideas that had previously escaped me. One can go through different junctions to get to the same destination – one can arrive at the same conclusion for different reasons. Most importantly, travelling a route is a *dynamic* process, it has to be travelled to be experienced and is not a fixed thing. In this sense, the process of thought is *distributed* across the journey rather than being located in any fixed place. In this distributed model, the process of travelling a route implies the process of being – thinking as movement through a medium. It makes the dimension of time integral to the process.

Given that a thought is activated, for whatever reason, it consists in a process of travelling through the cognitive medium. *A thought does not exist unless it is being thought* – otherwise it only exists latently, as a potentiality. When a thought is brought into being its potentiality has been actualised. In this way we can regard memories as the sum of the potential paths by which they might be actualised. These potential paths will be stable inasmuch as each memory is stable. Similar thoughts will take similar paths. Certain

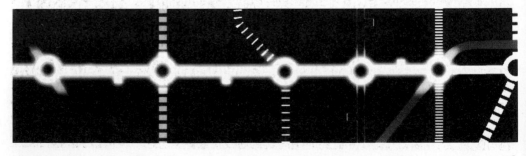

A route being travelled through our imaginary Underground map represented by the highlit areas

routes would be stable if they were often travelled which would help to reinforce stability and continuity. This relates to what was said above about the canalisation of input stimuli which allows recognition and learning.

In order to extend the usefulness of this model we would have to say that, in thought, routes are travelled in many different directions *simultaneously*. That is, the path that represents a thought is not linear in the sense that it travels from Ealing Broadway to Ongar on the Central line, or even that it might be diverted at some junction to a different line. The thought may travel from Ealing Broadway to Ongar *at the same time* as branching off at Notting Hill Gate to travel to Monument on the Circle line, *at the same time* as zooming off to Highgate from Tottenham Court Road on the Northern line, with another branch travelling to Covent Garden on the Piccadilly line. Each line represents an aspect of that which we perceive as a simultaneous thought. The more complex the thought, the more lines are simultaneously activated. Thought is not a one-dimensional line where concepts skip from one to the other along a path. Neither is it a two-dimensional circuit in which thought can skip from one line to another. It is not even a three-dimensional array in which thought can travel in opposite directions at once, but a four-dimensional process in which the dimension of time is integral. Thoughts and memories are not localised in time or space (as many of those who study the brain think) but distributed through time and space.

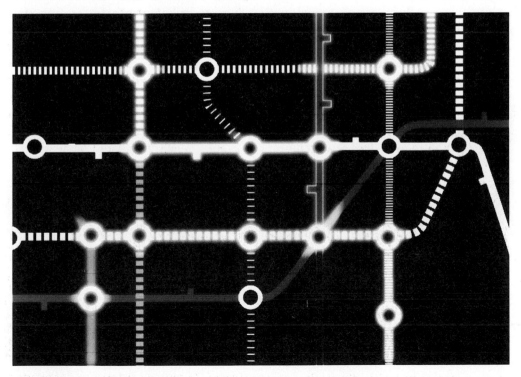

A number of different routes being travelled simultaneously

To complicate this further, we cannot say that all this activity is occurring in the brain alone as many who study thought believe. We would have to say that the 'lines' or 'routes' through which thoughts occur must extend throughout the whole nervous system and by implication the whole body. If someone takes us by surprise by tapping us on the back, the sensation through the skin is the 'start of the line' as far as the mental response to the tap is concerned.

This model of thought explains why all attempts to *localise* mental phenomena have thus far failed. In *Gödel, Escher, Bach*, Douglas Hofstadter summarises several recent attempts to determine where, in the brain, different thoughts occur (p. 342). The attempts have failed, not because we do not have very good measuring apparatus but because thoughts do not occur in any local place. They are distributed, not only throughout the brain, but the whole body.

Meaning

We can simply describe meaning as the process that occurs when thoughts connect with each other in a relatively continuous way. That is, if a human is presented with a set of signs, say a series of words, that can be linked together without too much effort then a meaningful articulation has occurred. When I say 'without too much effort', I mean that the paths through which the thoughts travel in the cognitive medium are easily accessible to one another. A great deal of energy is not required to connect them. In another case where the human is presented with a series of signs that are more difficult to understand, say something in an unfamiliar language, more energy will be required to make the necessary connections. In the case where a meaningless set of signs is presented the human may try to articulate them (that is, join them up) but will be unable to do so since the effort required is too great ('I didn't understand that differential equation').

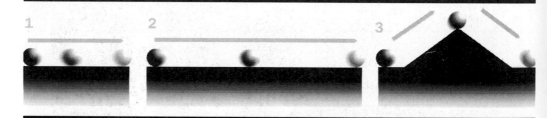

If we take a ball and an even surface and try to move the ball between two points it will require a certain amount of energy. If we extend the distance between the two points it will require more energy to move the ball between them. The total amount of energy expended in moving the ball is proportional to the distance between the points and dependent on any obstacles in between.

Using our Underground map analogy, the test of meaning is to judge whether there is sufficient energy available to travel the journey we are being asked to make and whether the route itself is one that is open for us to travel. That is, in order to be able to articulate a set of signs successfully, we need to be able to complete a journey and that requires *a.)* that the tube train has power and *b.)* that the tracks are clear and the stations open.

Continuity with the environment

There is little doubt that the human is sensitive to changes in their environment. Changes in environmental conditions are changes in energy states – electrochemical, thermal, kinetic, and so on. Given that these energetic changes occur within certain frequencies, and within a certain proximity, a correlated change will occur in the human body. In this sense the environment and the body are continuous. In principle this is no different from the tropism displayed by plants when they adapt to changes in their surroundings. Because the effect of environmental forces on the human is incalculably complex, and probably includes forces about which we are currently unaware, there is no possibility of producing a *complete* description of the processes of energy exchange between the human and their environment. The best that can be achieved is a model of human existence that is qualitative rather than quantitative. It is often implied that by studying highly specialised areas of the body with increasing resolution, we shall be able to create a full description of the whole organic process when all the pieces are joined together. Unfortunately, increasing specialisation tends to lead to increasing fragmentation and isolation. As we have learnt from complexity theory, one cannot understand a complex system by reducing it to its parts.

Energy can enter the body from the environment in a number of ways. There are the obvious channels of eyes for light, mouth for food, nose for smell, ears for sound and skin for touch. But there are also less obvious ways. The skin is sensitive to light as well as touch and heat. It not only adapts to light at the surface but allows it to pass through into the body to affect its biochemistry. Sound can affect the body by means other than the ears. Sound vibrations can be picked up by many parts of the body as anyone who has stood in front of a speaker stack at a gig will know. Some deaf people can 'hear' music through vibrations in their hands or feet. People can be affected by short wave radiation even though they cannot see or feel anything. The effect that energy will have on the body it enters will vary depending on the nature of the energy itself and the condition of the body.

The creation of memories

A memory or thought arising from an environmental stimulus may be analogous to a bolt of lightning. When energy enters at the sense organ it disturbs the array of sensory neurons and causes them to fire. In general, the greater the intensity of the stimulus the greater the rate of firing. 'The intensity of light seems to be coded by the frequency of firing of the ganglion cells: a bright light causes them to fire more' (Thompson, op. cit. p. 233). Having created an energy difference (potential) between the sensory neurons that received the stimulus and their immediate neighbours, the signal is passed on from one neuron to the next. Neurons will fire if their neighbour gives them sufficient reason to do so. In this sense, the original energy produced by the stimulus is passed through the web of neurons until the energy is dissipated in the cognitive medium – until the neurons see no reason to go on firing. Like all energy potentials, its dissipation will take the 'path of least resistance' until it is exhausted, that is, until a state of relative equilibrium is reached. In general, neurons at rest are in a state of equilibrium and are in a state of non-equilibrium when firing. They discharge their non-equilibrium state by passing signals through the 'out-tray', the axon, to other neurons and are brought into a state of non-equilibrium by receiving impulses from the 'in-tray' , the dendrites.

The energy that arrives from the stimulus is not the 'same' energy that dissipates through the neurons. Each sensory neuron acts as a transducer converting heat, light, sound, smell and force into chemical signals that neurons are able to pass to each other. Since energy is being converted at each stage, some is lost (entropy), which accounts for the fact that the signal decays to equilibrium over time.

The reason I suggested that lightning might be analogous to thought (a thought that arises from an environmental stimulus, e.g. 'There's my cat!') is that lightning can be described as *the dissipation of an energy potential through a complex medium*. In slightly clearer language, when there is a difference between energy in one place and another, the energy will be discharged through a suitable medium. If the medium has its own structure and form (i.e. it is at non-equilibrium), then it can be considered complex and will effect the way the energy dissipates. In the case of lightning, the energy potential is the huge electric charge that builds up in one place; the complex medium is the moist air through which the dissipation occurs. In the case of a thought arising from a stimulus, the potential energy is the sound or light or odour, and the complex medium is the web of nerves that transduce the energy and dissipate it through the cognitive medium.

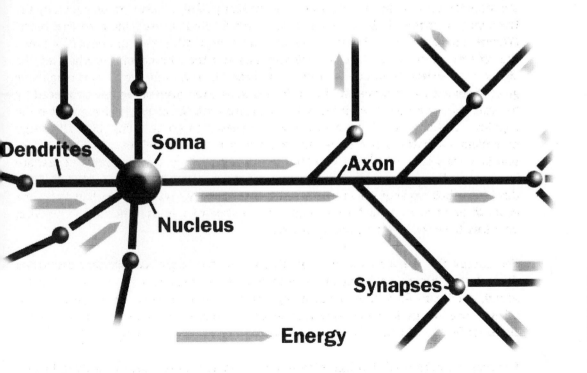

Schematic diagram of neuron absorbing and transmitting energy

The analogy can be useful in many ways. The path that lightning takes is essentially unpredictable. Describing the jagged appearance of lightning in *Chaos and Order,* Cramer says:

'At each point, an irreversible decision is taken as to the subsequent path to be taken. This decision is understandable only in statistical or quantum-mechanic terms. Whenever matter and energy are simultaneously transported through a medium in a system far from equilibrium, that is, at high energy level, such "lightning" occurs.' Cramer, *op. cit. p. 104*

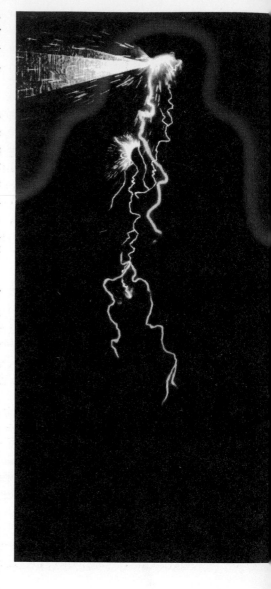

He then goes on to cite a number of examples of such 'lightning' occurring in river deltas, tree forms and electron paths in Plexiglas. Streaks of glass formed by lightning hitting sand have recently been found in American deserts. They look curiously like petrified, twisted branches. To this list of 'lightnings' we could add the path that energy takes through the cognitive medium. The trace of this path, inasmuch as it causes semi-permanent modifications to the neurons, could constitute the memory of the stimulus – a transformed potentiality. But this pathway is not necessarily linear. Lightning is known to travel in many directions at once in the same way that, above, we described thoughts occurring in many places at once.

Another property of lightning is that it can be conducted in a relatively predictable way given a suitable medium. A metal lighting conductor has a state which is in higher disequilibrium than the surrounding air. It is less random than its surroundings. The electrical charge is attracted to the atomic structure of the conductor and dissipated through it to the ground, hence the copper conductors on churches and high buildings designed to avoid damage to the structures. Referring to the mechanism of habituation we discussed earlier, a stimulus of type A, having once left a trace in the

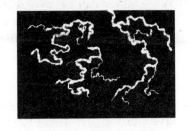

cognitive medium, on repetition may find that least resistance is met if the same path is followed. It is 'attracted' to structures of more order. A transformed potentiality can create a type of conductor that encourages similar stimuli to follow similar paths. As with a church conductor, this avoids damaging neural tissue through exposure to unnecessary repeated modifications. The sum of all the paths created by a stimulus generates an image that is 'burnt into' the cognitive medium in the same way that traces of lightning are left in the sand. By this principle we can learn what a cat is by seeing it on one day and recognise it by seeing it on another. We can even recall the image of a cat without necessarily seeing one with our eyes – 'Think of that cat we saw the other day.' By triggering a branch of the transformed potentiality, the rest of the thought may follow. This is the result of the path of altered synapses created by the original stimulus being activated. The transformed potential is the sum of heightened probabilities that certain neurons will trigger each other in a certain sequence. The ability of the cognitive medium to adapt in this way is often known as *plasticity*.

To summarise this analogy: A stimulus may travel through the cognitive medium in several directions at once, leaving behind it a trail of difference – a transformed potentiality – as it leaves some record of itself in the form of altered synaptic states. We may consider a memory of an environmental stimulus as the semi-petrified trace of an energy path in the cognitive medium. The experience is recorded as it occurs, i.e. as the input energy dissipates through the nervous system. It can be retraced via the path it describes, even though this path may have many simultaneous branches. The memory may be triggered by activating any one of the branches. Different thoughts may share branches or have roots in common – for example, all my memories of school have common roots although there are many of them that branch off in different ways.

' . . . one does speak of the speed of a thought; of how a thought goes through one's head like lightning; how problems become clear to us in a flash, and so on.'

Wittgenstein, op. cit. remark 318

Memory and thought fields

The combination of varied and stable stimuli to which we are exposed produces consequent changes in the cognitive medium that result in varying levels of probability that sets of neurons will fire. Very familiar stimuli will trigger paths of high probability, which is why they are *re*cognised. Very unfamiliar stimuli will either try to travel down existing paths (which is why we try to order information according to what we already know) or be forced to create new ones.

In order to be active a memory has to become a thought – in the jargon we have adopted, its potentiality will have to be actualised. When inducing a memory a number of paths will be triggered simultaneously, which may have the effect of creating a *field*, a field of transformed potentialities. The notion of a field is useful in suggesting something that is larger and more inclusive than might be implied by the notion of a single path. The actual field of a thought consists of all the simultaneous paths that are triggered during its occurrence. However, it is possible that the same or an almost identical thought could occur through other local pathways to reach the same result. The potential field of a thought consists of all the possible paths through which a thought or an almost identical thought, may travel as it is actualised. The field of any one particular thought may overlap with fields of other thoughts, so 'sharing' information that is common. Our experience of any particular thought derives from the simultaneous overlaying of many different impressions that are activated by the thought field. Proof of the fact that we can draw together disparate thoughts and hold them in unity is given by our ability to picture non-existent objects (something of which literature takes great advantage). If you can imagine a bright yellow vulture reading a cotton-wool bible in a tree made of sponge then you are constructing a composite image from component sources that are being shared simultaneously. Having invested energy in drawing all these sources together to form a composite image, we have created a new thought field that is partially new in its own right and partially the sum of the all the components that were united. Such fields of thought are consistent with the distributed model we are trying to describe. They avoid the necessity to specify exactly where in the brain a thought may be occurring and also take account of the fact that neurons in themselves cannot be solely responsible for creating thoughts. In our model, the field of thought is an event that occurs within the cognitive medium. This may seem a very imprecise way of describing thought, yet, I believe, we will always be denied a precise description of thought on account of the immense complexity involved.

Some thoughts on thought

I can imagine the future existence of a machine that would allow us to see this process. It would be a scanner able to detect energy changes in the cognitive medium to the resolution of a single molecule. Being able to view the whole body at once in three dimensions and in real-time we would see a constantly shifting pattern of multi-linear forks, particularly dense in the brain but spreading out to all parts of the body. The activity would show certain regularity but would never repeat. We would start to identify certain patterns with certain ideas, but we would be surprised to find that the same thing can be thought without necessarily having the same pattern. This would be so especially when different people were compared. We will find that certain areas of the brain are consistently related to predictable functions, but that these areas cannot be confined in anything but the most general way.

Something that we consider to be a discrete idea is actually a probability field in a very complex network. Given that you trigger part of it, it is probable that the rest will follow. However, as with all such things, this is not definite. You may start at one point on your route but get branched off onto another. You may arrive at the wrong destination. Mistakes are made.

With certain paths the probability that you will take a certain route will be very high, especially if it is a well established one. This would be the case with very familiar stimuli or associations. If it is an unfamiliar route, then it is likely that you may not get to your destination since there will be fewer paths leading to it, and you are less likely to find your way – you may get 'mentally lost'.

Consider the times when you are asked to identify something from a verbal clue, e.g. 'What's that stuff that cleans grease off hands called?' You can remember what it is, what it looks like, but you can't remember the name. In this case, certain components of the thought field are active whilst one is not – the one that attaches the name. After effort, or prompting, the link may be resolved. This suggests that the thought of a thing is held in separate components rather than as one complete entity, and that the process of thinking about it draws all the parts together simultaneously.

This method of storing thoughts as components would be efficient in that it would save space and avoid unnecessary complexity. If we take road signs as an example, one whole set of road signs consists of black and white images in a red circle. In memorising and recalling these it would be inefficient to remember each red circle individually. We might as well use a sample red circle and just remember the things that are different, the black and white images.

Saying that thoughts are stored in component form and reassembled under particular stimuli might mean that the various components of any one thought are located in diverse parts of the cognitive medium and ideas that are totally disconnected may be many millions of neurons apart. Therefore, the energy required to join them up – to make an associative connection – will be greater than that required to traverse two ideas that are much closer or better connected (see next section).

The cognitive medium adapts to familiar information so that it does not have to continually rearrange itself, thus conserving energy. Things are recognised, responses can be made reflexively or habitually as necessary. Yet it still has the ability to adapt to new, unexpected stimuli since there is a virtually infinite supply of neural connections that can be built. An ecologically successful cognitive medium is effective at dealing with both stability and change. Knowledge of stability is required for locating habit, food sources, offspring and mates. Knowledge of change is required for spotting prey moving in a landscape, spotting predators or dangers, adapting to shifts in the environment.

What we have outlined so far is a model of thought in which memories, ideas and concepts are stored as discontinuous thought fields (discontinuous inasmuch as they are distinct from each other) that require greater or lesser amounts of energy to navigate. Put another way, each concept is a probabilistic energy route insofar as it is distinct. Webs of such routes are formed (by learning, experience and physiognomy) so that networks of continuity evolve through which patterns of cognition are sustained – habits, reflexes, responses, etc.

An energetic model of human thought

It is clear that:

a. the human body absorbs energy, stores energy and expends energy
b. energy is absorbed via a number of different routes – eyes, mouth, ears, nose, etc.
c. the body stores and conducts energy using various biological mechanisms
d. the body consumes energy by transforming it
e. the body expends a variety of energy forms – heat, sound, kinetic etc

The human body can be considered as an energy-regulating mechanism of a very complex kind. It consists of a number of types of energy that are absorbed, stored, transformed, exchanged and expended.

Since the cognitive medium is an energy-regulating system there will be limits to its performance. The cognitive medium is no different from any other system in that it represents a particular process of energy transformations. In all such transformations some energy is lost and in any system that contains a finite amount of energy (as the cognitive medium does), lost energy will need to be replaced. If we attempt to bridge two concepts that are very far apart, more energy will be consumed (and lost) to achieve it. In the case where there is not enough energy, the connection cannot be made although the attempt to make it will still have some transforming effect on the cognitive medium. This might be termed the 'energetic limit to cognition'. Where two thoughts are continuous (for example, 'blue' and 'sky' in the sentence 'The sky is blue'), the pathway between each of these thoughts is well established. It will require little energy to pass from one to the other.

Where two thoughts are not well connected (for example between 'folk' and 'wheel' in the sentence 'The folk wheel') more energy is required to fuse the thoughts since they have less well established connections. Therefore, what we actually think, or what we are able to think, is subject to the constraints of the economy of energy in the cognitive medium.

Consider some expressions that are used when talking about thought. We 'concentrate' on something, implying a literal *concentration* of energy; we talk about 'flashes of inspiration' in the sense of lightning and of 'mental blocks' as inhibited flows. We talk about being 'excited' in the same way that neurons and sensory cells are excited when they are energetically stimulated, and about 'having no mental energy'. 'Mental exhaustion' is the exhaustion of energy and 'brain waves' suggest energetic propagation through a medium. Whilst some of these terms may have crossed into general usage from scientific terminology, they suggest an implicit understanding of the energetic basis of thought.

There is an established scientific principle by which energy moves through the path of least resistance in order, if possible, to reach a state of equilibrium. If we are to take this scientific principle at its word and remember that cognitive continuity is necessary for comprehension, we could draw the following conclusion: That energy passing into the body (environmental stimuli), being transported by the sense organs, is dissipated through the cognitive medium by the path of least resistance. In this way, the cognitive medium can be considered as a 'dissipative dynamical structure' as identified by Ilya Prigogine. In nature there are many examples of such structures in which complex media (in states of relative equilibria) which give spontaneous rise to patterns when supplied with the right amount of energy (relative states of dis-equilibria). A few have been mentioned above. If such patterns are 'recorded' into the media, then following influxes of energy are more likely to 'trace' those patterns as is the case with rivers or events in the cognitive medium.

> ' . . . the occurrence of dissipative structures generally requires that the system's size exceed some critical value. The critical size is a complex function of the parameters describing the reaction–diffusion processes. Therefore, we may say that chemical instabilities [such as those in 'fired-up' neurons] involve long-range order through which the system acts as a whole.'

> Ilya Prigogine, quoted in *Cramer,* op. cit. p. 108, (my remarks in box parentheses)

> The 'critical value', in the case of human thought, is the huge dynamic complexity of the cognitive medium.

The energetic action of recurrent, stable stimuli on a developing organism (e.g. a child), being dissipated through the cognitive medium by the path of least resistance, has the effect over time of creating *canals*. In the same way, water flowing along a featured terrain takes the path of least resistance. The effect over time of the water flowing through certain paths creates new streams and rivers of greater depth and width in existing ones. In an organism the development of such canals establishes a conduit through which further, similar, stimuli are channelled. This has the effect of decreasing the *significance* of recurrent information to the point where it might be ignored since the stimuli it presented have no differentiating impact on the cognitive medium (habituation). It means that we have learnt something about the world.

Further analogies

Let us address those energy input channels that seem to have most direct impact on thought, namely the *senses*. The senses can be thought of as conduits of energy between the environment and our cognitive medium. The camera metaphor is always instructive.

In a camera, if we have light of sufficient intensity, a lens of sufficient precision and some film of sufficient sensitivity, then opening the shutter for a certain period of time will expose an inverted image on the film emulsion. In other words, at the moment the shutter opens a simultaneous set of events occurs that result in a change in the chemical composition of the film emulsion, as will be *clear* when the film is developed. In energetic terms we can say that omni-directional rays of light energy have been focused by the properties of the lens onto a chemical compound that is altered in the presence of light energy such that when subjected to an energetic chemical reaction certain molecules are washed from the celluloid leaving those not affected by the exposure to form a negative image, semi-transparent, semi-absorbent to light.

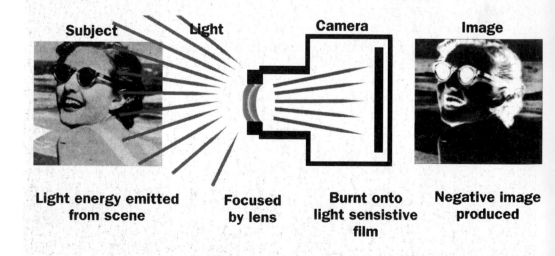

| Subject | Light | Camera | Image |

| Light energy emitted from scene | Focused by lens | Burnt onto light sensistive film | Negative image produced |

An appreciation of this will allow us, by way of illumination, to draw an analogy with human biology.

Say that, in our analogy, the light is an environmental stimulus and the lens is the sense organ through which the stimulus passes. The film represents the cognitive medium. We can now imagine that, in human biological terms, an environmental stimulus passing through a sense organ is 'burnt' into the cognitive medium in the way that images are burnt onto the retina.

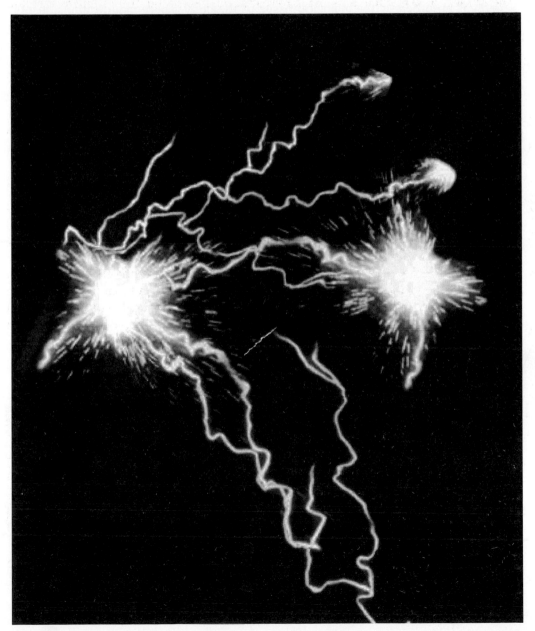

Our bodies are well known for their ability to adapt. There is no dispute about this. All human life is a process of adaptation, all human evolution is a process of adaptation and the human is an organism presented with greatly varying environmental stimuli. It is no surprise that, having existed so long, the human being displays such ability to modify itself in relation to its environment. Following this it could be argued that *all environmental stimuli cause the human to adapt* – in that all stimuli bring about change in the human state. Each set of stimuli that falls within the sensitivity range of the human will generate some modification as the incoming energy is absorbed by the biological tissue of the body. These modifications, insofar as the body adapts to them, can be considered to create *memories* and the reactivation of those memories, in the absence of the original stimuli, can be considered *thoughts.*

In another analogy, let us think in crude terms of the human organism as a lump of clay. The incoming stimulus is represented by pokes and prods with the result that the shape of the clay is changed. Each stimulus it receives in the form of a poke will leave an imprint – an inverted image of the stimuli. The magnitude of the imprint will be related to the magnitude of the stimulus. Imagine with this clay that a certain stimulus (a prod) is repeated consistently. Soon the clay will become immune to the prod since an imprint will have been established that allows the prod to have no effect on the shape of the clay. We could say that the clay had become desensitised – could we even say it had learnt something? Think of the phrase, 'She certainly left an impression on me.' The impression is the recorded trace that is left in the cognitive medium, the deformation of the clay.

As we have said before, it is necessary that organisms adapt to stimuli, even become immune to them through desensitisation. If this were not the case, they would be in a perpetual state of confusion and shock.

Consider a cat. When it is dozing it may be aroused by a finger scratching on the carpet. The scratch may represent a predator or a prey. Depending on the mood of the cat, and having established that it is my finger and not a mouse, it may become increasingly uninterested in my scratch. Ultimately it will be able to ignore the sound and return to sleep – until I make a hiss. In human terms, we can say that it is usually in our interests to deal with the energy introduced by external stimuli in such a way that we do not have to make a unique response to each occurrence of a repetition. This mechanism acts, in itself, to conserve the energy (and sanity) of the organism and has been referred to above as habituation.

The fact that we adapt to repetitious stimuli by being able to ignore them helps to confirm our faith in the relative stability of the world. We learn early on about the stability of the world and the fact that many things recur with varying frequency. Food arrives at certain times, it gets dark at certain times, you need the toilet at certain intervals, the wall paper next to your cot stays the same . . .

The net effect of all such repetitive stimuli on the developing organism is the creation of an image 'burnt' into the cognitive medium, an image made up of sounds, smells, textures as well as pictures. If the correlation of this image to future stimuli remains consistent then the sense of stability and permanence will be reinforced. The relatively stable energies radiated by the environment are translated, via the sense organs, into a relatively stable image 'burnt' into the cognitive medium. The cognitive medium, like our lump of clay, will adapt its form to accommodate the most powerful and persistent influxes of energy that act upon it. It is possible that a 'sense of order' is starting to emerge.

The first cut is the deepest

Returning to our lump of clay we must remember that, of a succession of repetitive pokes, the first will cause the greatest trauma and causes the largest modification in the form of the clay. Equivalent pokes that follow will have increasingly little impact. The first poke required the most energy, which means that it transferred the most energy to the clay. The clay had to make the largest adaptation to absorb the energy into its system.

This helps us to understand why the first occurrence of an event is the most memorable and also why experiences early in development have a profound impact on the rest of our lives. We can think of the cognitive medium as something that undergoes perpetual modification in response to environmental stimuli because it is constantly absorbing energy. The energy that is absorbed from the environment, along with the internal energy resources of the body, force transformations of the cognitive medium which leads the medium to adapt. This adaptation can be considered as a record of the stimuli – as a memory. It could also be thought of as an image, recalling our camera analogy. Any material which absorbs energy is changed by that energy. Having absorbed the energy from a certain stimulus, the cognitive medium will adapt in such a way that a trace of the original stimulus will be retained. Given that the same stimulus is repeated over a period of time, the need to make further adaptations will diminish. Therefore the first stimulus is likely to cause the greatest impact. We learn early on that something hot will burn us and many people can remember clearly the first time they were burnt.

There is, however, a complication to this. Whilst it may be easy to accept that we can become desensitised to a stimulus if it is often repeated (it is well known that during war participants can become immune to the most horrific experiences), we also know that repeated stimulation can cause irritation or pain and that even mild stimuli can sometimes give rise to panic or arousal. If a tap is dripping we may be able to ignore it for a while, but at some point it may become unbearable. If we hear a knock on the door in the middle of the night we might become very alert. A gentle kiss from a lover might lead to high arousal. In neurology this is known as *sensitisation,* the opposite side of the coin to habituation. Neurons are able to increase or decrease the likelihood of their firing by the mechanisms of *excitation* and *inhibition.* These processes are very complex but can be simply described as a feedback loop that attempts to regulate the state of the body, either to maintain homeostasis or to affect the behaviour in some way to the organism's advantage – to gain pleasure or avoid pain. In brief, habituation leads to a decreased likelihood that neurons will fire (they are more inhibited) while sensitisation leads to a greater likelihood that they will fire (they are excited). In the same way that we can become habituated to thoughts which occur regularly, we can also become sensitised to thoughts. Whether a stimulus leads to excitation or inhibition of neurons will depend on a large number of contextual factors that include the state of the organism and the type of stimulus. Sensitisation tends to amplify the response to stimuli and habituation tends to reduce it.

Consciousness and being

We have said that a sense of being is the sum of all active thought paths. This could equally well serve as a description of consciousness. Consciousness is the sum of all active thought paths, neural processes and sensory experience that may occur at any one time. Consciousness is the global effect that emerges from this set of occurrences. We have already said that this means we will never be able to find a 'seat of consciousness' in the brain or anywhere else, since consciousness is a function distributed over the whole of the being and intimately linked, via sense organs, to stimuli from the environment. The difference between consciousness and being could be described in the following way (although this does not mean that there are two separate things): Consciousness is the sum of all thoughts occurring at an instant. That is, a conscious thought need not necessarily be related to a prior or following thought. Being is the sum of all thoughts occurring over time when thoughts are built up into a pattern through negotiation with the environment and, having gained a certain level of stability, contribute to an on-going sense of existence. For most purposes we do not need to draw a distinction between consciousness and being and the two can be used interchangeably. It is assumed that during the normal course of events one is both conscious and aware of a sense of being. However, for a special case where one can be conscious without having a sense of being the distinction should be made. Such cases may occur when a subject is totally disorientated but remains conscious, that is, still thinking. They may not know who, why or where they are and may have lost the sense of on-going, stable existence. This may result from traumatic shock or neurological impairment. It can be said, however, that one cannot have a sense of being without being conscious.

The Post-Human concept of thought

We have described human thought, meaning and memory in terms of an energy regulating system. This means that the human is in essence no different from any other such system we may find in the universe. This does not deny that it is extremely complex, nor does it suggest that we will ever fully understand it.

What should be becoming clear is the divergence of this conception of human existence from the more traditional humanist one. If we can start to see how the most sacred of human functions, being and thought, operate in ways not dissected from other functions in the universe then we are moving away from the notion of humans as unique, isolated entities and are moving towards a conception of existence in which the human is totally integrated with the environment in all its manifestations – nature, technology and other beings.

I have discussed the complex and infinite-dimensional phenomena of human thought. I realise that it is not possible to make definitive and absolute descriptions of it. I have left out a lot more than I have put in. However, the ideas above allow us to understand how a useful model of human thought can be built up from such principles. It also allows us, in the next chapters, to speculate on the nature of consciousness and creativity, and how they might be synthesised.

'Human thought
is something
that occurs
within the
human body. It
is not
necessary to
identify
precisely where
it occurs
because it does
not occur
precisely in
any "part".'

The Post-Human Manifesto 5.1

What is art?
The only useful definition of art is that it describes any commodity of the art market. We must distinguish between an art object and an aesthetically stimulating object.

An art object is a commodity that is traded on the art market. An aesthetic object is one that is appreciated for its aesthetic quality. Something may be both an art object and an aesthetic object, such as Van Gogh's 'Irises', while something may be an aesthetic object without being art, like a sunset or an iris.

5. Art, Aesthetics and Creativity

The production of art, appreciation of aesthetic experience and the ability to create are particularly human faculties. They are often cited by the humanists as the highest expressions of human thought and the things which most distinguish us from machines. It would, therefore, be fair to admit that the Post-Human era cannot begin in full until we have met this challenge from the humanists – to make clear whether such processes are so mysterious as to be totally outside our realm of understanding or whether they can be understood sufficiently so that they might be synthesised by other means. In Post-Human terms the subject of art is interesting because it represents an area of human activity in which the processes of creativity and aesthetic production are highly concentrated and highly exposed. The study of art allows us to see more clearly how these processes operate, especially in light of the model of human thought we outlined in the last chapter.

Art

What is art? The only useful definition of art is that it describes any commodity of the art market. We must distinguish between an art object and an aesthetically stimulating object. An art object is a commodity that is traded on the art market. An aesthetic object is one that is appreciated for its aesthetic quality. Something may be both an art object and an aesthetic object, such as Van Gogh's 'Irises', while something may be an aesthetic object without being art, like a sunset or an iris.

Many people think that much modern art is not art because they consider it to lack aesthetic merit even though it commands high prices on the art market. They are simply confusing the art value and the aesthetic value of an object. These two values are quite separate, but of course linked. 'Art is a commodity like any other', said Henry Kahnweiler, Picasso's dealer. Art is an aesthetic commodity. Marcel Duchamp demonstrated very clearly the irrelevance of what the object is to the question of whether it is art. It is the process of its introduction into the art market that transforms an object into art. For example, in 1914 Duchamp designated a bottlerack as an art object. 'The choice', he claimed, 'was based on a reaction of visual indifference, with at the same time a total absence of good or bad taste, in fact a complete anaesthesia.'

In order to be clear, the art market can be defined as an identifiable set of institutions and commercial organisations which collectively, fund, promote and sell art.

Art must be (and always has been) elitist and exclusive in order to maintain its financial value and prestige. Many modern artists use aesthetic elitism to guarantee exclusivity which in turn ensures values are upheld. The main function of art is to distinguish rich people from poorer people.

Aesthetics

It is possible to distinguish between two types of art depending on the aesthetic qualities displayed. Good art is art that is aesthetically stimulating; bad art is aesthetically neutral. The criteria that determine whether something is aesthetically stimulating or aesthetically neutral are always changing.

Good art always contains an element of disorder (a late Turner landscape). Bad art simply reinforces a pre-existing order (Nazi-approved art).

Good art promotes discontinuity. Bad art enforces continuity. Discontinuity produces aesthetically stimulating experiences. Continuity produces aesthetically neutral experiences.

Discontinuity is the engine of all creation, but discontinuity disappears without continuity. Rich aesthetic experience is generated by the perception, simultaneously, of continuity and discontinuity in the same event.

'The serpentine line by its waving and winding at the same time different ways, leads the eye in a pleasing manner along the continuity of its variety, if I may be allowed the expression; and which by its twisting so many different ways, may be said to inclose (tho' but a single line) varied contents.'

William Hogarth, artist, quoted by Gombrich in The Sense of Order, *p. 137*

All successful design relies on balancing the relative quotients of order and disorder in the object. This also goes for the composition of music and literature. However, such judgements cannot be made in isolation from the fact that values of order and disorder are largely prescribed by social agreement. Beauty is not a finite and eternal truth that transcends the fluctuations of fashion and taste.

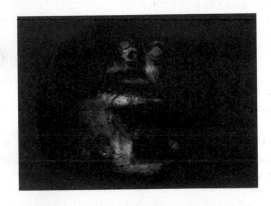

> *Beauty is ugliness repeated*

The process of aesthetic stimulation is heightened when concepts are forced together from relatively diverse locations. The amount of energy required to contemplate diverse concepts produces the rush of excitement familiar to lovers of art. Such an effect is often achieved when an object is taken from one context and placed in another. Or in the case of many Picasso pieces, we are asked to accept the presence of one object when we plainly see another.

'The greater and truer the distance between two juxtaposed realities , the stronger will be the image and the greater its emotive power and poetic reality.'

Pierre Reverdy, quoted by Breton in What is Surrealism?, *p. 282*

Discontinuity is the disruption in an otherwise continuous flow of signs that disorientates us within the chain of meaning. In this turbulence we find aesthetic experience and its associated joy for, although all discontinuity is not aesthetic experience, all aesthetic experience is discontinuous.

> The dream is a heavy
> Ham
> Which hangs from the ceiling
> > – *Pierre Reverdy*

> Your tongue
> The red fish in the aquarium
> Of your mouth
> > – *Guillaume Apollinaire*

> Guitar – a bidet that sings
> > – *Jean Cocteau*

Aesthetic experience – the joyous disruption that explodes from within that which we contemplate. The experience may be presented through many artistic forms although it is highly visible in art, where we find numerous examples.

The operation of aesthetics

'But however we analyse the difference between the regular and the irregular, we must ultimately be able to account for the most basic fact of aesthetic experience, the fact that delight lies somewhere between boredom and confusion.'   Gombrich, *op. cit. p. 9*

Remembering the model of human thought described in the last chapter, we stated that the human being is locked into a perpetual conflict between the need to maintain a sense of order and predictability on the one hand, whilst on the other being aware that such stability is vulnerable to dissolution and collapse. Thus, there is a continual need to draw threads of meaning together as a way of constituting the wholeness of the being, to assure oneself of existence. It is also true that to be in a constant state of predictability leads to boredom and, being conditioned to expect disruption, its absence may lead the person actively to seek it.

There is no doubt that humans like and need to be stimulated. There are numerous activities using touch, sight, smell, taste and sound in which humans engage for pleasure. From this we can deduce that the cognitive medium has a continuous demand for sensory input. If we are deprived of this for long periods we are seriously harmed (see the reference to sensory deprivation in Chapter 1). Given that the human is a system that demands a high level of sensory input, it is not surprising that we have developed so many means of providing it within our culture - music, films, books, sport, etc. However, just any old stimulation will not do. It is not enough to keep flashing a red light in someone's face to hold them intrigued. As well as the desire for pure sensory excitement (particularly in small babies), there is also the need for intellectual stimulation often linked directly to that of the sensory kind. This requires that the source of stimulation be complex enough to engage us at this level.

There are many examples of activities in which humans engage for pleasure where our physical sense of stability is threatened even though such a threat would normally be avoided. Some examples are mountain climbing, horse racing, motor racing, fair rides, hang-gliding and so on. Despite the obvious danger in all these activities, many people obviously feel that the risks presented are outweighed by the benefits of the pleasure to be gained. Even with activities of a less physical kind such as reading, film watching, computer games, looking at art, etc., there are many examples where our sense of mental stability is challenged, this of course being directly linked to our sense of physical stability. Books may contain complex and demanding ideas, films may terrify or try to offend us, computer games offer the option of watching ourselves die and art may confuse our perceptions.

What is common to all these activities is the simultaneous state of continuity and discontinuity to which the participant is exposed. Continuity of existence and meaning is maintained whilst, at the same time, discontinuity of existence and meaning is threatened. The fact that there is a conflict between these states gives rise to the excitement and heightened awareness that is experienced by the participant as they struggle to resolve this condition. In the case of the outwardly physical activities, the continuity of existence is maintained by knowledge that one is able to control the bike, horse or whatever. If one were not able to do this, then pleasure would turn to fear - the discontinuity, which is the threat of death or harm, may become a reality. With the more mental activities the guarantee of continuity lies in the knowledge that the author, director, game designer or artist has the power to resolve the disrupted threads of meaning to the satisfaction of the audience, to remove the fear, to explain the idea, to provide the means by which the game can eventually be won. Whether this is actually done or not differs in each case. But implied in the presentation of any work is the trust or belief that the author knows what they are doing whether or not the audience fully appreciates their intentions.

To return to purely aesthetic experience, we can say that humans find it stimulating to be put in a position where they can apprehend both stability and volatility in the same thing. In terms of our model of thought, aesthetic experience is induced when an idea can flow freely through the cognitive medium by a well established route in one direction while at the same time it draws in other notions or takes other routes which are dislocated. To take the example of an Impressionist painting, something which is generally regarded as having high aesthetic merit, we can look at this work by Claude Monet.

Claude Monet, *Impression - Sunrise, 1874*

The scene from which it is drawn may be familiar enough – some water, a rising sun and some objects in the fore and middle grounds. The fact that it is set in the very early morning may make it more significant to a viewer who is not used to such views, but on the whole it is not an outstandingly remarkable scene. Thus, we have established the context of continuity – it is a fairly standard view of Le Havre harbour and, as such, does not seem to deserve the astonishing attention that this painting receives in the history of art. What merits the fuss is the discontinuous way in which this scene has been represented here by Monet. This becomes even more true if we try to imagine looking at it in the context of other French painting of the 1870s. What Monet does is to suggest the presence of things by the use of marks which, in themselves, seem to bear only an approximate relation to that which they represent. Many marks seem not to represent anything at all. By this process Monet creates a level of confusion and disruption at the surface of the image that is in contrast to the placidity and simplicity of the subject. The artist has pictured a stable scene in a volatile way and has introduced a quotient of discontinuity into the otherwise continuous representation. It should be pointed out that, at the time it was painted, the idea that a matter-of-fact painting of a mundane port should be the subject of serious artistic attention was in itself discontinuous with the dominant conventions in art.

While it might be quite hard today to see this work as a culturally disruptive icon, as we have seen so much like it since, we are still able to appreciate the qualities of continuity and discontinuity it embodies. The fact that Impressionist works are amongst the most popular with the public does not rely solely on their historical value as art. As a body their function is to invoke images of pleasant environments and events which, for many people, are continuous with pleasurable things they have seen. At the same time they are slightly disruptive in that they do not merely produce photographic records of those scenes but use brushwork and palette effects to heighten illusions of shadow and light as well obscuring and blurring form. These techniques create a distance between the painting, which is present, and its imagined subject, which is absent, that is greater in Impressionist works than it is in a photographic record. The viewer is asked to recognise a scene which they plainly see being represented, that of water, boats, etc., but in doing so they are provided with visual clues which are clearly distinct from the things that they represent. In making the brush marks so bold we are forced to see the mark and its reference at one time. Looking at a detail of the water, we see many dark marks that are obviously those of a brush, whilst at the same time we see these as the shadows of ripples. This effect multiplied over the whole picture plane gives the painting its resonance, the discontinuity between that which we are being asked to see and that which we actually see. It is here that the aesthetic appeal of the painting lies. It is interesting to note that the contemporary art critic Frédéric Chevalier wrote in 1877:

'The disturbing ensemble of contradictory qualities which distinguish Impressionists . . . the crude application of paint, the down to earth subjects, the appearance of spontaneity . . . the conscious incoherence, the bold colours, the contempt for form, the childish naïveté that they mix heedlessly with exquisite refinements. . . '

quoted in Art of Western World, *p. 326*

In this passage the critic lists the elements of discontinuity as he perceived them in Impressionist works.

We stated earlier that whilst humans need to maintain threads of meaning in order to maintain their sense of being, they also actively seek stimulation of a kind which often threatens that sense of being and stability by exposing themselves to danger, confusion or fear. These two desires need not necessarily be seen as contradictory. Many people report heightened states of being and awareness having been exposed to volatility and confusion. The effect of discontinuous information on the person is to open up new pathways of neural activity that would otherwise have no need to be opened. Provided this stimulation is not excessive, the fact that neural activity is greater than it might be under more mundane circumstances actually brings more of the person into being, if we consider being as the sum of all active neural links. To maximise the number of active neural links we must maximise the stimulation required to activate them and so must expose ourselves to things that will produce this effect. For different people it will be different things. Some may use drugs, some music, some skateboards, some art. The effect in all cases is the same. By exposure to a source of stimulation that is discontinuous we transcend the mundaneness of ordinary existence where every thought is easily continuous with every other.

Aesthetic objects as emitters of energy

All perception of things in the environment occurs as a result of the energetic transformation that any thing is able to induce in our senses. Whether it is a sound, a vision, a smell, taste or touch, we are only aware of it in the extent to which it causes a modification in our sense organs, that is, an energetic modification. It is plain that the greater the amount of energy that is received from a stimulus, the greater that stimulus will be. One aspect of the apparently discontinuous effect of Impressionist paintings on the French public in the late nineteenth century was the use by artists of pure pigment and the juxtaposition of complementary colours. Compared to the standard 'brown' paintings of the French Academy which tended to mix and overlay colours, reducing their brilliance, the Impressionists were noted for applying dabs of unmixed colour in discrete brush strokes. This technique was developed by Seurat and the Pointillist school who made a virtue out of constructing images with small points of primary and secondary colour thus creating vibrant tonal effects when viewed from a distance. The use of pure pigment and contrasting secondary colours (particularly that of red against blue and yellow against violet) was developed strongly by Post-Impressionists such as Van Gogh, Gaugin and Cézanne and became especially apparent in the work of the Fauve School.

The effect of using colour in this way was actually to increase the level of light energy reflected by the painted surface. Bright colours reflect more light than dark ones. The effect on the viewer was to have their senses stimulated to a greater degree than normally would have been the case since the energetic modification upon their senses was much greater. Impressionist paintings produced an increased level of excitation. We can even speculate that name 'Impressionism' relates just as much to the enhanced sensory impression that the works leave on our senses as it does to the vagueness with which reality is represented.

We can understand the impact of many cultural products in terms of how much energy they present to the senses. Many people are particularly excited by the volume of music at concerts or raves. This excitement is often enhanced by the use of bright, flashing lights of vivid colour. The energetic input into the body is of a very high level, some might say dangerously high.

However, the effect of a particular stimulus cannot depend solely on the level of energy emitted from the object under consideration. One text may be more stimulating than another but both may be read from pages that reflect equal amounts of light into the eye. An exciting piece of music may be more stimulating played quietly than a bland piece of music played loudly.

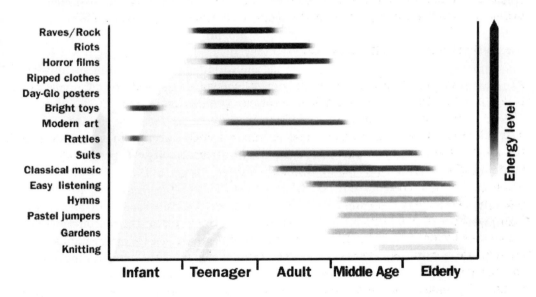

Diagram of different levels of energy excitement in the cultural products designed to appeal to different ages

The reason for this is that human stimulation is not wholly determined by the extent to which our surface sense organs are energetically modified (that is, the organs of sight, smell, touch, hearing and taste). The impact of an object may also depend on the extent to which it can induce energetic modifications in the cognitive medium. We have already described how thought is a process of energy transformations. Continuous thoughts require less energy to proceed than do discontinuous thoughts. If the effect of a cultural product is to induce discontinuity in the mind of a person, then a greater level of energy modification in the mind will occur. Thus, the mind itself could be thought of as a sense organ. There is no reason to suppose that it is, in essence, any different from any other sense organ. Indeed, we have stated on several occasions that the cognitive medium consists of all neural tissue necessary for the maintenance of a conscious being. In this way, energetic modifications brought about in the mind through the perception of semantically discontinuous stimuli are no different from the discontinuities of energy in the environment perceived by the surface senses.

The use of discontinuity

Art is an activity designed to heighten aesthetic experience. There are many others, including fashion, design, music, advertising, dance and architecture, which are intended to do the same thing. What is common to them all is that they are seen as productions of creativity. It follows that there is a link between the creative process of making these artifacts and the aesthetic experience of using or seeing them. The creative products of one set of people are used to generate aesthetic experience in others. We value the products of other people's creativity. There is a huge section of human society engaged in the design and manufacture of things that are intended to induce aesthetic experience in others. Many of these people (artists, pop musicians, film directors) are amongst the most highly paid (thus highly valued) in society. The fact that so much value is placed on the production of things that elevate our senses reinforces the idea that the demand for aesthetic stimulation is great.

And yet, while our culture elevates those products and producers who create aesthetic experience by exploiting our fascination with discontinuity, it prescribes strict limitations on what type of disruptions are tolerated.

We have shown that discontinuity is as important to the construction of meaning as continuity. And yet, in general, the continuum is privileged over the discontinuum by the dominant sections in society. Once a dominant group has become established it tends to reproduce a view of the world that serves it own interests and in doing so tries to establish this view as the definition of stability and continuity. Any threat to this system is perceived as a discontinuity in relation to the continuity that has been established. It must therefore be suppressed. We find countless examples in history. The persecution of witches and heretics, the suppression of popular revolt, legislation against raves, apartheid, Elvis televised above the waist. All are efforts to maintain the continuum of a specific authority against the threat of a discontinuity. And yet it is clear that discontinuity is inevitable, it cannot be eradicated, and indeed it is produced, defined, given its very form, by attempts to annihilate it. The authority of order pre-determines the possibilities of existence and belief. However, such authority can only hold for a time. As soon as any order is established it comes immediately into conflict with the forces of disorder and chaos which it will try to resist but will never remove. These discontinuous forces are represented variously by revolution, the avant-garde, magic, madness and by those who wish to extend their sense of being by subverting social continuities.

Post-Human art uses technology to promote discontinuity. Healthy societies tolerate the promotion of discontinuity because they understand that people need exposure to it in spite of themselves. Unhealthy societies discourage the promotion of discontinuity.

Creativity

Human society has distinguished itself from everything else on earth by its ability to create and innovate. The power to transform and recombine things, to invent, to improvise, is central to the success of the species. What will separate humanist era machines from Post-Human era machines is that the latter will be able to create, innovate, invent and improvise. Having reached this point, Post-Human machines will start to take over as the most successful species on earth.

It is tempting to think of creativity as a unique human faculty and, as such, distinct from other faculties like perception or intelligence. The fact that we have a distinct word to describe a phenomenon suggests that we are referring to a discrete thing. This is totally consistent with the humanist way of looking at the world. Humanists tend to compartmentalise phenomena, to create definitions and sub-definitions in an attempt to quantify or understand them. From a Post-Human point of view, creativity is no different from any other thought process. Creativity is thinking in general and thinking in general is creative. That is not say there are no exceptional thoughts, thoughts which expressed in the right way have a profound impact on culture.

Neither is creativity just about thinking; it is as much about doing. Since, as far as we know, we cannot read the thoughts of others the only way we can see the creativity of another person is through the things they produce. These might be words, music, paintings, games, clothes or any kind of product that involves a combination of thought and action to realise. Mental creativity of itself is of little use or interest to anyone unless it is expressed in some way.

A simple description (but not definition) of creativity might be that it is any act of transformation. This would include anything from turning the page of a book to painting the Sistine Chapel ceiling. Every time we transform something we create a new state in our environment. Of course, this does not mean that every act will be perceived as having created something of equal merit. It is up to the conventions of cultural mores to decide what act is, or is not, deemed to be significantly creative, and no fast definition of this can be made. Opinions will vary greatly depending on a large number of social factors.

Destruction may, on the surface, appear to be the opposite of creation. How we evaluate whether a particular act is creative or destructive also depends on the view of the person making the judgement. What is to one person the act of creating grazing land by clearing South American forests is to another the destruction of the rainforest. The dropping of the H-bomb on Hiroshima was conceived as an act of destruction, which indeed it was. But at the moment the bomb exploded it created the largest conflagration yet known on earth. Many argue that it later created the conditions for the Japanese surrender. The bomb itself was the product of many years of creative work by some of the most advanced scientific minds. Whilst we may take a position on whether a particular act is, in itself, creative or destructive we must remember that in doing so we are led by subjective concepts of good and bad. Creativity has connotations of goodness, whilst destruction has connotations of badness.

As Michelangelo carves the David he is destroying the marble in its original state. By this process of destruction (transformation) he has created something new. Trees are destroyed to make paper. Paper is used by James Joyce on which to write *Ulysses*. An egg is destroyed to make a cake. A cow is destroyed to create a pie. One may take a moral view of any act as to its desirability but it must be accepted that any transformation can be perceived as having properties of creation and destruction. The point of this is not to render the terms meaningless in a fog of relativistic word play.

Rather it is to look clearly at the process of creativity without the preconceptions of genius and elitism with which it is normally associated. Nature creates and destroys in equal measure. It is only we who, because of our linguistic make-up, classify those transformations according to what we believe to be good or bad.

As stated, we do not consider all transformations to be equal and the type of transformation we normally associate with creativity is that which produces something new. We think of human acts of thought and expression which bring something into existence that would otherwise not exist. Creativity, as we normally understand it, consists of acts of transformation that bring about something which is both new and beneficial. Destruction is usually an act of transformation that brings about something detrimental.

To be more specific, let us talk about the type of creativity associated with the generation of things that are new and beneficial since this is the most useful kind. What processes are at work when creativity becomes apparent? We have already stated that creativity is an act of transformation, but this is so general as to provide little illumination. What more can we say?

Creativity is not a thing but an experience; it has to be experienced in time to exist. This does not deny that the creative act may be embodied in an object or expression, but that object is not the creative 'thing', it is a creation. Imagine that I continually leave the bath running and forget about it so that it overflows. I invent a very clever but simple device that warns me of the danger. The act of making it may have been creative and the creativity it embodies may be apparent when viewing it afterwards, but the object or expression in itself cannot be creative, only a creation. This is true in all cases except one – when something is created which in itself is creative. A baby may be seen as the creation of a man and woman, but soon it becomes a creative being in its own right. A computer system may be developed that is shown to be creative, in which case it is both a creation and creative.

Since creativity is an act and not the product of the act, it can only occur as a process. It is important to stress the temporal nature of creativity to avoid confusion between the act of being creative and the product or expression of the act. It is obvious that many creative thoughts occur that are never committed to paper or keyboard. Creativity can still exist and be experienced without any material support, without any evidence that it ever occurred. If this is so how can our description of creativity as transformation hold true, if there is no evidence of any transformation having taken place?

Returning to the model of human thought offered in the last chapter, we noted that the cognitive medium is not a static system of memory and thought compartments but a highly adaptable medium that is constantly being changed by exposure to environmental stimuli. Within this medium lie paths that represent the probable routes a thought might take were it to be activated. It was proposed that these routes are not fixed and finite but open to reconfiguration in the light of new stimuli. Whilst the medium remains adaptable it also maintains a great deal of stability since without either quality it would be virtually useless in dealing with the coincident stability and volatility of the environment.

Any creative act is an act of transformation. It does not matter that the transformation might occur in the cognitive medium of a human mind or in the shape of a piece of marble. There are many times when we try deliberately to transform the layout of our mind. When we are learning, or trying to think of a new idea, trying to forget or to remember something, we are consciously attempting to transform the links between ideas and memories. Whether we are trying to think up an excuse for work or attempting to comprehend the ultimate nature of the universe, we are doing essentially the same thing: we are engaged in a purposeful attempt to generate new pathways and links within our mind. It is important to say 'new' because if such paths were already available there would be no point in trying to create them.

The establishment of a new link, or set of links, in the mind of the thinker is a transformation within the cognitive medium. To take an example. An entrepreneur who has made a great deal of money supplying organic foods to delicatessens wants to expand into a new market. One day they are asked to take their friend's daughter to a fast food restaurant. The restaurant is completely full of people of all ages and social classes. All are spending great amounts of money on food that the entrepreneur knows to be of minimal nutritional value and high fat content. The entrepreneur thinks, 'It's a very efficient operation and the food must taste good, but neither I nor most of my friends could eat here more than a couple of times a year. The food's so bad for you.' Several days later, after much thought about new markets, the entrepreneur is making a wholemeal sandwich, not having time to cook, when an idea strikes. 'What if there were a fast food restaurant that served tasty food which was also very healthy?' The benefits are immediately obvious. There is a huge international market for fast food, the unit costs are very low and prices can be premium. There is a great untapped market for health- and weight-conscious customers who would normally avoid fast food restaurants, and these are often the wealthier sections of society with more money to spend on going out. A name even presented itself – 'Whole Meal'. In this example the creative act of the entrepreneur was to draw a link between two concepts which had, until then, been incompatible in their own mind – fast food and health food. The new idea, Whole Meal, results from a transformation of these links into a new concept.

Creativity does not consist in the production of anything that is completely new since

there is nothing that *is* completely new. Creativity consists in combining elements that already exist but which have previously been seen as separate. Creativity and aesthetic appreciation are both functions of the human ability to modify the connections in one's thought paths, or to have them modified.

The question remains, how and why do such transformations occur? To take an historically famous example, Archimedes spent a long time trying to work out how to measure the volume of an irregular shape, one that did not conform to regular Euclidean theorems. After much mental effort he proceeded to take a bath at which point he noticed that the water in the bath was displaced by an amount equivalent to his irregularly shaped body. Simply by measuring the amount of water displaced he could calculate the volume of his body. Such was his joy at this realisation that he is said to have run from his bath shouting, 'Eureka'. There are many other such examples in the history of science and thought and they often follow the same pattern – a period of extended and frustrating struggle followed by a moment of realisation at a time of apparent relaxation or distraction.

We can speculate on a probable mechanism for this phenomena and this requires that we recall our model of the human cognitive medium as an energy-regulating system. You will remember I proposed that human cognition is a process of energy transformations, as are all other things in the universe. Any process of thinking requires and consumes energy. It is consistent with all other energy-regulating systems to say that extended periods of concentrated thought require more energy than short periods of absent-minded thought. Indeed, it is well known that mental activity can lead to exhaustion, a deficit of energy, just as physical exercise can. As with any energy-regulating system, there is a limited amount of energy that can be used at any one time. If a great deal of energy is invested in a confined part of the cognitive medium (for example, if one problem is examined again and again), then it is likely that the thought paths involved will become 'hot'. That is, they will constantly be receiving energy in a way that other parts of the mind are not and this causes them to adapt in the way that a muscle adapts if it is constantly used. At this point one of two things may happen. Firstly, the thinker may 'break through'. By forcing energy into a confined area of thought (thinking very hard) the build up of energy is such that there is nowhere else for the energy to go but to break out into a new location, thus forming a new path. Such is the case when someone has forgotten something and struggles very hard to remember. The link that could not be made initially is forced into existence by the application of energy.

The alternative thing that may happen is the thinker temporarily abandons the deliberate search for a solution and does something else. At some point whilst the thinker is distracted the solution arrives as if by magic. Many people have experienced this when trying to remember a name and, being unable to do so, give up. Only later does the name arrive when the question has been forgotten. Some people actually say,

'If I stop thinking about it, it will come to me.' In this case the energy regulating mechanism may work in the following way.

Energy is forced into a confined area of the mind as constant attempts are made to find links between a problem and possible solutions. Solutions may be found that turn out straight away to be wrong and so the process starts again. The fact that it takes a lot of time and effort suggests that the solution is actually located at a considerable distance from the problem since if it were close it would have been found quickly. Such is the case with problems of an extremely difficult kind where the thinker is trying to arrive at a solution to a problem that has never been solved before. Having abandoned the search for a solution, the thinker is no longer applying great amounts of energy to the thought paths in which the problem is being pondered. These paths, however, are used to receiving large amounts of attention and are now being ignored. They are still 'warm'. As the thinker starts to relax, the general demand for energy decreases in the mind as a whole. There is now a greater resource of energy which can be applied to the problem and it is this free energy that is used to form the distant connection which creates the solution. Whilst there was not enough energy to make the connection during the period of exertion, the surplus energy made available whilst the mind is relaxed makes the connection possible. Of course, this insight could not have occurred had the thinker not spent the long period concentrating on the idea. Just as a muscle which is never exercised will never need to grow strong, so a mind that is never exercised will never need to form new connections. Hence, 'Genius is 1% inspiration and 99% perspiration.'

Of course this model is very simplistic. It does not take into account, for example, that neural tissue is as likely to inhibit energy as it is to conduct it. We might say that any energy system in which large amounts of energy concentrated in small areas and which produce excessive potential differences ought to inhibit, fence in, those impulses in order to prevent damage. It may be that by concentrating too much energy on one problem the neural system is forced to prohibit what might be a dangerous link to another part of the system until such time as the problem is forgotten. At this point a smaller amount of energy might be allowed through to make a connection, it being less likely to 'blow a fuse'.

Note: The 'rate-limiting factor' in human cognition depends on a number of things including the speed that a charge can be conducted through the axon, the amount of neurotransmitters available and the production of energy in the form of ATP (adenosine triphosphate). The cognitive medium does not have an infinite supply of ATP. It has to be made in the little chemical factories (mitochondria) in the cell body, and this takes time. Therefore, if available ATP is consumed by intensive thought, time will need to elapse before more energy can be made available to continue. The neurons, however, having been 'exercised' in this way will have a greater potentiality to fire. Thus when they recoup their energy, they may be stronger than before and be able to 'push-through' connections that were not previously possible. It is interesting to note here that the cognitive medium, and the brain in particular, is the most voracious consumer of energy in the body.

Whilst this model may be simplistic it does conform with both our known experience and current scientific knowledge about the mind. The significance from the Post-Human point of view is that we can describe the operation of the thought processes, including things like creativity, in ways that are totally consistent with other systems we can study in the universe. There is no absolute reason to insist that the human mind is a freak of nature. Whilst the processes here described occur in a particular medium known as the human mind, there is no *a priori* reason why the same energy-regulating mechanisms could not occur in other media – say, computers.

Earlier I made a sweeping statement that 'Creativity is thinking in general and thinking in general is creative'. What I meant by this was that creative acts are not essentially different from other acts of thought. We are continually thinking new things, making up new sentences and concepts, being exposed to new stimuli without necessarily thinking we are being creative. Creativity in the traditional sense is taken to mean those exceptional acts that produce results having a significant impact our lives or on the course of human development. These acts may present us with a new idea, solve a problem, make us laugh, bring an invention into being, cure a disease. Creativity is the transformation of the mind, and, if it is to affect anyone else, must be done in conjunction with some transformation of the environment. But whether the product is of the greatest historical merit or of the most minimal personal value the processes by which it is produced are essentially the same.

Creativity and discontinuity

All creative ideas are discontinuous in that they involve divergence from a continuum. This is how we recognise them as something novel. However, it is not enough to say that one can simply diverge from a continuum to be creative. That way sits the monkey at the typewriter. We simply break up the flow of meaning. A truly creative idea diverges from the continuum without destroying it. It retains the continuum, albeit by transforming it. The effect to is increase the richness of the associative path of any particular idea, to link it up with a new idea or set of ideas. An idea of itself has no value. What is of value is the other ideas to which it is connected. In time the creative act that was originally seen as discontinuous forms part of a new continuum and so the process goes on.

Three levels of disruption

Continuous streams of signs can be disrupted by the insertion of discontinuities. The degree of interruption determines the level of creativity in the system. A minor interruption may be interpreted as a stylistic fluctuation, a variation on a theme. Truly creative interruption draws in a new meaning chain that enriches the currently operative continuity whilst allowing it to remain present. Extreme interruption leads to nonsense and the termination of the continuous chain.

Behold the difference between the crank and the genius! The crank's idea is disembodied and isolated, unable to be intelligibly linked to the rest of culture. The genius's idea, whilst it may be just as wild, has the merit of retaining the necessary links for their work to be taken seriously. Whether this is to do with the personality of the person, their status, communication skills, the set of beliefs prevalent at any one time is an interesting point for discussion. Van Gogh was the crank who turned out to be a genius. Forgotten are the geniuses who turned out to be cranks.

What we value in creative ideas is not just their novelty. Novelty in itself induces excitement because it has the effect of opening up pathways in the cognitive medium that have not been opened before. But having had this experience the excitement may be short lived. Once opened it is open and cannot be opened again. Richer creative acts lie in opening complex and far reaching new pathways, the more the better. Recalling our description of being, that it is the sum of *active* thought paths, we could say that the more active thought paths there are, the more we are being. With no active thought paths we cease to be. The more diverse and complex are those thought paths that are active at any one time, the more energy is required to travel through them. Thoughts that lie on a continuum are by definition closely located and require little energy to travel. By introducing discontinuity, a divergence from the continuum, without deactivating the continuum we are increasing the total amount of active conscious area. The greater the area of active consciousness, the greater the sense of being. The rush of energy through the cognitive medium required to travel many pathways at once is a tangible effect of the heightened state of being.

How does discontinuity arise in the mind? Surely, if thoughts normally move in a continuum, by the path of least resistance, there is no need for them to diverge in a discontinuous way. How can creative acts emerge? At this point it will become clear

why I have insisted at all times that the brain, body and environment cannot be separated. Whilst the mind may be an energy-regulating system, it is not a self-contained regulating system. The mind is something which is at all times sensitive to fluctuations in the environment through the activity of the sense organs. The sense organs, which are intimately connected to the mind, are themselves involuntarily responsive to fluctuations in the environment. These fluctuations are not all regular, nor are they wholly irregular. Were the world a totally regular place there would be no need to diverge from any continuity of thought because one would not expect any discontinuous stimuli. Were the world a totally irregular place there would be no opportunity to develop continuous thought since there would be no continuous stimuli.

The mind is not a sealed unit. It is forced to respond continually to variations in sensory stimuli and, in being so, forced continually to reconfigure itself. This being the case, the mind can never remain static. Thinking can never stop. And every thought is a change. No thought can be thought twice in an identical way. Thought is, to some extent, dependent on the environment which is never static. By the same token the body is never static; things may seem the same but time will have moved on. Each heartbeat is one closer to death and one further from birth. It may be that we try to regulate our environment to smooth out unwelcome fluctuations of stimuli. We regulate our temperature, noise levels, odours, tastes. We try to make the world as continuous and predictable as possible. Yet at the same time this bores us. We seek excitement and stimulation to maintain our sense of enjoyment and our sense of being alive – the cold sea, the hot sun, the loud music, the strong tastes, the exciting film, the stimulating art.

To answer the question of how discontinuities arise in thought: The mind, being a highly complex set of connective tissues, can never be said to be fixed. This does not mean that, like all other organic matter, it does not display a considerable amount of stability. One thought that may lead to another thought on a particular day may lead to an entirely separate thought on another day given that the structure of the mind may have changed in the intervening period. Several things may have changed it – new set of experiences which cause new learning paths, the body may be in a different state, a drug or stimulant may have been introduced into the system.

All this does tend to imply that all such mental fluctuations are out of our control, that we are simply weather vanes that blow in the wind. Isn't our notion of creativity that it is something we deliberately choose to do? Of course the human mind is not simply a barometer that responds blindly to prevailing conditions. The fact that we can act to change things in our environment, for better or worse, is something we learn at a very early age. Why should we choose to draw an arbitrary division between acting to change things in our environment and acting to change things in our mind? They are, after all, part of the same thing.

Aesthetic experience and creativity have something in common: they both serve to activate pathways of cognition that would otherwise lay dormant. The pathways they activate are richer and more complex than those associated with more mundane activities thus leading to heightened senses of being and awareness. Both use discontinuity as a way of diverging from the continuous but neither, if successful, deactivates totally the continuum from which they diverge. This explains why creativity is needed to generate objects of aesthetic stimulation and why many creative acts are regarded in themselves as objects of aesthetic pleasure.

Creative selection

'What appears at first glance to be an error – namely, the mutation resulting from a copying error or the chemical instability of the nucleic acid – is, in the final analysis, a gain in flexibility and adaptability. Indeed, it makes the evolution of the genetic system possible. Gain through error.'
F. Cramer, op. cit. p. 48

Any act of design, creation or invention consists in generating a set of possibilities bound by a set of requirements and restraints. The creative process involves testing possible outcomes against the limitations imposed by the structure in which one is working as well as the requirements one has in mind.

A simple form of such a process is the game where one is required to match a set of variously shaped pegs with variously shaped holes in a piece of wood. The requirement is that each piece is fitted into a hole. The constraint is that there is only one hole into which each piece will fit. It is through trial and error that one finally succeeds, trying different pieces in different holes until the task is complete.

This procedure is not unlike that which happens in other, more complex, forms of creativity such as painting, music, design and business ideas. In setting out to create, say, a piece of music, one is aware of the almost infinite possible combinations of notes, chords and expressions that are available to a composer. However, there is a whole set of constraints imposed on anyone who wishes to create an original tune.

1. The composer is likely to be working within the constraints of a particular musical genre such as jungle, rap, serial, folk or some combination thereof. The genre imposes its own constraints of rhythm, melodic structure, instrument sounds etc.

2. Since music is a time based art, any piece will have a beginning, middle and end. (Even the silent piece *4'33"* by John Cage conforms to this). A piece of music is likely to be longer than one second and shorter than one day. Of course there are exceptions but these are very rare. Therefore, there is a time constraint on the length of the piece. The ability of humans to concentrate on one thing continuously is limited (some claim to around 90 minutes, the length of many football matches, films and symphonies).

3. An original piece must not exactly reproduce another piece. This does not mean that one cannot be creative when producing a variation of a piece, or that one cannot use sections of other pieces in an original work. Most pieces of music contain elements of other pieces of music and one could argue that some styles of music all sound the same. However, no composer would be satisfied with producing a work which copied exactly that of another composer.

A composer, then, is put in the position of having, on the one hand, a series of almost infinite possibilities whilst, on the other, having a set of limiting constrains within which to work. Many composers work by improvising with combinations of notes and rhythms until a sequence is arrived at which is satisfactory. The process of improvisation involves generating sequences that do not have a prescribed order but which are not wholly random. Many composers claim inspiration from things they hear in their mind. Mozart claimed to have seen whole symphonies appear at once as a revelation. These cases must be counted as exceptional since, for most composers, the original product comes from many hours of practice and improvisation. Given that a composer is writing through improvisation it will be the case that many sequences may be generated before one is chosen to be retained as part of the composition.

We could draw a comparison between this and the process of evolution through natural selection. Simply put, evolutionary theory states that organisms have the capability randomly to generate new characteristics (by genetic mutation) which may make an organism more of less viable in relation to its environment. If a new characteristic emerges that makes the organism more suited to its environment then it will be more likely to survive, thus passing the new characteristic (via its genes) to the next generation. If the new characteristic makes the organism less suited, then it is more likely to die and less likely to reproduce the mutation through the next generation. Mutations occur randomly but those best fitted are reproduced and those least fitted die out. There is an almost infinite number of possible mutations but only certain ones fit the requirements of the organism and the constraints of the environment.

Applying such a mechanism to the process of creativity we could say that whilst it is possible to generate a seemingly infinite number of new combinations (of paint, sounds, words) only certain of these will fit the requirements and constraints imposed by the medium in which we are working. Therefore it is only these that will be selected – a process we could call *creative selection*.

chapter

6

Automating
Creativity and
Synthetic Beings

6. Automating Creativity and Synthetic Beings

Having suggested ways in which some of the most complex and mysterious of human thought processes – aesthetic appreciation and creativity – might be modelled, we can speculate on some ways in which these processes could be synthesised in other media. In addition we can look at some of the arguments relating to the possibility of producing conscious beings in a non-human media.

Automating creativity

There are many products coming onto the software market that are intended as aids to creativity. Some examples are the graphics packages produced by Kai Krause such as 'KPT plug-ins' for Adobe's Photoshop which create customised textures and patterns. Some professional music programs such as Cubase now include an algorithmic pattern generator, which allows a program to generate sequences of notes and chords. There are a number of public domain text editors that take in phrases and 'randomly' edit them so as to produce new combinations of words. Some 3D packages such as 3DStudio have modules that generate trees and plants of varying shapes and complexities. The word processor I use can suggest improvements to my grammatical structure. One can imagine some developments that may occur very soon: a design program that lays out elements and chooses fonts, a video editing program which cuts pop video footage to the rhythm of the track, programs that generate realistic images from algorithms to produce image libraries that attract no royalties. It is not a huge step from this to imagine synthetic actors and pop stars, computer generated pulp fiction (I have heard of a program which generates Mills and Boon-type romantic novels) and computer synthesised artists.

We should distinguish between aids to creativity and things that are truly creative. There are very few examples of computer programs currently existing that many people would claim are sufficiently interesting to be called truly creative. There are programs that imitate the results of human creativity and some do this very well; for example, the AARON program used by Harold Cohen. This program produces totally credible line drawings of which many artists would be proud. For a description see Margaret Boden, *The Creative Mind*. Most of the programs we have mentioned above are used as aids to help speed up the productivity of people in creative industries. They may help to inspire new ideas but it cannot be said that they have actually thought up the idea. So what is the distinction between a computer that is truly creative and one that imitates creativity?

There are two limitations placed on the ability of the current range of computers that prevent them from becoming truly creative. All the examples mentioned above consist of linear computer code running on serial machines. Serial computers can only execute one command at a time and therefore linear code can only issue one command at a time. They are essentially long strings of commands that, even running on the fastest machine, can only 'think' one thing at a time. Secondly, they are programmed by humans. Even using the largest team of programmers on earth there is a theoretical limit on the complexity of any executable program that could be written. To write a program that approached anything like the complexity of even the mind of a cat would require more time in design and debugging than is left in the universe (this is a guess, I have not worked it out but if you do, and I am wrong, let me know).

At the time of writing this book digital computers have existed for about 50 years. Humans, or something like them, have been around for millions of years. Humans have had a lot longer to evolve than computers have had. Yet, which is now evolving the faster? Humans have not changed much in the last five thousand years in terms of their anatomy and mental capacity, to judge by archaeological evidence and fossils. Within a fraction of that time, computers have evolved from nothing to a point where they densely populate our lives.

It is a fair bet to say, then, that given the same rate of growth in complexity there will come a point within the next five hundred years when the computer will reach such a phenomenal state of intricacy that its workings will be wholly beyond human comprehension. It might even be that they have mental capacities equal or superior to our own. Some might say, 'That's a long time away so I don't need to worry about it.' Others, like Roger Penrose in *The Emperor's New Mind*, might say that it is mathematically impossible for any machine ever to replicate the complexity of the human mind. And others might say, 'It's going to happen a lot sooner than that.' Take your pick. My own inclination is towards the last view and for the following reason.

Complex machines

The linear computers we described earlier are due for redundancy, as are many of the people who program them. The new generation of digital computers work in parallel rather than series and the new way of programming them is to let them learn for themselves. We are now designing machines that emulate much more closely the complex systems we see in organic beings. A parallel computer is one that consists of an array of processors each linked to the other in a network. The more processors it has, the more parallel it is. Current machines may contain many hundreds and are consequently called 'massively parallel'. In simple terms these machines can think of many things at once and they can execute more than one command at a time, as many commands as there are processors. There is no obvious limit to the number of processors that can be combined into such a machine, although the current state of electronic engineering makes practical limitations necessary. Given that such limitations are gradually overcome in time, the computers of the future are likely to be not only individual machines with huge numbers of processors but banks of these joined together with high speed lines forming global networks.

It will be impossible to apply traditional software engineering techniques to such platforms if their power is to be exploited fully. Even the smartest anorak in the world would never be able to comprehend the behaviour of a program running on several hundred thousand chips simultaneously. Rather than writing and running one single program that takes over the whole computer, it is more likely that the frighteningly parallel machines will run several (maybe thousands of) different programs at once.

Such machines would be able to deal with extremely complex data and this may come from a wide variety of sources. It may include visual data from cameras and imaging equipment, audio data from microphones and receivers, sensory data from robots, linguistic data from other machines and people. These machines may be able to retrieve as much, or more, sensory data as humans can from the environment – they could be as aware of what is going on around them as anything else. But could they learn about what is going on – could they know?

Complexity theory states that given a simple behaviour pattern multiplied through a large set of operands, each of which can affect the other, a global behaviour pattern will emerge which is essentially unpredictable. An example is the computer simulated flock of birds (or 'boids') of Craig Reynolds discussed in Chapter 1. He constructed a computer environment with boids, each of which had a very limited set of instructions: each was to fly in a certain direction without hitting an obstacle or another boid. The behaviour of any one boid on its own was highly predictable. It always took the same route. However, when all the boids flew at once and took references from each other, a complex global behaviour occurred that was not predictable. A flock is a complex phenomena (see Stephen Levy, *Artificial Life*, p. 76).

It is possible to think of many human mental functions as the global behaviour of large numbers of quite simple events working in parallel. It is well known that the human cognitive system relies heavily on the activity of many single cells known as neurons. The behaviour of neurons is very simple – they either fire or don't. The complex issue of how they determine whether or not to fire is another matter which depends on their relationship to each other. We also know that we cannot observe the effects of individual neurons firing but we know that the sum effect of many such simultaneous events produces thoughts, memories, emotions, etc. These sum effects may be seen as global properties that emerge from the relatively simple behaviour of millions of individual neurons (with connections throughout the body), just as we see the global effect of a flock that is actually the sum of many individual birds performing a simple task.

If we construct a computer system that is made up of many thousands of individual components each of which operates in a predictable way and then allow them all to work together on a task in reference to each other, the global behaviour that emerges will be unpredictable if the laws of complexity theory hold true. By unpredictable is meant that the observer cannot say in advance exactly what will happen; one can only guess at the probability that certain things will happen. Some measure of responsibility for what is occurring is passed over to the computer. The frighteningly parallel computer will be one such machine. The internal workings of all the thousands of processors calculating and referencing at rates close to the speed of light (optical computers based on light waves rather than electrical impulses are now being developed) will create a machine of such complexity and speed that its global behaviour is bound to be unpredictable.

Other developments in computer design suggest further convergence of organic processes and machine processes. There has been a recent revival of interest in the analogue computer, which treats information in a way similar to the human sensory organs. Most of today's computers are digital – they store and manipulate information as a series of binary codes. To a digital computer there exist only two states – 'on' and 'off', or '1' and '0'. All the information the computer deals with is stored as strings of 1s and 0s. From these basic strings are built up logical operators that perform tasks on strings of data. Any input or output from a digital computer must be encoded into a stream of 'bits' or binary digits, a process known as *digitisation*.

Compact-disc players are digital devices in which the variable sounds of music are turned into strings of numbers that are stored on a metallic plate. The CD player reads these numbers and turns them back into sound waves which pass through the speakers. Analogue computers, on the other hand, deal with information that *varies*. Rather than handling information encoded as a series of discrete 1s and 0s, an analogue machine responds to variable data that can have values *between* 1 and 0. Record players that produce sound from vinyl discs are analogue machines. The groove in a record is a wavy line that does not have discrete states, unlike the CD which is a string of separate numbers. Therefore, in theory, a record can contain more information than a CD, since it holds all the information that a CD contains in 1s and 0s, and all the information in between. Many hi-fi buffs still claim that vinyl records give superior reproduction of sound for just this reason. Virtually all processes in nature are analogical. The sound coming through the air from your speakers travels in waves that have variable frequency, even if they are generated from the binary information on a CD. The human ear is sensitive to a huge range of variable frequencies which affect neurons in the auditory canal. Analogue computers are able to deal with information of infinite variability, although in practice this is limited by 'noise' generated by the system. Although neurons in the brain are often compared to transistors in digital computers, it is more likely that they behave in an analogical rather than a digital way. Optical computers (those that use light or laser beams instead of electronic pulses) are a type of analogue computer that use variations in light intensity to transmit and process information. Such computers are still in their early stages of development but could supersede digital electronic computers within 50 years. An interesting suggestion, which relates to our earlier discussion of non-

linearity in Chapter 1, is that optical analogue computers, unlike digital computers, would be essentially non-linear because of all the variables at work within the system. Thus, they could give rise to huge levels of complexity with relatively few cells (see Kreinovich and Sirisaengtaksin).

What is a complex machine? A complex machine is one that displays global behaviour which cannot be reduced to any of its parts. Its global behaviour is essentially non-deterministic and unpredictable. It is likely to produce unpredictable complexity, even though each component may be seen as deterministic. To remind us of how this might happen, think back to the examples of unpredictability emerging from determinism in Chapter 3.

Learning

Since the ability to learn is something that has obviously evolved in nearly all animal species (albeit at different levels), there is no reason to suppose that a similar process could not emerge in a machine of the complexity we are currently contemplating. If the ability to learn is a faculty beneficial to an organism (which, since it exists, it must be, according to the laws of evolution) then it would be equally as beneficial to a machine of the complexity we are describing. Which brings us back to why today's programmers could find themselves redundant in the age of complex machines. Since it will be too complex to program them in the linear sense we now employ, the computer operator may take more the role of a teacher than a programmer. There are significant advances being made in the field of computer learning. Neural networks are arrays of computational elements known as nodes connected together so that they can affect each other in a dynamic way. This approach to machine learning is sometimes called 'connectionism'. The use of neural networks (systems that mimic the structure of organic neurons) has enabled many machines to acquire capacities similar to those endowed on humans. The work of Marvin Minsky at MIT (see Marvin Minsky, *The Society of Mind*) has often been cited in this regard. The ability to recognise faces or buildings, the ability to decipher handwriting, to learn game rules are some of the abilities that machines can now be said to possess. Whilst such programs still require a programmer to set up the conditions in which the machine learns they are not actually coding in the information that is learnt. They make it possible for the machine to learn and provide it with information but the act of learning itself is a function of the neural network and not of the direct input of the operator.

In *The Brain*, Richard Thompson describes the work of Rumelhart and McClelland who used neural networks to allow a machine to decipher the past tense of verbs by example:

'The astonishing result was that the network seemed to learn the past tenses of verbs much as young children do. It learned the general rules for forming regular past tenses before it had learned to form the past tenses of irregular verbs correctly. Thus, during the learning process it formed regular past tenses for irregular verbs, for example "digged" rather than "dug". This result had profound implications for the nature of language. The network had no deep grammatical structure built into it. Rather, it formed the abstract rules for forming past tenses strictly from example; it learned the rules by "inference". If a simple neural network with a few hundred units can learn this way, so can the vastly complex human brain. Perhaps there is no deep language structure built into the brain.'   Thompson, *op. cit. p. 409*

The question of whether such a network is truly learning, in the sense of 'understanding' what is learnt, is one I shall address later. The clear implication of the work cited above is that a property can emerge from a system that was not necessarily programmed into it, and which cannot be reduced to a function of any of its parts.

Adapting machines

To make a machine that is truly creative rather than one that mimics creative acts we need two things – a machine that is sufficiently complex to produce global behaviour which is emergent, and sufficient time for it to learn. If we had such a machine (and they are being designed as we speak), and were able to allow it time to gather a great deal of information, and then allowed it time to find links and meanings among those pieces of information, we would have started to create an artificial mind. Given that this mind would be forced to make conceptual links among pieces of information and to retain those links, it would be starting to learn. Given that this mind would be constantly fed new sources of information (sensory data) that could not be guaranteed to fit into a predefined path but about which the mind had to make judgements it would begin to become creative. It would have to create new conceptual links based on the modification of existing concepts in order to 'understand' the information it was receiving. In short, it would have to be able to adapt.

Several mechanisms for adaptation are well understood. Using principles of feedback, similar to those observed in organic neurons, allows nodes (the 'neurons' of a neural network) to change their connection strength. They can either be inhibited or excited in the same way that organic neurons can, and the thresholds at which they fire can be altered. Since in most neural networks the modification of thresholds is under the control of the program, the level of determinism in the system is quite high. A lot of 'control' has to be programmed in. Another approach to adaptability, which often complements the one just described, is the use of genetic algorithms, pieces of code that randomly mutate and mate until a good match is found.

The basic mechanism of organic evolution is the random mutation of DNA, the 'code of life'. In plants and animals, the DNA in cells that controls growth and behaviour can change randomly owing to various factors – it can mutate. This may produce new features in the species which may either help or hinder its 'fittedness' for the environment. Those features that help are kept (since those organisms are more likely to survive) and those features that hinder are lost (since those organisms are less likely to survive). The beneficial features are passed on to the next generation through mating, and over time the species appears to adapt. Genetic algorithms are mathematical models of this process that offer new possibilities in designing complex, adaptive systems. In *Out of Control*, Kevin Kelly describes the work of John Holland, who was amongst the first to see the potential of modelling evolutionary mechanisms:

'The evolutionary approach, Holland wrote, "eliminates one of the greatest hurdles in software design: specifying in advance all the features of a problem." Anywhere you have many conflicting, interlinked variables and a broadly defined goal where the solutions may be myriad, evolution is the answer.'

Speaking of Holland's work in breeding virtual life forms (code strings) to perform well in an unpredictable landscape, Kelly says:

'In Holland's scheme, the highest performing bits of code anywhere on the landscape mate with each other. Since high performance increases the assigned rate of mating in that area, this focuses the attention of the genetic algorithm system on the most promising areas of the overall landscape. It also diverts computational cycles away from unpromising areas. Thus parallelism sweeps a large net over the problem landscape while reducing the number of code strings that need manipulating to locate the peaks.'

Kelly, *op. cit. p. 376*

These adaptive processes are things we understand and know how to simulate. They mirror processes that occur in nature and which, in human beings, have led to our higher faculties of consciousness and self-awareness. We learn and we mutate. We already have machines which, within a limited environment, can learn through neural adaptation and genetic mutation.

Uncontained machines

A problem arises, however, if we imagine that we can rely on self-contained systems spontaneously to generate faculties of consciousness and creativity. Self-contained systems, those which use very limited information from outside themselves, can generate extraordinary levels of complex behaviour, but nowhere near as complex as the behaviour of which humans are capable. We know from what was stated in Chapter 1 that consciousness does not spontaneously arise in the brain. It emerges as a result of the co-operation between the cognitive medium and the environment. Speaking of the primacy of visual stimulus in human brain development, Richard Thompson says:

'The fact that the critical period for vision in humans lasts for six years [from birth] implies that the circuitry [of the brain] is growing and the fine tuning of its patterns of interconnections is taking place. Normal visual experience has profound effects on the development of circuitry in the visual brain . . . the message is clear: normal sensory experience is critically important for the normal development of the brain.'

Thompson, *op. cit.* p. 318 (my remarks in box parentheses)

This is not to say that people who are blind from birth cannot become conscious. They still have many other stimuli which the cognitive medium can use to develop consciousness. However, it is very unlikely that consciousness, as we know it, could emerge in the case of an unfortunate person who is born without any sensory faculties at all. Therefore, the human faculties of consciousness and creativity, which we are suggesting could emerge in a non-human media, rely to a huge extent on the information that is received from the environment. Not only is the human mind changed by the environment, it also produces changes in the environment. The human mind is not a self-contained system, it cannot be localised in any one part – it is uncontained.

The effect of environmental stimuli is, as we have noted before, both predictable and unpredictable. The effect on the cognitive medium is, therefore, to produce a mixture of stable and adaptive thought paths. In Chapter 5 we saw how critical to the process of creativity it is that humans receive unpredictable input. Without this, the scope for

'Currently the output of computers is predictable. The Post-Human era begins in full when the output of computers is unpredictable.'

The Post-Human Manifesto 8.1

re-configuring pathways, or the connections between pathways, is limited. With such volatile stimuli the need to adapt, which is central to creativity, is continually reinforced. In order to model human creativity in a non-human medium and, by implication, to automate it we need to ensure that the system is prone to random fluctuations. Such fluctuations are not however random in the sense of noise, but complex in the sense of both stable and instable.

Those systems described as containing artificial life, cited above, are often seen as the precursors of more complex machine life in general, and 'machine consciousness' in particular. However, they do have the limitation that they are bounded by the parameters of the machine in which they live. Real life is bounded only by the universe, a somewhat larger system. It has often been noted in A-life research that systems reach a certain level of growth and then seem to stabilise or atrophy. This is because all current artificial life machines are hermetically sealed. They are limited by the complexity of the calculations our machines can perform so they are only sensitive to a finite number of stimuli. The quotient of randomness intruding upon them is relatively small and thus they are able to reach a state of order or equilibrium. As we have seen previously, life is essentially a state of disequilibrium. As energy is dissipated through an appropriate medium it produces forms that represent a state of non-equilibrium. Life in the universe is seen as an example of this. No living system is in equilibrium since equilibrium is death. Disorder, in the form of new energetic stimuli, is needed to maintain the disequilibrium of life. Like all other features of life, human thought is not a hermetic system and a mind cannot exist in a state of equilibrium.

What is essential to the functioning of human consciousness is that the mind receives a continuous input of random stimuli from the environment. The human mind has evolved to absorb the unexpected – the discontinuous stimulus. We know that it is the compulsion to reassert order in the face of random stimuli that generates our sense of being. Therefore, it is obvious that if we are to create any synthetic intelligence with a sense of being like that which we recognise in ourselves, then it must be sensitive to

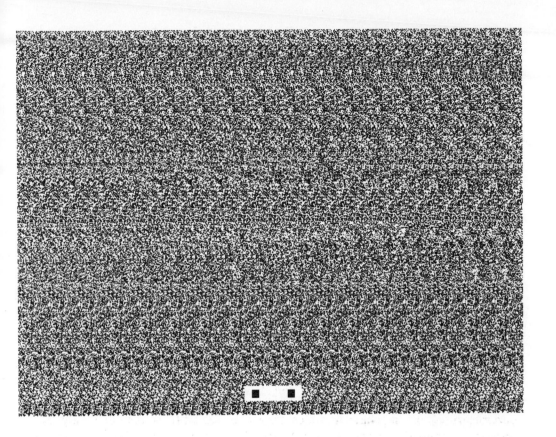

The intrusion of disorder avoids equilibrium, thus preserving life

the same level of random interruption that humans are. It must have a compulsion to reassert meaning in the face of both stable and unstable input. If we wish to produce a synthetic intelligence that displays creativity then we need it to be able to establish connections between its thoughts in a discontinuous way. This will be achieved by making it perpetually sensitive to unpredictable stimuli.

If we wish to produce a synthetic intelligence that displays aesthetic appreciation then it should be able to sense continuity and discontinuity simultaneously – without crashing. Whilst this would cause excitement in the machine it is yet to be determined to what extent it would be pleasurable.

Automated creativity in the short term

In the future what is certain is that the demand for creative aids will be immense as soon as people realise that the potential exists. The creative people in our culture are some of the most highly paid. Musicians, film directors, advertising creatives, scriptwriters, designers, actors are all, if successful, able to command huge salaries. From the point of view of a publisher or film producer, these people are very expensive. They require a lot of money, their work can be erratic and they can be temperamental. From the point of view of the people who pay creatives, it would be great if they could get the same results from a machine and avoid having the high costs and high risks associated with humans. As in many areas of the economy, expensive tasks that can be automated and have quality improved are ripe for mechanisation. Imagine a film star who is as successful as Arnold Schwarzenegger but who only exists as a piece of code on a huge super computer. After development costs you wouldn't have to pay him any fees, he would never get old, unless you wanted him to and he would never turn down a role, unless you decided he should. Imagine that you ran an advertising agency but instead of employing all those art college drop-outs you had a shiny machine in the room into which you fed all your clients' briefs and out of which came a whole set of brilliant pitches complete with story boards and artwork. Since some of these examples may appear very distant, we can briefly consider a few examples of computer aided creativity which, I believe, are due soon.

1. For a number of years we, at Hex, have been producing interactive music CDs. These are basically albums of music which, when played on an appropriate machine such as a PC, have a set of computer generated visuals to accompany the music. These visuals act essentially as pop videos for the tracks. But they differ in that they are both interactively controlled by the user and randomly generated. They never appear the same twice. Since visuals are now an essential accompaniment to music in clubs, bars and on MTV, we can imagine the pop video of the future not being a fixed film which is always the same, but a mutating series of images partly under the control of the user and partly controlled by the machine. Thus the locus of creativity has shifted from the video editor to the machine and the user (via the programmer, of course).

2. We can imagine an album of the future which consists of a CD-Rom containing sound samples, midi sequences and compositional rules for generating certain songs. The album would not be a fixed recording of an artist's performance, but would be generated each time the CD was played or, more accurately, run. Whilst the album would be generally the same each time is was played, it could also vary so that, for example, guitar solos or bass lines could change. The artist would set the parameters of change but the machine would carry out the mutations. Some part of the musical creation would only occur at 'run-time'. Many CD players have a very rudimentary version of this with the 'random play' button – the listener can listen to the tracks in a order different from that intended by the artist. The order is chosen by the machine rather than any human.

3. An extension of the above idea would be the 'live' album. Whilst an artist or band was performing live a program could monitor the variations in performance from

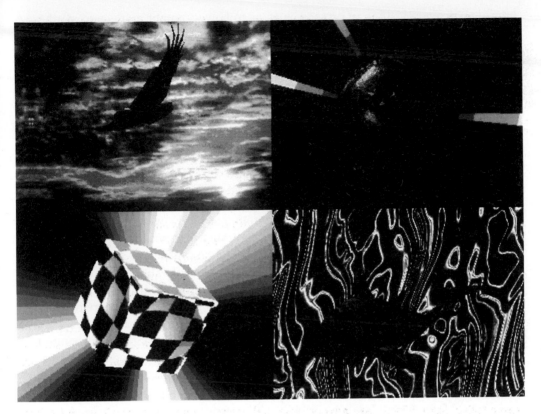

Screen shots from the PC version of Hex's Digital Dreamware CD-ROM

night to night and encode these as rules. Using samples or sound synthesis, the program could then 'recreate' the live performance through a computer so that the listener would get that spontaneous 'live' feel when they listened to the album. Something like this already exists in embryonic form in that some professional music sequencers have 'humanness' controls that can be applied to computer generated sequences. These produce slight variations in tempo and pressure to give the sequence a more natural feel.

These are examples of computer aided creativity that are possible with current, or soon to be current, technologies. They all either exist now or in some emergent, prototypical form. The degree to which they are taken up by artists and the public will depend on how exciting they are to use, how effective they are at enhancing aesthetic experience.

As for those creative systems that lie further in the future, we can speculate on how 'deeper' levels of creativity might be encoded into machines. From our general discussion of creativity we can see how the Post-Human era, the era of non-deterministic complexity, can provide clues as to how we might model and synthesise creativity. Creativity, like language, is something so complex that we could never formalise a set of rules by which it could be fully quantified. By its very nature it is temporal and erratic. We don't know when it's coming or exactly what it looks like. Yet we know what qualities it possesses – we can recognise it. In the short term (that is, short of the existence of complex machines) the best hope for modelling creativity lies in a combination of neural nets and genetic algorithms running on digital computers. It is possible to model a useful type of creativity within the constraints of today's machines, programs that will aid human creativity but will not be truly creative in themselves.

The principle lies in designing systems which have a set of rules that provide coherence coupled with the ability to mutate randomly within a machine, thus providing unpredictability. In the future, however, such systems would have to be able to deal with information that is both continuous and discontinuous and would have to 'learn' the difference between them. There are a number of ways this principle could be implemented in programs to aid the composition of painting, writing, designing, music, video editing and advertising. For example, given a particular genre of music, a program could learn the rules of melody, harmony, rhythm, structure (the continuity) by example and then have the ability to mutate part or all of the rules (discontinuity) to a degree that produces novelty without decaying into noise. A program that simply knew all the rules without the ability to mutate them would just be a database. A program that simply generated random notes would be a pain. It is unlikely, however, that we would be able to teach a computer all the subtleties of the rules pertaining to, say, reggae music without it having access to all the cultural influences which humans are able to assimilate. At this point we would need a complex machine that was able to learn all about the cultural subtleties associated with a particular genre.

Machines and rules

Reminding ourselves of the notion of creative selection outlined in the last chapter we said that it is possible to produce any number of random variations on an idea but it is only those that are best fitted to the requirements and constraints that will succeed. Applying this to a computer model, we soon realise that it is not producing the infinite and random variations that is hard, it is letting the computer know the requirements and constraints by which to choose the best solution. Random mutation is relatively easy, it's the selection part that is difficult. How do we feed into the computer all the necessary rules of requirement and constraint for it to be able to make a judgement on whether the randomly seeded data is useful? This is why most creative programs in near future will be creative aids rather than fully creative tools. We will still need the human to interpret the results in order to see whether they are good because currently the machine does not 'know' all the rules. It would take too long to put them in manually.

There is a long history of creative works that are produced according to well understood rules. Bach was famous for using strict mathematical formulae to produce canons. The constructivist painters of this century used sequential formulae to produce abstract paintings and the Fibonacci sequence has been used for centuries as a means of generating balanced designs. Whilst the application of such rules has produced some very beautiful compositions that would be quite straightforward to replicate with computer programs, the rules themselves are the product of human invention and not those of a machine.

The rules by which humans evaluate the worth of any piece of work are so complex, being intricately bound up with other social values, that a set of rules which are mathematically deducible are only a small subset of all the rules we use to judge creativity and aesthetics. The problem with the formulaic approach is that we may be able to get a machine to create works according to rules we put into it, but could the machine generate new rules that would produce works which we would consider to be creative? Bach did not compose all his works using formulae. Many were composed as the result of countless hours of improvisation at the organ keyboard. In doing this he redefined many of the rules by which subsequent music was composed.

News rules regarding the requirements and constraints of creative works are emerging continuously. In fact, it seems to be the case that as soon as a new set of rules become widely recognised, a group of people come along who wish to change them. This is particularly noticeable in the fashion industry, where sets of rules about colour, shape and fabric arrive each season only to seem out of date within a few months. No doubt this is due to the market forces exerted on and by the fashion industry itself, but the process occurs with the complicity of the fashion buying public who want to present an image of themselves as up to date. One may be able to deduce patterns in the emergence of such rules (the cyclical nature of taste, the development of new materials, etc.) but no one would claim that such trends are completely predictable. Who in 1976 would have predicted the worldwide influence of punk and the consequent overturn in the status of flares?

The successfully creative person is one who has an implicit understanding of the rules (requirements and constraints) pertaining to a particular medium and yet is able to generate new works that display enough variation so as to produce excitement and social stimulation. In addition this may have the impact of causing a change in those rules such that the old rules may seem redundant. The Cubists working in 1909 had a great understanding of the rules pertaining to the contemporary art world (Picasso had produced work in a huge number of contemporary styles) and yet were able to alter those rules so substantially as to create a completely new style, indeed a new movement in culture. The Cubists' works, however, were not dissociated from other works of their time. They were essentially a fusion of the influences being exerted on young Parisian artists at the turn of the century – later work of Cézanne, the startling exoticism of African sculpture and Gaugin's Polynesian compositions, the mechanisation of modern life, and so on. This is to say that Picasso and Braque were not randomly rewriting the rules of modern painting and sculpture but were changing them substantially in the light of a complex set of rules and constraints that were present at the time. It was only their understanding of these rules that allowed them to be altered. Picasso and Braque were conscious mediums through which the complex influences of their time were synthesised into the works for which they are now famous.

In order then to have a machine that would be able to produce works of creation to rival those of Picasso or Braque, we can see that it will need to be as aware of all the complex social and aesthetic criteria of today as they were in their time. Otherwise the works may be highly creative as far as the machine is concerned, but of little value to anyone else. The problem of creating a machine that is aware of all the complex rules governing our sensibilities is not insoluble. Remember that we described a type of computer that has many millions of parallel processors, the ability to learn and a huge range of sensory inputs – the complex machine. It is conceivable that such a machine will have access to much more sensory stimulation than we do (or that Picasso may have had). It may have the ability to learn more quickly and remember much more than we can. So, whereas it might take a human being 30 or so years to mature to the point of being creatively consistent and successful (to become aware of all the rules and nuances), a complex machine may be able to assimilate equivalent experiences in a much shorter time. As well as being able to scan all magazines, articles, plays, etc. very quickly, it may have the ability to scan human thoughts and download the accumulated experiences of highly trained people. Such systems already exist in a rudimentary form as Expert Systems for dealing with medical, engineering and legal knowledge.

Rules and continuity

It would be consistent with everything said so far to equate the rules of cultural production with the continuity of thought paths described in previous chapters. That is to say, we are able to perceive the connections between various components of a creative work insofar as the different stimuli it presents cause activity in thought paths that are relatively close to each other in our minds. If we are expecting to hear a romantic symphony then the combination of strings, brass and melodic structure will activate responses in the cognitive medium that have a certain level of consistency and stability. These responses will be similar to, though not identical with, any other work of that genre. If, in the middle of Beethoven's Third, we were to hear an accelerated drum break at 160 beats per minute we would be surprised. This would not be the case if we were listening to a pirate Jungle station in South London where such drum breaks are the staple fare. We would be somewhat surprised to hear the whole of the Third symphony on the pirate Jungle station although we would probably put this down to the fact that the frequency had been intercepted. Either way, the rules and structures governing the perception of any cultural product are those that we learn and which are etched into our conscious mind so that we may recognise and distinguish information of different types.

If we call the rules that govern our perception of cultural products the fabric of continuity (which is represented in our minds as the connections between thought paths), then we can call any deviations from these paths discontinuity. We have already said that continuity and discontinuity are present in all things depending on how they are viewed. But this does not mean that we cannot distinguish between them. The sum of rules give any genre or form its continuity – whether it is Jazz or pop art or flower arranging. The extent to which those rules are varied and reconfigured gives rise to the level of discontinuity in a work. Inasmuch as each work is distinct from another, it will display discontinuity – the discontinuity which allows us to distinguish it. But greater levels of discontinuity may be present, such as in a painting that does not represent anything. It has taken many years for the general public to accept that a square canvas on a wall in a gallery need not necessarily represent something else, such is the overwhelming historical continuity of representational art.

We have already said that the perpetual reproduction of a continuum, whether in art or anything else, leads to dissatisfaction and boredom. Whilst we like continuity insofar as it confirms our sense of being, we are attracted to discontinuity and its associated excitement – excitement that can lead to a heightened sense of being. We have described successful creation as that which presents us with a sense of continuity whilst, at the same time, introducing a level of disruption that does not cause the continuity to evaporate.

Take three musical examples:

1. The standard Eurovision Song Contest entry. Such entries are almost invariably conservative in nature, probably being the results of committee-processed compromises. These songs, and performers, are usually formulaic and display little variation or originality whilst insisting on seemingly endless repetition. Thus we have a genre that displays excessive continuity and virtually no discontinuity.

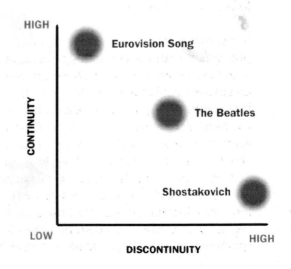

2. The Beatles. Taking the whole of their musical output, it can be said of the Beatles that their work contains high

levels of continuity and high levels of discontinuity. From 'Love Me Do' to 'Revolution No. 9' they produced a spectrum of music from conventional pop to avante-garde soundscapes. On the whole their songs displayed continuity in the form of strong melody and harmony, strong rhythm and musical structure, and discontinuity in the form of surreal lyrics, mixed musical genres and experimental aural effects.

3. Shostakovich. Here we could talk of any modern composer who rejects the traditional musical forms and uses broken rhythms, atonality and unusual orchestration as displaying high levels of discontinuity in their work. The apparent continuity of melody, scale and harmony is almost totally displaced, leaving many to ask 'Is this music at all?'.

This does not tell us which type of music is best, but it is clear which is the most popular with the public – that is, which mixture of continuity and discontinuity has the most universal appeal.

The benefits of automated creativity

Is it a good thing that we are suggesting the possibility of a machine acting as creatively as humans? Are we not in danger of displacing one of the most valued of human attributes?

It is likely that, initially at least, many people will be sceptical about the merits of computer generated creativity. In the early days of electronic music, the 'synthetic' sound of instruments like the Moog were derided by many serious musicians and members of the public. The attempt to mimic the sound of violins and trumpets exposed the limitations of synthesisers trying to be something they were not. Yet in the late 1960s and early 1970s a new generation of musicians exploited the synthetic sounds for what they were – noise generators. A new aesthetic emerged around the music of Kraftwerk, Eno, Pink Floyd in which the synthetic sound actually became an integral part of the aesthetic.

I imagine the same thing will happen with synthesised creativity. A number of products will emerge claiming novelty for having been generated using computers. A small group of 'leading-edge' technophiles will like what is generated *because* it is synthetic, but the rest of the public will compare it unfavourably with the human generated version. Gradually, however, the huge cog of taste will turn another revolution and the new generation, partly to disassociate itself from the previous one, will embrace the products of automated creativity and a new aesthetic will be established. It will become acceptable to go to a bar where all the music, visuals, cocktails and bar staff are created in real-time by a bank of transputers.

Creativity is not a one way process. It is not the case that creativity is the preserve of a deified elite whose deeds we anticipate with awe and whose work we admire with blind adulation. The creative process is only fully consummated when the creative work of one person induces a sense of creativity in another. That is not to deny that many people produce creative work that no one else ever sees or hears but the majority of creative work is *intended* to be seen or heard, even if it never is. Regardless of whether or not it is meant to be seen, or heard, the *successful* creative work is able to induce a sense of pleasure or excitement in the recipient (viewer, listener, reader) as well as the creator – something which we have described as aesthetic experience.

Many artists have commented on the way in which the creative work of another has inspired them to their own creative acts. The Beatles responded to the work of Chuck Berry and Buddy Holly. Picasso responded to the work of Matisse and Cézanne. I know from personal experience the degree to which seeing the work of others can produce a strong sense of creative possibilities. Just as the aesthetic sensibilities of artists are heightened when producing a piece of work, so the aesthetic sensibilities of the viewer are heightened when contemplating it.

True creativity arises in a machine that knows the rules as well as we do. It has to be able to understand everything that pertains to a creative piece.

The result, then, of producing a machine able to act in a truly creative way would not necessarily be just to make human creativity superfluous. This would only be the case when humans themselves are superfluous – a point which may eventually arrive. In the meantime, such machines could be used to increase generally the level of creativity in society, just as cars and planes have increased generally the level of our mobility in society. The consequences that will flow from this cannot be predicted, but if we are to follow the example of past developments, they will be both beneficial and detrimental depending, to some extent, on who you are.

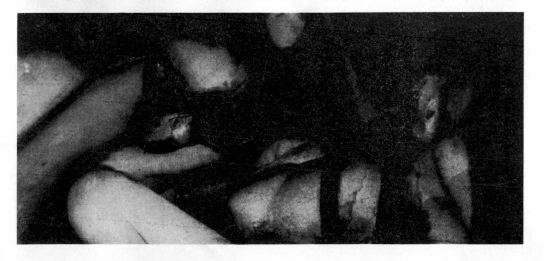

Synthetic beings

How would it be possible to create a sense of being in a medium other than the human mind? With the huge computational power now available to us, could we produce a sense of being in a machine?

Synthetic beings will have to evolve from the 'bottom-up' – they cannot be programmed from the 'top-down'. No human, or group of humans, will ever be able to construct a computer program containing sufficient complexity and unpredictability to replicate that found in a human being. In the same way that 'true' creativity, as described above, must emerge in a machine that learns about the world to same level of complexity humans do, so a machine that has a sense of being must evolve it as humans do, by negotiation with the environment in all its complexity.

Our working description of being is that it is the sum of all active thought paths in the cognitive medium. Above we have outlined the type of machine that could conceivably support activity of sufficient complexity to enable thought-like processes to occur – the complex machine. If the machine had enough stimulation, enough capacity to process information in the way described above and enough time to learn, we might say that any active program in such a machine would be analogous to a thought path in a human. That is, a program that is running and actively processing data, transferring it from one point to another or causing a new link to be made between programs, has characteristics similar to that of human thought. If enough such 'thoughts' occurred simultaneously (and collectively) in our machine so as to allow it to reach a critical mass of complexity – the point at which global behaviour emerges – then we could say that a number of thought paths were active. The state of being of that machine would consist in the sum of all those active paths. Whether or not this means that it would be a type of being that we would immediately recognise as a human-type being is another question and one that will be addressed.

The state of being is one that we recognise easily in other humans and in ourselves. There is little dispute that we have such a state even if we cannot agree on exactly what it is. Could we accept that creatures other than ourselves have a sense of being? Only the most arrogant humanist would argue that it is humans alone who share this sense. Most of us accept that monkeys, dogs, cats, cows, dolphins have some idea of their own existence, even if it is not of the highly self-reflexive kind that we enjoy. The problem of attributing a sense of being to ants and spiders is more acute. They have complex neurological systems, but are they complex enough to support a sense of being or are such creatures mere automatons with no sense of existence? Opinions vary as to what extent different creatures in the biological spectrum are endowed with a sense of being but there is no clear line of demarcation to which we can refer for a definitive answer. The source of this problem is that, until now, we have had only a very vague notion of what being is.

If we accept the working description of being as the sum of all active thought paths occurring over time, then we could say that any entity that can lay claim to at least one active thought path can be attributed a sense of being (a thought path may consist of many active neurons). We do not have to claim that all senses of being are equal in the same way that we do not regard the level of intelligence in all species as equal. A cat that has a well-developed neurology could be attributed a sense of being that would include its reflexes and sensory functions, behaviour and body regulating mechanisms. We do not regard the cat as having any powers of conscious thought to match our own but we must nevertheless admit that the richness of its behaviour and sensory capabilities merits it some degree of sentience. If I call my cat, it knows I am referring to it.

If we cannot draw a clear demarcation between the occurrence of being in humans and other species then we must accept the possibility that a sense of being could arise in any system that meets the necessary conditions – namely, the ability to have a number of active thought paths. Provided that a machine could meet this requirement there is no reason to exclude it from having a sense of being.

However, what separates the simplest organism from the most complex computer is this: organisms are continually responding to their environment in a way that computers are not. Computers are contained systems and organisms are uncontained. The crux of this distinction is *motive*. Organisms need to be aware of their environment since it is that environment which either sustains or destroys them. Even plants devise strategies for self-protection and propagation. Computers only need to be aware of their environment insofar as we tell them to be. They have no motivation for awareness 'hard-wired' in, they do not complain if we try to kill them, they do not need to feed or reproduce.

This crucial distinction is often overlooked by those enthusiastic about machine learning and artificial intelligence but it is crucial when we come to examine to what extent 'meaning' can be said to be present in any neurological process. Meaning only occurs as part of some wider context; it always results *from* something or *in* something. The wider context, as far as an organism is concerned, is the on-going process of existence conducted in an environment that is both hostile and supportive. This is the sense in which meaning occurs in humans. In its most basic terms it is the following: 'That big, stripy thing with fangs coming towards me *means* I am going to be killed.' In such a situation one need not argue about the semantics of meaning.

Therefore, any sort of machine, or non-human medium, which we wish to endow with a sense of being must have a motive. Without any motivation the system will have no need to 'know' anything, for knowledge is the currency of survival. Without any purpose the knowledge in a machine remains abstract and self-referential. It is merely the 'waging of mathematics by other means'.

Synthetic beings and logic

'The so-called *computational approach* to brain function was pioneered by the school of *cognitive science*, a cross between psychology and artificial intelligence. It states quite simply that for the brain to arrive at any kind of understanding, whether the recognition of a face or the proof of a mathematical theorem, it must go through a series of simple logical steps.'

Eric Harth, *The Creative Loop, p. 154*

Is creativity logical? Is human thought logical? Will synthetic beings be logical? The assumption of artificial intelligence (AI) research is that human cognition can be formalised in logical symbols which can be manipulated without reference to the neurological structure of the brain. Because the huge complexity of the brain is difficult to understand, the modelling of logical processes in symbolic form seems more 'do-able'. Having deduced such logical rules in the abstract, the aim is to compute them on 'hardware' other than the human brain. The view that *all* human cognition can be expressed this way is known as 'strong AI'. Prominent advocates of strong AI include Marvin Minsky and Douglas Hofstadter. Supporters of strong AI hold that there is no essential difference between humans and machines. In this sense, they are intellectual descendants of eighteenth century mechanism. On the possibility of creative machines Hofstadter writes:

'It is obvious that we are talking about mechanisation of creativity. But is this not a contradiction in terms? Almost, but not really. Creativity is the essence of that which is *not* mechanical. Yet every creative act *is* mechanical – it has its explanation no less that a case of the hiccups does. The mechanical substrate of creativity may be hidden from view, but it exists.'

Douglas Hofstadter, *Gödel, Escher, Bach, p. 673*

It would be interesting to ask Hofstadter if a mechanical process is also a logical one. That is, do machines act in a logical way? If so, then one could substitute the term *logical* for *mechanical* in the above extract and reach the same conclusion. This should pose no problem to supporters of strong AI. As we have suggested in previous chapters, creativity is describable, even reproducible given the right conditions, but it is not *mechanical*; that is, if we mean by mechanical, fully understandable in terms of logic. For we can imagine machines whose working we do not fully understand. We have called them complex machines. But complex machines are radically different from the types of machines which supporters of strong AI enthuse about, those which we might call 'complicated logic machines'. Whatever behaviour a complicated logic machine might exhibit, supporters of strong AI will assume that, ultimately, it will be operating according to logical functions that are algorithmic. This is fundamental to their whole case.

There is much debate between those supporters of strong AI who believe that human thought can be expressed algorithmically in appropriate machines, and their opponents such as John Searle and Roland Penrose who dispute this. Much of it centres around the 'limits to computability' of algorithms revealed by Kurt Gödel and Alan Turing (for an account of this see *Gödel, Escher, Bach* or *The Emperor's New Mind*). The consequence, in brief, is that there are theoretical limits to what any formal logic machine can compute, as shown by Gödel and Turing. Yet there are no theoretical limits to what a human can think, at least there is no way of finding out what they are. Hence, the possibility that there might be an 'algorithm for human thought' is ruled out since there are classes of human cognition that cannot be expressed algorithmically. Finding an algorithm for human thought is what strong AI claims as its goal. The Post-Human view is this: algorithms are not reality. They can be used to describe aspects of reality, sometimes with remarkable precision, but they are in themselves constructions of the human mind. This is not to suggest that constructions of the human mind are not real. But they are not a type of reality in which *all* other aspects of reality can be found. Our mental construction of reality is only part of the total reality in which we are immersed (although strong idealists would dispute this).

Algorithms are logical and, as Post-Humans know, logic is an idealisation which has been developed by human imagination. The formal project of logic is to eradicate contradiction. The work of Bertrand Russell and Alfred North Whitehead in *Principia Mathematica* was such a project – a project that failed. It failed because contradictions arise only in language (or, more precisely, human thought) and do not exist in any other form. And, as we have shown in Chapter 4, language is not consistent. Nor is mathematics, that particularly aesthetic form of language, free from contradictions as Kurt Gödel showed in his paper on 'Incompleteness Theorem':

'This paper revealed not only that there were irreparable "holes" in the axiomatic system proposed by Russell and Whitehead, but more generally, no axiomatic system whatsoever could produce all number-theoretical truths, unless it were an inconsistent system! And finally, the hope of proving the consistency of a system such as that presented in *Principia Mathematica* was shown to be vain: if such a proof could be found using only methods inside *Principia Mathematica* then – and this is one of the

most mystifying consequences of Gödel's work – *Principia Mathematica* itself would
be inconsistent!' Hofstadter, *op. cit. p. 24*

Russell and Whitehead tried to eradicate paradox. Paradoxes are constructions of the
type:

Epimenides was a Cretan.
Epimenides said, 'All Cretan are liars.'
Was he telling the truth?

But a paradox, in that it is circular, does not represent any rupture in the fabric of the
space-time continuum that demands explanation. It is simply a function of the
exclusive operation of human language in which a word with one meaning (in this case
'liar') is excluded from meaning its opposite. It is taken as axiomatic that something
cannot be true and false at the same time. Yet nothing in reality is as clear cut as this;
such judgements are always context sensitive. There are plenty of examples of
indeterminate states where something is true and false at the same time – the case of
Schrödinger's cat is often cited. A cat locked in a box with a poison pellet is both 'dead'
and 'alive' until an observer opens the box. The release of the poison is dependent on
the decay of an atomic particle that cannot be predicted exactly, but only calculated
as a probability. It is only when one opens the box that the probability wave function
collapses and the 'deadness' or 'aliveness' of the cat is determined. Prior to opening
the box, the statement 'The cat is dead' is as true as the statement 'The cat is alive'.
(For a further description of this 'paradox' see *Schrödinger's Cat* by John Gribbin.) This
is the case that is often cited from the 'hard' world of physics, but language itself is
riddled with ambiguities, inconsistencies, interpretations of fact, which defy all logical
analysis.

'Art is a lie which lets us see the truth.' Picasso

Logic is an extension of the rationalist humanist project in which the universe is
assumed to obey consistent laws that humans shall, one day, be able to understand.
The paradox of logic is that it is always expressed in language and language itself is
illogical. To hope, as many in the AI community do, that human language can be
successfully modelled using logical operators is bound to lead to frustration. To take
this further, and hope that the rules governing human thought can be modelled from
a logical model of language will lead to even greater frustration. Since there are few
things less logical in behaviour than humans, any machine that is restricted to using
logic as its base will never display fully human characteristics.

But we are left with an apparent contradiction that seems to point to an illogical hole
in the Post-Human argument. It has been argued all along that those attributes that are
essentially 'human', such as creativity, consciousness, aesthetic experience and a sense

*Logic may be a
construction of humans
but this does not mean
humans are logical*

of being, could be replicated in non-human media. By non-human media we are
assuming that we mean computers. This is a view which supporters of strong AI would
approve of. Yet we also seem to be siding with the opponents of strong AI, those who
claim that certain 'higher' human faculties are not algorithmic, are not prone to logical
decomposition and, therefore, would resist replication by any other means. Can both
views be right? The controversy surrounding whether or not machines will be able to
think is known as the strong AI debate.

The strong AI debate

As is usual with such tightly fought debates, both sides are right but for the wrong
reasons. The solution to this conundrum, simply put, is this: Yes, the things we now
call computers will evolve into beings which, if necessary, will have attributes of
consciousness, creativity and aesthetic sensibility. But, no, they will not predicate such
abilities on purely logical or algorithmic functions. They will not be things which any
human can fully understand. Why is this so? To back this up we have the most
compelling evidence that one could want – the human condition.

Humans are humans because of what they are. They display all the faculties we are
able to recognise as human. The fact that we are here and that we display those
faculties is not in doubt. It clearly shows that, given the conditions that exist in the

universe, it is possible for entities to emerge that display all those faculties and weaknesses we know as human. It has been done once, it can be done again. This does not mean that, in producing the faculties in another medium, we should have a complete understanding of how they work. Many common electrical devices work on the basis of applied quantum mechanics, yet there is no suggestion that quantum mechanics is fully understandable, or even that it is essentially logical. The physicist Richard Feynmann claimed that those who think they understand quantum mechanics don't understand it. The true test of an intelligent machine is one that can think it's being logical when it isn't. Truly intelligent machines, those with human-like capabilities, will be just as confused as we are.

The confusion arising from the debate as to whether machines can think or not is central to the notion of synthetic beings and the whole Post-Human condition. One of the most provocative ideas put forward recently (to judge by the amount of debate it has caused) is the Chinese Room hypothesis proposed in 1980 by John Searle. He imagines a thought experiment in which he sits in sealed room, sealed except for two slots. In the room is a basket full of cards with symbols on them and a big book of rules. From time to time a card is passed through slot A. His job is to match the symbol on the card which has passed through the slot with another symbol from his basket. The symbol he chooses is determined by the rules in the book in front of him. Having determined the correct symbol, he passes it out through slot B. Unknown to him, the symbols are actually Chinese characters, a language of which he is completely ignorant, and the symbols passed through slot A are questions posed by fluent Chinese speakers to which they are requesting answers. These symbols chosen from his basket and passed out of slot B are the answers, presented in fluent Chinese, to the questions which came through slot A. Searle's case, intended to refute the claims of the strong AI community, is this: The fluent Chinese speakers may think they are in the presence of a machine that can understand Chinese as well as they can since every time they ask a question, they receive an intelligible answer. However, Searle does not understand any Chinese. He is merely carrying out instructions written in English in a book of rules. He distinguishes between the syntax (the book of rules) and the semantics (that which is understood by the Chinese) in order to show that a machine can seem to be understanding a language that it actually isn't. This scenario is an analogy of the Turing test, named after the famous English mathematician, in which a challenge is set to produce a computer program which, when interrogated by a human, produces answers that are indistinguishable from those that would be given by another human. In the Chinese room Searle and his book of rules simply become this computer and program. The expectation of those who take up the Turing test is that, one day, a program will be able to think like a human so that the age old quest of machine thought can be realised. Such contests are actually held annually, and there is a considerable prize for the first program that meets the requirements. Searle argues, however, that even if it were to meet all the requirements this would not prove that the machine actually has a semantic grasp of the conversation, no more that he does in his Chinese room. It would just be a clever trick of symbol manipulation.

Searle's argument seems to have particular force. It has certainly raised a lot of opposition from those who believe machines can be programmed to think in the same way that humans do. The fact that the argument rages on suggests that the Chinese room hypothesis has still not been discredited sufficiently to allow it to be dismissed.

As has been suggested many times in this book, Post-Humans believe that machines (or what we now know as machines) will acquire mental capacities comparable to those we recognise in humans. In this sense Post-Humans agree, in principle, with the advocates of strong AI, but disagree on how this will happen. Unlike the advocates of strong AI, Post-Humans do not accept that algorithmic models of 'the brain' programmed on digital computers will be able to think, for these reasons:

1. As we have said many times, there is more to thinking than just that which goes on in the organ of the brain. AI programs of today, and the near future, will proceed under the delusion that the 'mind is caused by the brain', and will waste a lot of time trying to simulate the brain whilst forgetting the role of that which is around the brain in producing thought.

2. Algorithms are totally logical, digital computers are totally logical and humans are not totally logical. The existence of logic is an assumption held in language. It works in many cases but everything cannot be reduced to logic. Mathematics, a form of language, cannot escape the fact that since language contains illogical loops it too must contain them. Hence, any model of thought based on logic cannot contain a complete description of human thought.

3. It is beyond the capacity of any human programmer to implement the complexity of the human mind. The belief that an algorithm might be devised that contained a complete description of human thought, which is an aim of strong AI, rests on the hope that, were such an algorithm devised, it would be intelligible by those who devised it. This hope rests on finding an algorithm that only models the brain, it does not take account of all the other complexities introduced by the body and the environment, which takes us back to point 1. The complexity of an algorithm that models a confined brain is nothing compared to modelling an active brain that is operating in the world.

You will note that in this list we have not mentioned Searle's syntax/semantics argument against the declared aims of strong AI. This is because I think his argument has been generally misunderstood by both him and those who have sought to attack it. The strong argument against strong AI is actually contained within his parable, but hidden slightly from view. In fact, it is by exposing a mistaken assumption in his hypothesis that the real objection to 'programmed thought' emerges. Searle is right,

but for a different reason than the one he proposes. In *Minds, Brains and Science*, he outlines the Chinese room hypothesis, much as we have above, and in doing so makes this crucial statement:

'Suppose for the sake of argument that the computer's answers are as good as those of a native Chinese speaker.'

Searle, *Minds, Brains and Science*, p. 32

Here, before he has even started passing symbols through slots or looking up correlations in his book, his hypothesis is shattered, although, paradoxically the outcome of his argument is not altered. For any machine, whether it is Searle as an automatic sign passer or a complex digital computer, to give answers that 'are as good as those of a native Chinese speaker' it would *have* to understand the questions. It is simple. No book of rules devised by even the cleverest human(s) could account for all the intricacies of human language. No such book could exist! By the same token, as we have said above, no humans (or even AI researchers) could produce a set of rules running on a computer that were able to account for meaning as perceived by humans. As we spelt out in Chapter 4, language and human thought are far too slippery and mobile in operation to be encoded in a formal set of logical operations. Language changes every day and no two occurrences of a linguistic event are identical. It is true that certain aspects of language can be modelled in a limited way, but to hope to make this anything more than an approximation is as misguided as it is to hope that we could produce accurate long-range weather forecasts. Language is non-linear, complex-dynamical and turbulent. It changes from person to person, from region to region and among classes and age groups. All these groups may have linguistic and conceptual structures in common, but there are just as many differences of such subtlety that they are barely perceptible, yet contribute just as much to the 'meaning', the 'semantics', of any conversation that is going on. Searle premises his argument on the fact that the Chinese interrogators have full confidence in the ability of the machine to understand the questions they are asking and to give fluent answers even though the machine itself (the interrogatee) does not have any understanding of the language employed. I would argue that the only way such confidence could be sustained is if the interrogatee actually *does* understand, for nothing short of full understanding would allow the interrogators to maintain their confidence. Therefore, the Chinese room as described by Searle could not work according to one of his own premises, yet this does not invalidate his claim.

However, if we take Searle's claim to mean that there will *never* be machines that can think like humans, we must disagree with him. In this sense, Post-Humans agree with strong AI enthusiasts when they imagine that, someday, machines will be able to think. But, as has been spelled out above, this day will only come when machines are able to engage with the world in the same way that humans do. Machines that are able to do this are some way off, but we have outlined above some of the principles along which they might be constructed. Searle counters this argument by stating that it does not matter how complex the machine is, or how many causal links it has with the world, it will never be able to understand in the sense that we do. We can agree with him here if he means machines that are programmed by other humans according to formal, logical rules. But we must disagree with him if he means (as he does) all machines of any type, for these reasons:

1. It is no longer clear that the distinction between machines and natural things can be perpetuated indefinitely. As outlined in the introduction, there are many emerging technologies that blur the distinction we have, up until now, been able to maintain. To take an example, is a man with a mechanical heart, an artificial eye and a nerve-connected robotic hand (incidentally, all technologies which are currently available) a man or a machine? Clearly he is a bit of both.

2. Searle's argument is directed against digital computers. Yet there are machines, as we have already said, that could, in principle, overcome the limitations of the digital architecture. We have mentioned analogue computers, organic and optical computers, massively parallel transputers, learning and adaptation systems. The machines under development now are likely to be some hybrid of such technologies, possibly directly linked to organic structures such as brains or skin. One cannot rule out the possibility that, in such a complex environment which so closely parallels the conditions of human existence, a sense of meaning could emerge.

3. We have found that meaning and understanding do not arise in an isolated system but through motivated interaction with the environment. Given that there are certain technologies under consideration (such as microrobots – microbots) that are intended to exist and survive in the environment independently of human control, and that these technologies would have to be aware of their environment in order to be effective, we cannot rule out that a sense of motive might emerge, just as is has in organic entities.

4. Searle does not know what meaning is. Neither he, nor anyone else, has an objective, quantifiable definition of semantics as opposed to syntax. If he is claiming (as he is) that he can refute the claims of strong AI on the grounds of a distinction between 'syntax' and 'semantics' then he should, at least, be able to give a quantitative definition of these qualities. For, if he has no means of measuring 'meaning', how can he assure himself that it is, or isn't, happening in any particular case. He can never actually tell whether something else, other than himself, is enjoying a sense of understanding. He can only assume they are, or are not, from the qualities they display. The distinction between syntax and semantics is an arbitrary one devised by linguistic philosophers in their attempts to formalise language. It is an academic tool, not an *a priori* fact.

Louis Istvan Designer Room, Second Floor

Undoubtedly this argument will continue for some time to come, though it need not. In Post-Human terms the argument is somewhat academic. Taking the last of those four arguments we see that the only way we can tell if something else is enjoying a sense of meaning is from the way they act towards us. Given certain responses and clues, we use our subjective judgement to attribute to them a sense of meaning, or not. But this is never totally assured, even in our dealings with other humans. There are plenty of examples of conversations between humans where one party does not understand what the other one is saying. I might believe that what I am saying to person *x* is making sense. They may nod in encouraging agreement, but I find out later that, contrary to my impressions, they understood not one word. Does that mean that during the conversation person *x* was reduced to the status of a digital machine, all syntax and no semantics? In fact, the whole of this argument could have been avoided if we simply said, 'It does not matter whether something which I believe to be enjoying meaning *actually* is or not.' For *as long as the illusion is maintained*, as far as I am concerned, the thing has got a sense of meaning since there is no way of objectively verifying whether it has a sense of meaning, other than the impression it gives me.

The Post-Human conception of synthetic beings

Imagine that you are a combatant soldier taking part in a war in 50 years' time. You are separated from your unit and picked out by a hostile anti-personnel microbot. You see it coming towards you, firing its laser, but you manage to take shelter in a large building. Whilst hiding you hear the microbot searching the building, over-turning sheets of metal and boxes to find you. Observing the microbot through a hole on the floor you see it using scrap metal to block all the exits. It knows you're in the building and it doesn't want you to escape before it can kill you. Finally, realising you are cornered, you attempt to jump out of a window but you immediately find that the microbot has communicated with several other comrades who have now surrounded the building. At this point, the question going through your mind would not be 'Does that machine really understand what it is doing, or is it merely following a set of symbolic procedures?'

'In adversarial situations, being forced to treat a machine as an intentional system may be considered as a good criterion for mechanical intelligence. In the case of predatory machines, not only would we have to fight them on the "intentional plane" but we may also assume that they would treat us, their prey, as predictable assemblages of beliefs and desires. It would be, then, a clash of "minds" or of "rational wills".'

Manuel de Landa, *War in the Age of the Intelligent Machine, p. 157*

The real trajectory of machine intelligence in the foreseeable future is one of machines which, through clever programming techniques and adaptation abilities, will give the strong appearance of 'understanding', whether they actually have it or not. Humans will attribute a sense of understanding to machines that display sufficient complexity and responsiveness. Machines will learn what humans respond to well and adapt their internal state accordingly – they will start to seem more natural. In order to accelerate this process, engineers will adopt mechanisms and strategies from nature such as the abilities to reproduce, to repair, to adapt to changes in the environment. This will further reinforce the sense of something that is alive and understands what is going on around it. At some indefinite point in the future it might be possible effectively to argue that a machine is thinking, even that it has a sense of being. But by then it will be too late. No one would doubt that it had.

To outline the Post-Human conception of synthetic beings: Firstly, machine intelligence, using traditional AI methods, will develop in the near future to such a degree that we will come to regard certain types of systems as having a high level of intelligence which is comparable or superior to our own. Such machines will perform a limited range of functions which will complement human skills rather than replace them. These might include military weapons, intelligent agents, creative aids, simulated realities and knowledge databases of great sophistication. Although these machines will create the strong impression that they are thinking, they will not generally be considered by society as sentient beings which experience pain, emotion or pleasure. Secondly, there will be developments in the engineering of machines that will mark an evolution from digital computers as we know them today. In order to increase the effectiveness of intelligent machines, researchers will increasingly adopt strategies of design based on organic models. This is because organic models are the best systems we know of when it comes to information manipulation, self-replication and survival.

Therefore, we will develop systems that have adaptive learning capabilities, high levels of sensory awareness, self-repairing and self-reproducing capacities and distributed processing. Such machines, based perhaps on optical analogue or molecular architectures, will be of sufficient complexity to allow the emergence of global characteristics that will be unpredictable. They will not be 'deterministic machines' in the sense that digital computers are today. They will be too difficult to program so we will have to teach them, or allow them to learn.

Complex machines, as we have called them, will gain increasing autonomy from direct human control and support. To do this they must become aware of environmental influences and self-perpetuation demands such as the need to acquire energy. To achieve this they may need to be motivated, in the same way that organic species are, and through this motivation they may acquire characteristics that we could regard as animate. It will be harder to dismiss the notion that such machines have an sense of understanding since they may be able to experience pain (which would be a motivating factor in self-preservation) or may have some notion of their own existence as distinct from other things. Given a neural system of sufficient complexity and adaptability, and sufficient access to rich sensory data, we might judge that they are able to have thoughts in the sense that we described thought in Chapter 4. That is, they may be able to encode their sensory data into memories that can be recalled by prompting. Not only this, but they will be able to draw associations between those memories and relate them to their negotiations with the world. Their thoughts would acquire a sense of meaning. These thoughts, taken as a whole, could satisfy our criterion for something having a sense of being. Thirdly, we can anticipate the 'mechanisation of the human' in which certain aspects of the human constitution are replicated or enhanced by artificial means. We have already mentioned hearts, eyes and hands but there are a number of other techniques under development that could accelerate this process.

Nanotechnology, mentioned in the introduction to this book, would allow the introduction into the human of microscopic machines which may alter body processes and affect disease, memory capacity, ageing and so on. DNA manipulation, also mentioned, would allow the modification of the very chemistry that determines our humanity. DNA can be considered as a very complex molecular machine that controls our development and characteristics. To gain control over our genetic make-up could dramatically alter the course of human evolution. We could, in effect, 'select for' certain characteristics or 'select against' others from one generation to the next thus greatly increasingly the speed at which we evolve. There is no reason, in principle, why we should not harness the information stored in genetic code for other purposes. For example, we could use the capacity to generate complex organisms contained in DNA to design new machines which have an organic base which would be part-human part machine. We could not deny that such machines would have a sense of being and understanding as long as we retained those human elements which gives rise to them.

In short, it could be said that machines are gradually acquiring human characteristics and humans are gradually acquiring machine characteristics. It is almost inevitable, at some point, that the two will merge to the point where we cannot be absolutely sure of the distinction between them.

'If we wish to produce a synthetic intelligence that displays aesthetic appreciation then it should be able to sense continuity and discontinuity simultaneously - without crashing.'

The Post-Human Manifesto 8.7

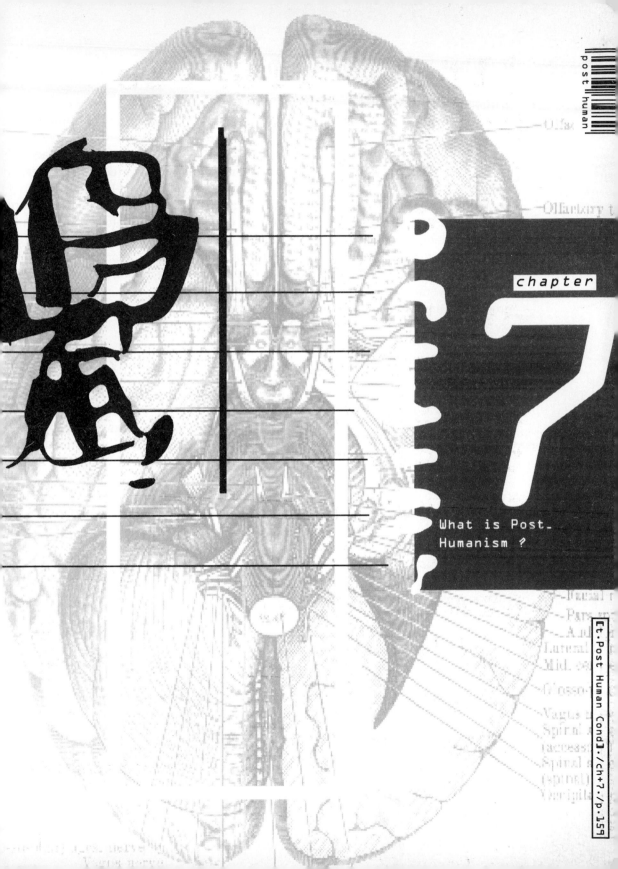

chapter

7

What is Post.
Humanism ?

7. What is Post-Humanism?

In the last chapter we gave an outline of the course along which technology might proceed in the future and, from this, it clear what is meant by Post-Humanism. Humans will, in some sense, merge with machines to the point where they may become indistinguishable. We are obviously not at this stage now. However, it has been argued that the Post-Human era has already started, and even that it started some time ago. If this is so, when can we say it did start? The emergence of the Post-Human era cannot be said to have happened suddenly at any particular point in history. There are examples of Post-Human thought that can be traced back to the ancient Greeks and there are examples of classical humanist thought that are with us today. However, if we had to set a time that marked the general break from a humanist view of the universe to a Post-Humanist one, it is probably at the beginning of the twentieth century. Several events occurred around that time which, as we shall see, were profoundly important in the development of Post-Humanism as we are coming to know it today.

The human condition

For much of history there have been three notions central to the human condition – the notion of God, the notion of man and the notion of nature. Each of these entities was thought to stand in distinction and in opposition to each other. In the minds of those who believed in them, they were arranged hierarchically with God at the top, His favourite creation man below and the lower forms of life sprawled throughout nature at the bottom. The deep impact this belief has had on our understanding of what it is to be human is hard to overstate. Even today many are inclined to believe that those distinctions are valid despite all the progress made in science and technology which might seem to invalidate them. What has changed, however, is the relative prominence each one is afforded at different stages of history. It is important for an understanding of the Post-Human condition that we appreciate it in its historical context.

Humans and theism

The debate about the human condition, at least over the last eight hundred years, has been intimately bound up with the Christian church. From Thomas Aquinas to Nietzsche and beyond, most of the dominant philosophical disputes have been deeply rooted in theological discussions about the relationship between humans and God. Even if this has meant rejecting the actual existence of a Christian God, as in the case of Marx and Nietzsche, it has often meant dealing with the social consequences of belief in a deity. The Christian church has long perpetuated a separation between God and humanity and this has deeply affected Western thinking. An opposition between these entities has been upheld also by institutions of state, law, science and art for many centuries largely because of their dependence on the power of the church.

History is commonly divided into eras according to whichever type of wealth production predominates in a period of time. In the era up to the sixteenth century when the agricultural mode of production was paramount, the political system was largely feudal and the authority of God was used by the ruling élite to justify the social order. Virtually the only recorded intellectual debate we have of the medieval time was centred around theology and interpretation of scriptures. Whilst there was considerable argument amongst philosophers and theologians as to the precise meaning of various religious doctrines, the actual existence of God was rarely questioned from within the institutions of power such as the church, court, judiciary or executive. The church maintained a virtual monopoly on ideas and information since reading and writing were skills restricted largely to the clergy. The overwhelming effect of official intellectual debate was to perpetuate and support the feudal Christian social order. For example, the Crusades, which were early colonial adventures, were justified as Christian missions, as were the later Spanish inquisitorial interventions in South America. The burning of witches to prevent female succession to property was justified on religious grounds in Puritan settlements in the New World (see *The Devil in the Shape of a Woman* by Carol Karlsen) and the line of succession of the royal houses was secured through reference to divine ascendancy. The churches were able to justify all this in the name of God in return for the support they received from the ruling establishment via donations to church funds and influence on the legislature. From this we can see how important it was from the point of view of maintaining order in a feudal society that a God could be invoked who was always right, whatever happened, and who supported implicitly everything the establishment did, since the establishment included the church, which interpreted the word of God via theology and philosophy. Deeply engrained in our culture, therefore, was the notion that the human condition is defined in relation to the will of God and his earthly representatives.

The human experience of nature during feudal times must have consisted of a brutal set of uncontrollable events (diseases, floods, droughts) which could only be explained with reference to supernatural entities. Such entities could use nature as a conduit for their wrath ('acts of God', the 'work of the devil', the plague as divine retribution) and humans were in a very precarious position when it came to dealing with natural forces. Genesis I makes it clear that God spent much longer making nature in general than he spent on making humans, even though it was of humans he was supposed to be most proud. This points to human vulnerability and vanity. Humans were inserted into nature, the Garden of Eden, and given a chance to live in harmony with it, which they squandered. The consequence was perpetual conflict with nature, and alienation from God himself. Natural disasters emanated from God as punishment for sin, sin as defined by the church. Nature must has seemed to act upon humans in a violent and unpredictable way, with little hope on the part of humans that they could exert any significant control over it, except possibly by pleasing the church. Therefore, the feudal view of the human condition must have been based on the apparently real distinction between God, humans and the conflict with nature. This was the view supported by the intellectuals of the day, such as Thomas Aquinas, in deference to the political structure which dominated. To some extent we still retain remnants of this view today.

Humans and humanism

As the mercantile economy became established in seventeenth century Europe, followed by the industrialisation in the eighteenth century, societies grew increasingly bourgeois and urbanised, and a city-based middle class started to evolve. The political structure which until then had prospered, came to face serious threats throughout the eighteenth and nineteenth centuries (protest came in the form of the Levellers' movement, the French Revolution and Chartism) as the wealthier middle and lower classes challenged the political privileges of the landed nobility. The intellectual order which had once accompanied this ancient structure of landed privilege was increasingly challenged and the edifice of accepted ideas started to shift. During the era that saw the Enlightenment and the rise of materialism, new, more accurate, scientific instruments were developed. The telescope, the microscope, the mechanical clock were developments that provided new sources of empirical evidence about the nature of the universe. Above all, the arrival of mechanical printing saw a huge growth in the spread of ideas, and printed pamphlets were often used to spread ideas that subverted the establishment line. Science became sceptical about the discrepancies between observable phenomena and the church view of how nature worked.

For most of its history the Catholic church propagated the view that the earth was the centre of the universe. Thinkers and astronomers who did not believe this had to renounce their views on planetary motion for fear of excommunication or death. Galileo had to recant his heretical views on planetary motion in 1632, yet his ideas were already gaining wide acceptance since they proved useful in improving navigation. Gradually philosophy and intellectual debate started to detach itself from the direct control of the church. To the newer bourgeois ruling classes, religious fidelity was less important than technical and scientific progress since it was through such progress that they enjoyed increased wealth and power. Better clocks and astronomical charts allowed for better navigation which meant shorter voyages and fewer lost cargoes. Better machines allowed for increased productivity in mills, mines and factories. Along with the development of scientific materialism various strains of materialist and anti-religious thought grew, leading in the nineteenth century to the radical political materialism of Marx, Engels and Feuerbach. Since God did not enjoy the overriding prominence he once had, and tangible steps were being made through scientific endeavour to exert control over nature, or at least mirror its achievements, the humanist view developed which perceived humanity in direct conflict with nature without the intervention of God. Gradually, through scientific progress nature could be overcome and tamed, like the alien cultures in the far off colonies. The 'clockwork' view of nature as a logical machine that followed its own predetermined laws, gradually being uncovered by science, came to be the official view endorsed by the establishment in the form of the Royal Society.

The humanist view had its origins in the science and philosophy of ancient Greece and Rome. The early Greeks and Romans obviously did not consider the world to be subject to a Christian God, yet documents discovered and translated in the late medieval period, notably by Erasmus, pointed to the existence of a pagan society of great sophistication and technical prowess. Many of its ideas, such as theories of gravity and mathematics, proved contradictory but, nevertheless, superior in explanatory power to those embodied in Christian ideology. These ideas were taken up with much enthusiasm in the Italian Renaissance and greatly influenced the neo-classical culture that arose in parallel with mechanisation in the eighteenth century. A 'Faith in Progress', meaning human progress, largely usurped the 'Faith in God'.

During the industrial era of the nineteenth and early twentieth Centuries great political and economic forces influenced the general content of intellectual activity. Whilst the name of God was still invoked to justify wars, living conditions, colonisations, etc., progressive intellectual forces were openly challenging his existence and curbing the extent of his influence. It is true that Christian fundamentalism enjoyed a significant revival in the nineteenth century, especially in England, where the Pre-Raphaelites and Gothic revivalists were promoting a utopian and guilt-free haven, based on misconceptions about early medieval history, from which to escape the horrors of Industrial capitalism. However, it was no longer necessary to gain the approval of the church to conduct scientific experiments or publish discoveries, as it had been for

many years previously. The idea that humans are responsible for their own living conditions became widespread. It was found that plagues could be controlled by quarantine and improved housing, that diseases were not 'punishments for sin' but could be cured or avoided, and that humans evolved from primates rather than having been spontaneously created some five thousand years earlier. As far as practical scientific and intellectual debate was concerned, God was no longer the sole authority.

The human condition, under the influence of scientific materialism, came to be one in which the universe could be seen as consisting of two things – humans and nature. Humans were seen to be part of nature (especially when the views of Darwin gained wide acceptance) but increasingly in control of it. Again, this view still has strong reverberations in today's culture.

The cover pages of Francis Bacon's secular humanist work 'Novum Organum' printed in 1620, using a naval navigational metaphor to show the ship of knowledge setting out on the uncharted ocean of science

Humans and Post-Humanism

As we enter the technological era, which is marked by increasing automation (as opposed to the mechanisation of the industrial era), we can see that the perceived relationship between nature and humans is changing. For example, we now know that natural phenomena are infinitely more complex and unknowable than Laplace believed in the early eighteenth century. The evidence of Quantum theory, suggestions of Chaos theory, deep space probing and sub-atomic research all provide more problems about nature than answers, and no scientists can confidently say that the final answer to the structure of the universe is anywhere in sight. At the same time, the technological advances multiply exponentially in the fields of micro-electronics, gene manipulation and communications, leading to possibilities of synthesising, or even surpassing, aspects of nature which until now have been closed off. The tendency towards the development of artificial life, synthesised intelligence, instant telecommunications and virtual reality means that we are now aware of a disappearing barrier between 'natural' and 'human-made' phenomena. It is not at all unfeasible to think of ourselves communicating with a synthetic intelligence on another planet, swapping samples of digital artificial life through interplanetary cyberspace. Once we can conceive of such activities, and understand how they might be realised, the need to impose a fixed distinction between nature and humans diminishes. We will simply cease to think in those terms. The Post-Human era begins fully when we no longer find it necessary, or possible, to oppose humans and nature. This is the point at which we move from thinking about the human condition to thinking about the Post-Human condition.

The modern origins of the Post-Human era

Ferdinand Léger
'Seated Woman'
(1913), Oil on canvas

Historically, we could say that the foundations for our modern conception of the Post-Human condition were laid in the period leading up to the First World War, since this was the time we were introduced to relativity, quantum physics and Cubism. The consequences of these made one thing clear: in the words of Heisenberg, 'There are no things, just probabilities.'

Relativity and Cubism

Within a small number of years before the outbreak of World War I the whole structure of Western science and culture was disturbed by a sequence of scientific discoveries and artistic innovations.

In 1911 Ernest Rutherford postulated his theory of atomic structure and in 1912 the invention of Wilson's cloud chamber confirmed the existence of protons and electrons. In 1913 Niels Bohr formulated his radical theory of atomic organisation. In 1914 Jeans published 'Radiation and Quantum Theory' while Einstein put forward his General Theory of Relativity in 1915. At the same time, Picasso and Braque were consolidating and extending their Cubist techniques. 'L'Homme à la Pipe', often considered a seminal Cubist work, was painted by Picasso in 1911. A year later new media were introduced to the canvas such as chair caning and paper cut-outs, exemplified by works such as

Pablo Picasso
'Still Life with Chair Caning'
(1912), Oil and mixed media on
canvas

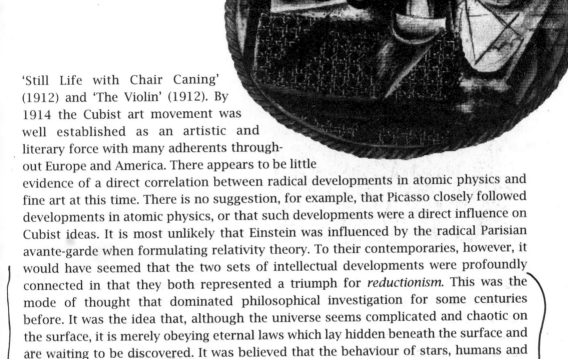

'Still Life with Chair Caning'
(1912) and 'The Violin' (1912). By
1914 the Cubist art movement was
well established as an artistic and
literary force with many adherents throughout Europe and America. There appears to be little
evidence of a direct correlation between radical developments in atomic physics and
fine art at this time. There is no suggestion, for example, that Picasso closely followed
developments in atomic physics, or that such developments were a direct influence on
Cubist ideas. It is most unlikely that Einstein was influenced by the radical Parisian
avante-garde when formulating relativity theory. To their contemporaries, however, it
would have seemed that the two sets of intellectual developments were profoundly
connected in that they both represented a triumph for *reductionism*. This was the
mode of thought that dominated philosophical investigation for some centuries
before. It was the idea that, although the universe seems complicated and chaotic on
the surface, it is merely obeying eternal laws which lay hidden beneath the surface and
are waiting to be discovered. It was believed that the behaviour of stars, humans and
atoms could be understood in terms of regular patterns and rules that determined
how everything worked and it was felt that a complete understanding of the universe
would be achieved if everything could be reduced to its essential building blocks.

Such was the enthusiasm for pinning down the ultimate nature of the universe that
some scientists were led to declare in the late nineteenth and early twentieth centuries
that high level physics was complete and subsequent research lay in merely refining
those principles already understood. In *Dreams of a Final Theory*, Steven Wienberg
quotes physicist Albert Michelson, speaking in 1894:

' . . . it seems probable that most of the grand underlying principles have been firmly
established and that further advances are to be sought chiefly in the rigorous
application of these principles to all the phenomena which come under our notice.'

Quoted in Weinberg, *op. cit. p. 9*

Such views were echoed well into the twentieth century when optimism about the findings of quantum physics led, in the 1920s, to the belief that all the hard questions had been answered and 'the rest was chemistry'.

Art critics of the period (and many since) regarded the Cubists as illuminators of the 'essence of Nature', the underlying reality and structure of the material world. It was felt that such artists had revealed a hidden truth by reducing visual phenomena to their basic components of construction, i.e. Cézannian cubes, cylinders and spheres. Of the Cubists Michel Puy wrote:

'They are hungry for objective truth . . . they aspire to the essence, to the pure idea . . . Their wish has been to reduce the universe to a conjunction of plane-faceted solids. By reducing the beauty of a landscape or the grace of a woman to precise geometrical bodies, one is led to give more vigorous definition of the planes, to establish the structure better, and to penetrate more deeply into the relationships between form and colour.'

Michel Puy, 'Les Indépendants', *Les Marges*, Paris 1911, quoted in E. Fry, *Cubism*, p. 65

I would argue that there is a profound link between the discoveries in atomic science, which were to become known as relativity, quantum physics, and the Cubist art movement. It is not, however, that they represent a triumph for reductionism. Rather, it was the introduction of *relativism* into Western culture through the agency of scientific exploration and artistic innovation that links the two sets of investigations and which provides their most lasting impact on our thought today.

Relativism is obviously central to relativity theory as postulated by Einstein. It contains the fairly well accepted idea that space and time cannot be measured as absolutes in isolation but gain their value from their relationship to each other, a concept known as the 'space-time continuum'. It is exemplified by the idea that a watch hand on a train platform rotates at a relatively different speed to an equivalent watch hand on a train speeding through the station. The distance a watch hand has to travel on a speeding train will seem greater to an observer on the platform than it will to an observer on the train.

This can be likened to putting a golf ball on an aeroplane. To the observer on a plane the ball might seem to travel a few metres, but the distance the ball travels as viewed by someone on the ground may be hundreds of metres since the ball also has the momentum supplied by the plane. Relativity theory is full of ideas that run counter to our everyday intuition of reality because its effects are not normally noticed at the human scale. Yet the theory has been shown to accord with many aspects of cosmic reality and is now accepted as accounting for many phenomena which could not otherwise be explained. Our notion of everyday reality is further subverted by

Ball hit on aircraft

Ball hit on ground

quantum theory, which holds that deciding the position and velocity of a particle must remain essentially ambiguous (see below). When we reduce the atom to its components we get more ambiguity, not more accurate measurement. As we has said above, this subverts the classical assumption of a universe that can be quantified by accurate measurement. What emerges is a new way of thinking about reality which suggests that as we try to 'reduce' the universe to its components, we are forced to accept greater levels of uncertainty. We can only measure with relative precision. In the case of atomic physics the process of reduction leads to relativism in that values can only be defined in relation to some other force, and cannot be isolated in themselves. Quantum reality is a 'field' of interrelated forces. The standard critique on Cubist painting emphasises the reduction of complex objects to simple forms. It is often informed by Cézanne's assertion that he wished to depict the underlying essence of nature through the simplification of a subject. The very name Cubism (which was not coined by any of the artists themselves) suggests the reduction of varied forms to basic blocks. The name can justifiably be applied to the landscape

Relativity – two golf balls, hit with equal force will seem to travel different distances depending on the position of the observer. To the observer on the ground the actual distance travelled by the ball in the air will be greater than the distance observed by the person in the plane

paintings rendered by Picasso at Horta de Ebro and those of Braque at L'Estaque in 1908-9. These owe much to the later landscapes of Cézanne (which had recently been shown at his retrospective) and the primitivism that was fashionable in Paris around this time.

However, when we study the later work of Picasso and Braque, particularly that of the period 1912 to 1914, there is very little evidence of box- or cube-like structures at all. The

Pablo Picasso, *Houses at Horta, (1909)*

still lives and portraits are rendered with flat, interconnecting planes which suggest the *possibility* of forms and edges. There are curly hints of violin *f*-holes and tuning keys, oblique references to bottles and glasses, tentative moustaches and fleeting fingers. In fact, what Picasso and Braque produced is more radical than

the mere reduction of complex forms to simpler ones. It is even more radical than the idea that one can represent a thing from more than one point of view. They were giving pictorial expression to the ambiguity and uncertainty that was simultaneously emerging in the physical sciences. What was so revolutionary about Cubism in the period 1912 to 1914 was that it challenged the idea that a picture should represent a finite object or person.

Pablo Picasso, *Violin, (1914)*

Any object or person in a painting from this period is not *absolutely* there, it is *possibly* there. Indeed, it is a powerful way of expressing the notion that there are no finite objects or people that exist absolutely in space. There is no absolute measure of matter, space or time. The only absolute against which things could be measured was the speed of light which, Einstein argued, was the fastest thing in the universe and which remained constant. Yet, even this absolute has now been rendered questionable. Recent developments in particle physics suggest that there are events in the universe that cannot be measured against the speed of light. The effect of 'non-locality' states that a particle can 'exist' in more than one place at a time. Causing a change in a particle in one location will cause an equivalent change in its counterpart *immediately*, regardless of the distance between them. Somehow the effect is transmitted without being subject to the constraints of acceleration. The stability of things that might exist only in one place and at one time cannot be taken as given. In such circumstances objects, rather than being fixed things, become clusters of probabilities that mutate over time and which are dependent on the viewer for their perception. The Cubists introduced an ambiguous contingency into pictorial representation which was analogous to the contingency to be found in advanced physics.

'It is hardly just to look at Cubism mainly as a device to increase our awareness of space. If that was its aim, it should be pronounced a failure. Where it succeeds is in countering the transforming effects of an illusionist reading. It does so by the introduction of contrary clues which will resist all attempts to apply the test of consistency. Try as we may to see the guitar or jug suggested to us as a three-dimensional object and thereby transform it, [in Cubist works] we will always come across a contradiction somewhere which compels us to start afresh.'

E. H. Gombrich, *Art and Illusion, pp. 238-40 (my remark in box parentheses)*

The similarity between such a reading of a Cubist work and the attempt to pin down the exact position of a sub-atomic particle is acute. The thing we look at, or investigate, is there. It has a recognisable form and structure, yet we cannot precisely state where it is, or where it will be. We cannot define its edges or boundaries. Each process of looking will be different, each process of looking will be probabilistic.

The huge implications of the pre-World War I investigations into atomic structure and pictorial representation are only now, I believe, being fully realised. Contemporary interpretations of both quantum theory and Cubist images were hampered by an enthusiasm for reductionism which clung to the idea that they were part of some search for the essential truth about reality. This reductionism was part of a larger paradigm which is generally labelled humanism – a way of looking at the world which is now becoming redundant. From our position in the late twentieth century we can see that these pre-war ideas were to lay the foundations for the demise of humanism and the shift into Post-Humanism, the shift from a universe of certainty and predictability to a universe of uncertainty and unpredictability. With this change we will all realise that our capacity to order and control the universe is ultimately limited, that randomness, ambiguity and disorder are as integral to the cosmic process as their opposites. They cannot be eliminated or ignored. The universe cannot be reduced to anything other than itself, which is irreducible. It means that we should learn to accept unpredictable events as quantum physicists have done since the 1920s and, even better, to harness them to our own ends. If we wished to model human creativity, as physicists model sub-atomic reality, should we consider building a system which was totally coherent and predictable? Or should we allow the system a certain autonomy, the option to be influenced by randomness and apparently unconnected events? Which would be the richer, the more 'realistic'?

Uncertainty

The humanist era was characterised by certainty about the operation of the universe and the place of humans within it. Great confidence was expressed in the transformatory power of science and the ascent of man. The Post-Human era is characterised by uncertainty about the operation of the universe and about what it is to be human. Science may now seem fragmented, flawed and limited. There is no longer any guarantee that the world will be ruled over by men.

There is a principle of quantum mechanics which illustrates clearly the divergence from a view of the universe that is certain to one in which the universe is inherently uncertain. Heisenberg's *Uncertainty Principle* states that it is impossible to measure the location and velocity of a sub-atomic particle (an electron) at the same time. The principle is very simple. If we wish to measure the position or speed of an electron we must bombard it with some energy source, usually light particles, so that it can be seen. Wherever the electron we wish to measure is located will be the point at which some of our light particles will be bounced back. Thus we have the location. But the light particles themselves will disturb the path of the electron under investigation, thus altering its velocity. We can imagine this as a kind of radar beam sent out to track aircraft. Yet the aircraft in our model is so small that the radar waves move the aircraft around thus giving our measurement an inherent level of uncertainty. This gives rise to the probabilistic nature of quantum measurement. If we cannot know the speed and direction of travel of an electron at the same time, then we cannot predict where it will travel next. We can say that given a certain position and an uncertain velocity it will probably move to one of several locations. We cannot determine exactly which one. To the physicists of the 1920s this ran directly counter to the intuitive operation of the universe that classical mechanics presupposed. In classical mechanics, it was assumed that we could determine the future position of any particle, be it electron or golf ball, by calculating the path it would take given a certain position and velocity. This assumption led to the notion that it would be possible in theory to predict the whole future of the universe if we could measure the state of all particles at any one time – one of the great mistakes of humanist science. Built into this assumption was the desire on the part of the humanists to exert human control over the whole universe and to achieve the eradication of uncertainty.

The age of uncertainty

Questions arise in the Post-Human era that would have not troubled us in the humanist one – What is a human? Is there such a thing? We have our bodies, our anatomies with well defined features. But these can be changed with chemicals and plastic surgery. We have our books and our music and our art. But these can be mass produced, sampled and distributed in mangled form across vast galaxies of media, or synthesised in vats of digital creativity. We have our feelings and emotions, our responses to the world and other people. Feelings and emotions can be controlled by drugs and cosmetic pharmacology, any experience can be synthesised from the right virtual stimuli, people are falling in love on-line. We have our genes, they are mapped out clearly by the Human Genome Project and stored as digital data which can be experimentally recombined. We have our minds. That is why we are humans. But remember human history, where the mind was anything we wanted it to be, where people could be made to think and do anything. Where does any*one's* mind exist in the virtual matrix of the cyberverse? 'There is no there, there.' said Gertrude Stein.

Uncertainty is becoming familiar. There is uncertainty about life-time employment due in part to the automation of many jobs, about political and economic theory, about choices of medical treatment which is undergoing huge technological changes. There is uncertainty about what is happening to the environment, about whether scientific progress is always beneficial and about where technology is leading us. But couldn't we say that this uncertainty has always been with us? It has, but until now we have always had the hope that it would end. Either God would end it for us if we did the right things, or science would end it for us by making everything work. We are like children who have lost their parents. There is nothing, and no one to turn to.

What can we say is certain? Only that which we have to *accept* as certain for some other reason. There is nothing that we can say that in itself is certain. It is not certain that things have opposites – randomness and order, truth and falsity, natural and artificial, material and immaterial. It is not even certain that we *need* to die. This genetic disorder may be cured.

In Post-Human terms uncertainty is nothing to fear. The world has always been as uncertain. What has changed is that it is now much harder to impose certainty. Therefore, we have less *false* sense of certainty in the age of uncertainty. Certainty, like belief, only arises in the absence of full information.

Whilst the tendency of humanist science has been to avoid uncertainty, it is now obvious that no life-like system can be designed that does not include a fundamental level of uncertainty which we will never be able fully to control. Computers and computer software that act in predictable ways are mere machines. That is what they are now. The real fun begins when the computer output becomes a *probability and not a certainty.*

Other eminent Post-Humans

I do not claim any originality for the use of the term Post-Human. The concept of a future state of humanity in which biology is merged with technology has tentacles going back at least to the 1940s with the cybernetic movement inspired by Norbert Weiner. This idea has been variously named as the Post-Biological, the Transhuman and the Post-Darwinian stage of human development. But there is no doubt that, in whichever form it exists, it is gradually gaining a hold on the imaginations of many people including artists (see the catalogue to the 'Post Human' exhibition held in 1992 by Jeffrey Deitch), science-fiction writers (Bruce Sterling has recently made frequent reference to 'Posthumanism') and philosophers. In particular it has been enthusiastically supported by those who call themselves Extropians and whose ideas are carried in the philosophical journal *Extropy*. The Extropian view can be summarised as an optimistic belief in the power of technology to transform, for the better, that which we now know as human existence. Extropy is the opposite of entropy, the pessimistic principle that all of the universe is decaying into chaos. Extropians seek to affirm, in a Nietzschian way, the self-organising qualities of life, that order which emerges out of chaos. They imagine the indefinite extension of human life, deep space exploration and the alteration of human neurobiology by chemical and genetic means to overcome our limitations. One of the founders of Extropianism is Max More and it is worth quoting a passage in which he describes Transhumanism and Posthumanism.

'Q: What do "transhuman" and "posthuman" mean?

'A: TRANSHUMAN: We are transhuman to the extent that we seek to become post-human and take action to prepare for a posthuman future. This involves learning about and making use of new technologies that can increase our capacities and life expectancy, questioning common assumptions, and transforming ourselves ready for the future, rising above outmoded human beliefs and behaviours.

'TRANSHUMANISM: Philosophies of life (such as the Extropian philosophy) that seek the continuation and acceleration of the evolution of intelligent life beyond its currently human form and limits by means of science and technology, guided by life-promoting principles and values, while avoiding religion and dogma.

'POSTHUMAN: Posthumans will be persons of unprecedented physical, intellectual, and psychological ability, self-programming and self-defining, potentially immortal, unlimited individuals. Posthumans have overcome the biological, neurological, and psychological constraints evolved into humans. Extropians believe that the best strategy for attaining posthumanity to be a combination of technology and determination, rather than looking for it through psychic contacts, or extraterrestrial or divine gift.

'Posthumans may be partly or mostly biological in form, but will likely be partly or wholly postbiological — our personalities having been transferred "into" more durable, modifiable, and faster, and more powerful bodies and thinking hardware. Some of the technologies that we currently expect to play a role in allowing us to become posthuman include genetic engineering, neural-computer integration, molecular nanotechnology, and cognitive science.'

Max More, taken from *The Post Human Sub-page* on the World Wide Web

Further references for Extropianism and Transhumanism can be found in the Reference section in this book. There are some points of emphasis by the Extropians with which I would not wholly agree, but these are not significant enough to unravel here. For most purposes we can say that the Post-Human condition and the Extropian vision share a common idea of the future of humanity.

The Post-Human condition

Post-Humanism is not about the 'End of Man'. The 'End of Man' is a concept that has been proposed since, at least, the time of Nietzsche, yet now, with the technologies we have described, it looks increasingly probable. The possibility that machines may evolve which 'out-do' humans, or even replace them, immediately suggests our ultimate erasure. This implication is naïve. Post-Humanism not about the 'End of Man' but about the end of a 'man-centred' universe or, put less phallocentrically, a 'human-centred' universe.

Firstly, it is about end of 'humanism', the long held belief in the infallibility of human power and the arrogant belief in our superiority and uniqueness. This 'end' will not happen abruptly. Belief in the ideals of humanism have existed, at least, since the fourteenth century and will continue to exist well into the future.

Secondly, it is about evolution, a process that started at the beginning of life and has no reason to stop. If life can run more efficiently and become 'fitter' inside things we think of as machines, then it will do so. By the same token, if humans are able to evolve more effectively by acquiring machine-like enhancements, or by DNA modification then they will do so. But this does not necessarily mean the end of humans. If life does emerge in machines (or machines emerge in life) there is no reason to suppose that this should replace other forms of life which may carry on indefinitely. Earth still abounds with species that predate humans; evolution does not necessarily discard old models when it generates new ones.

Thirdly, Post-Humanism is about how we live, how we conduct our exploitation of the environment, animals and each other. It is about what things we investigate, what questions we ask and what assumptions underlie them. The most obvious manifestations of the end of humanism are those movements that resist the worst aspects of humanist thought: feminism – the movement against the domination of women; animal rights – the movement against human exploitation of animals; environmentalism – the movement against human exploitation of the earth; anti-slavery – the movement against human exploitation of other humans. The fact that all these movements exist suggests the gradual overturning of a hu*man*-centred world is well underway.

This is why Post-Humanism is not just about the future, it is also about the present and the past. The past determines our view of the future just as the future will determine our view of the past. To some extent we live for the future; it promises better things. But this can lead us to forget that the future, and whatever benefits it may bring, is not something that just happens *to* us – we create it by our conduct in the present. We *all* have an influence now on the way the future will turn out. One reason for writing this book is that most people remain unaware of the huge implications of the technologies that are now being developed, and very few of us are invited to take an active part in those decisions which will profoundly affect the course of human development. Who is in charge of the future?

The awkward question posed by the changes we have labelled Post-Humanism, is not 'Will we develop machines that are equal or superior to humans?' We have already described how this will happen. The difficult question is, 'Why do we want to develop such machines – to what ends will they be put?'

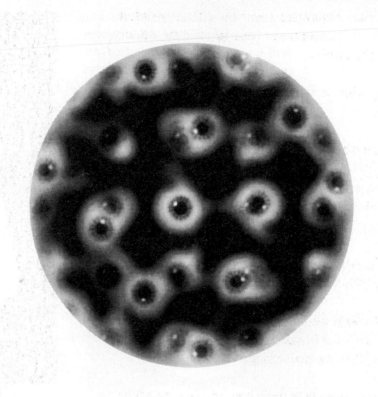

The Post-Human Manifesto (version 1.0) is printed here in full. It summarises many of the ideas contained in the book.

A version of this manifesto is posted as a Web document at:

"http://www.southern.com/PIPE/01phmfaq.html "

It is intended that those who are interested in the ideas dicussed can e-mail comments or criticisms to the author at:

manifesto@hexhq.demon.co.uk or
manifesto@ae47.cityscape.co.uk

These contributions will be included in later versions of the manifesto which will be kept updated and will include credits for the contributors.

The pages also include a number of links to other sites of interest.

chapter

8

The Post_Human
Manifesto

8. The Post-Human Manifesto

Post-Humanists are people who understand how the world is changing. By understanding this they are changing the world.

1. General statements

1. It is now clear that humans are no longer the most important things in the universe. This is something the humanists have yet to accept.

2. All technological progress of human society is geared towards the redundancy of the human species as we currently know it.

3. In the Post-Human era many beliefs become redundant – not least the belief in human being.

4. Human beings, like gods, only exist inasmuch as we believe them to exist.

5. The future never arrives.

6. All humans are not born equal, but it is too dangerous not to pretend that they are.

7. In the Post-Human era machines will be gods.

8. Intelligent agents will be the religious authorities of the information age. We will ask them to interpret the chaos of the god machines for us.

9. It is a deficiency of humans that they require others to tell them what they already know. It is only then they will believe it. The Post-Human avoids excessive scholarship, preferring to spend one hour thinking rather than ten hours reading.

10. Post-Humanists do not fall into the trap of imagining a society where everything works well. Economic and political theories are as futile as long-range weather predictions.

11. Surf or die. You can't control a wave, but you can ride it.

12. We now realise that human knowledge, creativity and intelligence are ultimately limited.

13. Complex machines are an emergent life form.

"SOCIETY IS MORE COMPLEX THAN ANY OF OUR THEORIES ABOUT IT"

14. A complex machine is a machine whose workings we do not fully understand or control.

15. As computers develop to be more like humans, so humans develop to like computers more. This is especially apparent in youth culture where the aesthetic value of what the computer does, in music, in image generation, in design, in games is increasingly appreciated.

2. Statements on consciousness, humans and philosophy

If consciousness is a property that emerges from a specific set of conditions, in order to synthesise it we do not need to re-model it from the 'top-down'. We only need to recreate the conditions from which it might emerge. This requires an understanding of what those conditions are.

1. Consciousness is not exclusively restricted to the brain.

2. Consciousness is the function of an organism, not an organ.

3. One does not understand consciousness by studying the brain alone.

4. The mind and the body act together to produce consciousness. If one is absent consciousness ceases. There is no pure thought, isolated from a body. In order to function the brain must be connected to a body, even if the body is artificial. Consciousness is an effect which arises through the co-operation of a brain and body. We think with our whole body.

5. Consciousness can only be considered as an emergent property. In this sense it is like boiling. Given sufficient heat, gravity and air pressure the water in a kettle will start to boil. We can see what boiling is, we can recognise it as something to which we give a name. We do not consider it mysterious. Yet we cannot isolate it from the conditions which produced it. Consciousness is a property which emerges from a given set of conditions.

6. To say that conscious thought is not *exclusively* a function of the brain does not deny that the brain has a significant part to play.

7. Human bodies have no boundaries.

8. No finite division can be drawn between the environment, the body and the brain. The human is identifiable, but not definable.

9. Consciousness (mind) and the environment (reality) cannot be separated. They are continuous.

10. There is nothing external to a human, because the extent of a human cannot be fixed.

11. If we accept that the mind and body cannot be absolutely separated, and that the body and the environment cannot be absolutely separated, then we are left with the apparently absurd yet logically consistent conclusion that: *consciousness and the environment cannot be absolutely separated.*

12. First we had God, humans and nature. The rationalists dispensed with God, leaving humans in perpetual conflict with nature. The Post-Humanists dispense with humans leaving only nature. The distinction between God, nature and humanity does not represent any eternal truth about the human condition. It merely reflects the prejudices of the societies which maintained the distinction.

13. Idealistic and materialistic philosophical views both assume a division between the thing that thinks and the thing that is thought about – between the internal mind (brain) and external reality (environment). Remove this division and both views become redundant.

14. The idealists think that the only things that exist are ideas; the materialists think that the only thing that exists is matter. It must be remembered that ideas are not independent of matter and that matter is just an idea.

15. Most philosophical problems are debates about language. They arise because of the mistaken assumptions *a.)* that language is consistent and *b.)* that because a word exists there must exist a 'thing' that it represents and *c.)* that the things that are represented should, in themselves, be consistent.

16. Post-Humans never get bogged down in arguments about language. The scholars and humanists will always try to restrict debate to the battleground of language because they know no one can win.

17. Scholastic philosophers are disqualified from saying anything of interest. We need recombination, not regurgitation.

18. Logic is an illusion of human imagination. Truth and falsity do not exist in nature – other that in human thought.

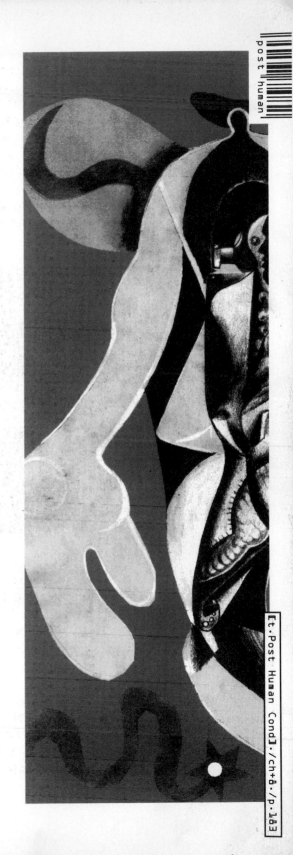

3. Statements on science, nature and the universe

1. Science will never achieve its aim of comprehending the ultimate nature of reality. It is a futile quest, although most scientists do not acknowledge this yet. The universe will always be more complex than we will ever understand. It is dishonest of scientists not to admit that total understanding of the universe is their aim. It is even more dishonest not to admit that it can never be achieved.

2. The Post-Human abandons the search for the ultimate nature of the universe and its origin (thus saving a lot of money in the process).

3. The Post-Human realises that the ultimate questions about existence and being do not require answers. The answer to the question 'Why are we here?' is that there is no answer.

4. To know the ultimate nature of the universe would require knowing everything about the universe, everything that has happened and everything that will happen. If one thing were not known it would imply that all knowledge of the universe is partial, potentially incomplete and, therefore, not ultimate.

5. No scientific model can ever be complete. It will always be partial and contingent. For any model to be complete it would have to take all influential factors into account, no matter how insignificant. Since this is impossible, the scientist must make an arbitrary decision about which ones to ignore. Having ignored some factors, their model is incomplete, although this does not mean that it is not useful.

6. The Post-Human accepts that humans have a finite capacity to understand and control nature.

7. All origins are ends and all ends are origins. Chaos theory has often been illustrated with the image of a butterfly's wing-flap causing a thunderstorm on the opposite side of the globe. Whilst this might illustrate the sensitivity of systems to initial states, it does not take into account what caused the butterfly to flap its wings – a gust of wind?

8. Logic that seems consistent at the human scale cannot necessarily be applied to the microcosmic or the macrocosmic scale.

9. Our knowledge about the universe is constrained by the level of resolution with which we are able to view it. Knowledge is contingent on data – data varies with resolution.

10. Scientists give privilege to order over disorder on the assumption that they are gradually discovering the essential laws of nature. This is a fundamental error; nature is neither essentially ordered or disordered. What we perceive as regular, patterned information we classify as order. What we perceive as irregular, unpatterned information we classify as disorder. The appearance of order and disorder implies more about the way in which we process information than it does about the intrinsic presence of order or disorder in nature.

11. Science works on the basis of an intrinsic universal order. It assumes that all phenomena are subject to physical laws and that some of those laws are well understood, some partially understood, and some unknown. The Post-Human accepts that laws are not things that are intrinsic to nature, nor are they things which arise purely in the mind and are imposed on nature. This would reinforce the division between the mind and reality which we have already abandoned. The order that we commonly perceive around us, as well as the disorder, is not a function exclusively of either the universe or our consciousness, but a combination of both, since they cannot really be separated.

12. Everything that exists anywhere is energy. Energy has four properties:

a. It is everything and everywhere
b. It is manifested in an infinite variety of ways
c. It is perpetually transforming
d. It always has been, and always will be, the above

13. The appearance of matter is an illusion generated by interactions among things at the human level of resolution.

14. Humans and the environment are different expressions of energy. The only difference between them is the form that energy takes.

15. The Post-Human is entirely open to ideas of 'paranormality', 'immateriality', the 'supernatural', and the 'occult'. The Post-Human does not accept that faith in scientific methods is superior to faith in other belief systems.

4. Statements on dis|order and dis|continuity

1. Order and disorder are relative, not absolute, qualities. The proof that order and disorder are relative qualities lies in the fact that they define each other.

2. Anything we perceive can be considered to contain different degrees of order and disorder. The perception of order and disorder in something is contingent on the level of resolution from which it is viewed.

3. What we perceive as ordered and disordered is often culturally determined. Logicians will assert that there are mathematical ways of defining disorder, entropy and complexity – ways that are independent of human subjectivity. Whilst these definitions may be useful in certain applications they remain open to relativistic interpretation.

4. In Post-Human terms, the apparent distinctions between 'things' are not the result of innate divisions within the structure of the universe, but jointly a product of:

a. the way in which the sensual processes in living entities operate.

b. the variety of ways in which energy is manifested in the universe.

5. The ways in which energy manifestations are perceived by an observer can always be described with two simple qualities – continuity and discontinuity. Continuity is non-interruption of

space-time. Discontinuity is a rupture in space-time. Both qualities can be discerned in all events depending upon how they are viewed.

6. Energy manifestations should not be thought of as intrinsically continuous or discontinuous, that is there are no absolute qualities of energy. Energetic states will appear as either continuous or discontinuous to an observer depending upon their viewing position. The quality of dis|continuity is context sensitive.

7. What distinguishes things from one another is the perceived discontinuity that they display. The difference in manifestations of energy between a philosopher and a chair allows them to appear distinguished.

8. In Post-Human terms we can see that, whilst there may be no intrinsic divisions between things (since all things are expressions of energy), an organism will perceive differences since energy is manifested in different ways and an organism is sensitive to different levels of energy. These varying manifestations of energy can be perceived as either continuous or discontinuous, these qualities being entirely relative to each other. Things appear to be distinct from each other. The existence of order or disorder is, therefore, a function of both the perceptual apparatus and the energetic expression of that which is perceived. Order does not exist separately from its perception.

9. The level of complexity in a system cannot be defined in objective (that is, absolute) terms. Complexity is a function of human cognition, not an intrinsic property of anything we might look at.

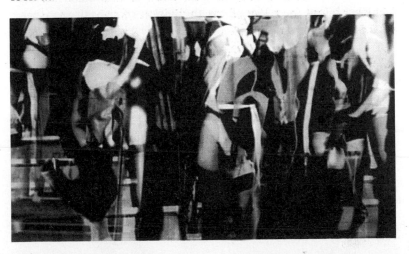

5. Statements on thought, meaning and being

As long as models about how the brain might work are defective (being based on fallacious assumptions), the creation of a synthetic consciousness will be impractical.

1. Human thought is something that occurs within the human body. It is not necessary to identify precisely where it occurs because it does not occur precisely in any 'part'.

2. The combined biological processes that give rise to thought could be spoken of as a 'cognitive medium'. At our current state of knowledge this would include neurons, the nervous system, the brain, various hormones, bio-feedback mechanisms as well as others as yet unknown. Speaking of the cognitive medium allows us to locate thought in the biological processes of the human body (i.e. thought is not independent of the body) without falling into the old trap of locating it exclusively in the brain.

3. Inasmuch as each thought is distinct it will occur as a distinct event within the cognitive medium.

4. It is tempting to think of thoughts as blocks of data in the brain. This would be a mistake since it reinforces a static view of mental activity. A thought is a path through the cognitive medium. Think of it like this. Taking the London Underground map as an analogy of how the mind works, many people would say, 'Each of the stations on the map represents one of our thoughts and the lines represent the links between them. The lines are what enable us to get from thought to thought.' The Post-Human would say, 'A thought is not a station on the map but the route from one station to another.' That is, a thought is the action of travelling rather than a particular destination.

5. Given that a thought is activated, for whatever reason, it consists in a process of travelling through the cognitive medium. A thought does not exist unless it is being thought. The most likely journey that a thought may take once it has been activated defines its path. Similar thoughts will take similar paths.

6. Such paths can be created in a number of ways – direct experience, learning, pre-wiring, the act of thinking itself. The paths are described in neuro-physiological terms as the

connections between neurons and the probability of their firing. The cognitive medium is not a static substance. It is continually changing in response to stimulation and activation. The cognitive medium is prone to adaptation just as the skin or muscles are.

7. The path that a thought takes is not uni-linear in the way that we normally think of paths. It takes many different routes simultaneously. The occurrence of one particular thought may require that we bring together many different thoughts in combination.

8. The fact that different thoughts may lie in different paths, each of which are distinct insofar as each thought is distinct, shows us how we can imagine things we have never seen. We have never seen a 'girl with kaleidoscope eyes' but we can imagine what she looks like by making a composite image of the components, i.e. travelling through several distinct thought paths at once.

9. The activity of thinking is regulated by the conduct of energy in the cognitive medium. The cognitive medium is no different from any other system in that it represents a particular process of energy transformations. Where two thoughts are continuous (for example, 'blue' and 'sky' in the sentence 'The sky is blue'), the pathway between each of these thoughts is well established. It will require little energy to pass from one to the other. Where two thoughts are not well connected (for example, between 'tree' and 'sardine' in the phrase 'The sardine-tree') more energy is required to fuse the thoughts since they have less well established connections.

10. Ideas that can proceed from one to another with relatively little effort (energy) can be considered continuous. Ideas that require great effort to travel between can be considered discontinuous.

11. The presence or absence of 'meaning' is determined by the amount of energy required to pass from one concept to another. Difficult meaning arises from the co-existence of concepts that are semantically distant, that is, when there is not a well established connection between them. However, the path between concepts that have little or no connection may be too difficult to travel. For example in the phrase 'The yesterday of refractive stepshine', whilst not meaningless, is certainly awkward to assemble by the standard of most phrases.

12. In order to maintain a sense of being the human tries to build up continuity through the stimuli it receives from the environment. Such stimuli are both stable and unstable since the environment displays different amounts of both. The development of stable thought paths which correspond to stable stimuli generates a sense of order. Over time such stability develops into a sense of being.

13. Were the sense of order not perpetually threatened by the recurrence of random stimuli, there would be no compulsion to reassert order. As it is, since humans are continually faced with random stimuli, it is necessary to keep reasserting order (maintaining meaning) so that we do not dissovle into chaos, thereby losing our sense of being.

14. In Post-Human terms it is unimportant through what mechanism this process of being occurs. The same effect can be achieved in a number of different ways. It is true that we can learn from the human being how being occurs, but this does not mean that it is the only way it can be done.

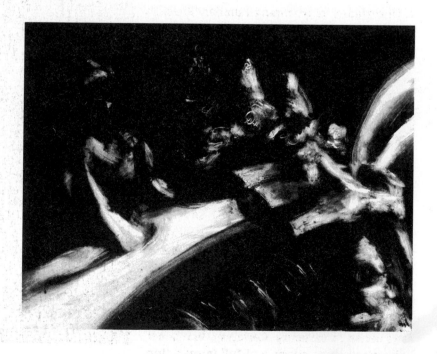

6. Statements on uncertainty

1. The humanist era was characterised by certainty about the operation of the universe and the place of humans within it. The Post-Human era is characterised by uncertainty about the operation of the universe and about what it is to be human.

2. Questions arise in the Post-Human era that would have not troubled us in the humanist era – What is a human? Is there such a thing?

3. Historically, we could say the Post-Human era, the age of uncertainty, was born in the period leading up to the First World War since this was the time we were introduced to Quantum physics and Cubism. The consequences of both made one thing clear. In the words of Heisenberg, 'There are no things, just probabilities.'

4. Uncertainty is becoming familiar. There is uncertainty about life-time employment, about political and economic theory, about choices of medical treatment. There is uncertainty about what is happening to the environment, about whether scientific progress is always beneficial and about where technology is leading us.

5. What can we say is certain? Only that which we have to *accept* as certain for some other reason.

6. In Post-Human terms uncertainty is nothing to fear. The world has always been as uncertain as it is now. What has changed is that it is now much harder to impose authority since increased information flow diminishes authority. Therefore, there is less *false* sense of certainty. Certainty, like belief, only arises in the absence of full information.

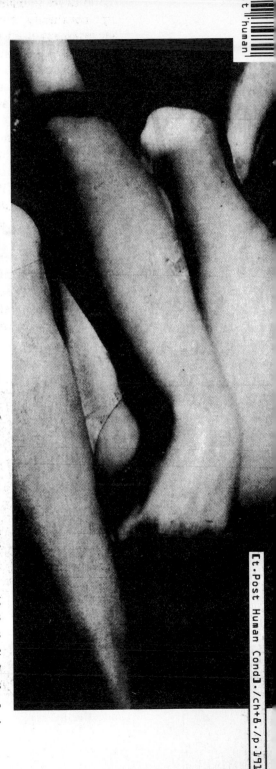

7. Statements on art and creativity

The production and appreciation of art is a particularly human faculty. It is often cited by the humanists as the highest expression of human thought and the thing that most distingushes us from machines. It would, therefore, be fair to admit that the Post-Human era cannnot begin in full until we have met this challenge from the humanists. In order to develop a machine that can produce and appreciate art we must first have a clearer understanding of what it is.

1. What is art? The only useful definition of art is that it describes any commodity of the art market. We must distinguish between an art object and an aesthetically stimulating object. An art object is a commodity that is traded on the art market. An aesthetic object is one that is appreciated for its aesthetic quality. Something may be both an art object and an aesthetic object, such as Van Gogh's 'Irises'. Something may be an aesthetic object without being art, like a sunset or an iris.

2. By the way, many people think that much modern art is not art because they consider it to lack aesthetic value even though it commands high prices on the art market. They are simply confusing the art value and the aesthetic value of an object. These two values are quite separate, but of course linked. 'Art is a commodity like any other,' said Henry Kahnweiler, Picasso's dealer. Art is an aesthetic commodity. Marcel Duchamp demonstrated clearly that the object itself is irrelevant to whether it is art. In 1914 he designated a bottlerack as an art object. 'The choice', he claimed, 'was based on a reaction of visual indifference, with at the same time a total absence of good or bad taste, in fact a complete anaesthesia.'

3. In order to be clear, the art market can be defined as a identifiable set of institutions and commercial organisations which collectively fund, promote and sell art.

4. Art must be (and always has been) elitist and exclusive in order to maintain its financial value and prestige. Many modern artists use aesthetic elitism to guarantee exclusivity which, in turn, ensures values are upheld.

5. The main function of art is to distinguish rich people from poorer people.

6. Good art is art that is aesthetically stimulating. Bad art is aesthetically neutral. This applies equally to all art forms.

7. The criteria that determine whether something is aesthetically stimulating or aesthetically neutral are always changing.

8. Good art always contains an element of disorder (discontinuity). Bad art simply reinforces a pre-existing order.

9. Good art promotes discontinuity. Bad art enforces continuity.

10. Discontinuity produces aesthetically stimulating experiences. Continuity produces aesthetically neutral experiences.

11. Discontinuity is the basis of all creation, but discontinuity is meaningless without continuity.

12. Rich aesthetic experience is generated by the perception, simultaneously, of continuity and discontinuity in the same event.

13. All stimulating design relies on balancing the relative quotients of order and disorder in the object. This also goes for the composition of music and literature. However, such

judgements cannot be made in isolation from the fact that values of order and disorder are largely prescribed by social agreement.

14. Post-Human art uses technology to promote discontinuity. Healthy societies tolerate the promotion of discontinuity since they understand that humans need exposure to it in spite of themselves. Unhealthy societies discourage the promotion of discontinuity.

15. Creativity does not consist in the production of anything that is completely new. Creativity consists in combining things that already exist, but which had previously been held as separate. Creativity and aesthetic appreciation are both functions of the human ability to modify the connections in their thought paths or to have them modified.

16. The process of aesthetic stimulation is heightened when concepts are forced together from relatively diverse locations (discontinuity). The amount of energy required to contemplate diverse concepts produces the rush of excitement that is familiar to lovers of art. Such an effect is often achieved when an object is taken from one context and placed in another. Or in the case of many Picasso pieces, we are asked to accept the presence of one object when we plainly see another.

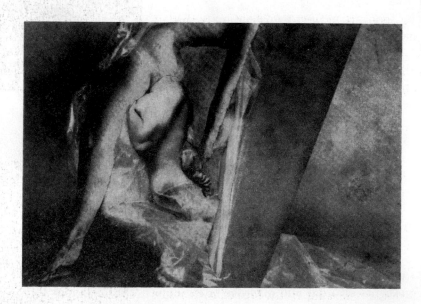

8. Statements on synthetic beings

We already have machines that can learn. However, their abilities are currently limited by the fact that they are logical. As we know, logic is an idealisation which has been developed by human imagination. Since there are few things less logical in behaviour than humans, any machine that is restricted to using logic as its base will never display human characteristics.

1. Currently the output of computers is predictable. The Post-Human era begins in full when the output of computers is unpredictable.

2. All current artificial life machines are hermetically sealed. They are limited by the complexity of the calculations our machines can perform. They are only sensitive to a finite number of stimuli. The quotient of randomness intruding upon them is relatively small.

3. Human thought is not a hermetic system. Since we know that the mind, body and environment cannot be separated, we cannot rule out the impact of any environmental stimuli on the process of thought, no matter how minute it might seem.

4. What is essential to the functioning of human consciousness is that the mind receives a continuous input of random stimuli from the environment. The human mind has evolved to absorb the unexpected – the discontinuous stimulus.

5. We know that it is the complusion to reassert order in the face of random stimuli that generates our sense of being. Therefore, it is obvious that if we are to create any synthetic intelligence that has a sense of being like that which we recognise in ourselves, then it must be sensitive to the same level of random interruption that humans are. It must have a compulsion to reassert meaning in the face of both stable and unstable input.

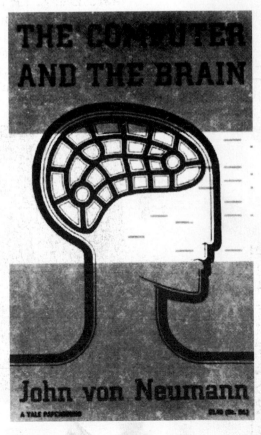

THE COMPUTER AND THE BRAIN

John von Neumann

6. If we wish to produce a synthetic intelligence that displays creativity then we need it to be able to establish connections between its thoughts in a discontinuous way. This will be achieved by making it perpetually sensitive to random stimuli.

7. If we wish to produce a synthetic intelligence that displays aesthetic appreciation then it should be able to sense continuity and discontinuity simultaneously - without crashing. Whilst this would cause excitement in the machine it is yet to be determined to what extent it would be pleasurable.

1

BLAST Post (the inevitable) HUMAN

CURSE THE MACHINE FOR ITS GRAPHS AND LOGIC

TEPID THINKER, SET around scriptures
of intricate dull masters.

FRANKENSTEIN DEV, the LOCAL wet sucks
the CLIENT'S brain

A 1024 MB LONG, 32 DATASTRING Wide

STREAM OF DATA even, is pushed against us

from the Floridas, TO MAKE US COLD.

OFFICIOUS SCHOLARS keep back INFECTIOUS HEAPS

SO MUCH VAST IMPOVERTY TO PRODUCE

THE READER of "Æsthetics"
LEARNED WORM
IRRITANT OF NATURE
DEPARTMENTAL
                    IMPERSONATOR
MULTI USER DUNGEON
SOCIAL-REMARKER
THE BEST ICE CREAM
EXPLOITING THE OLD
A GOOD REST

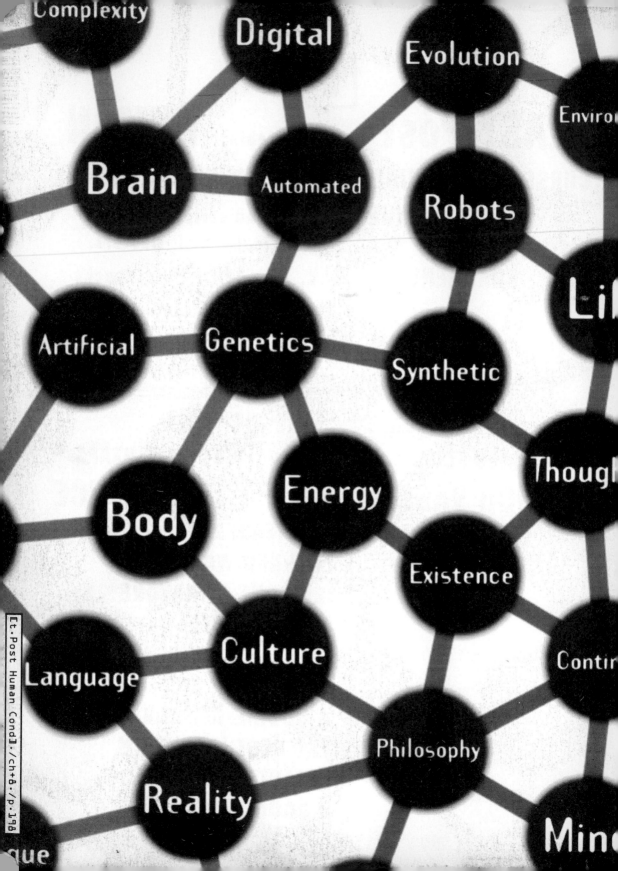

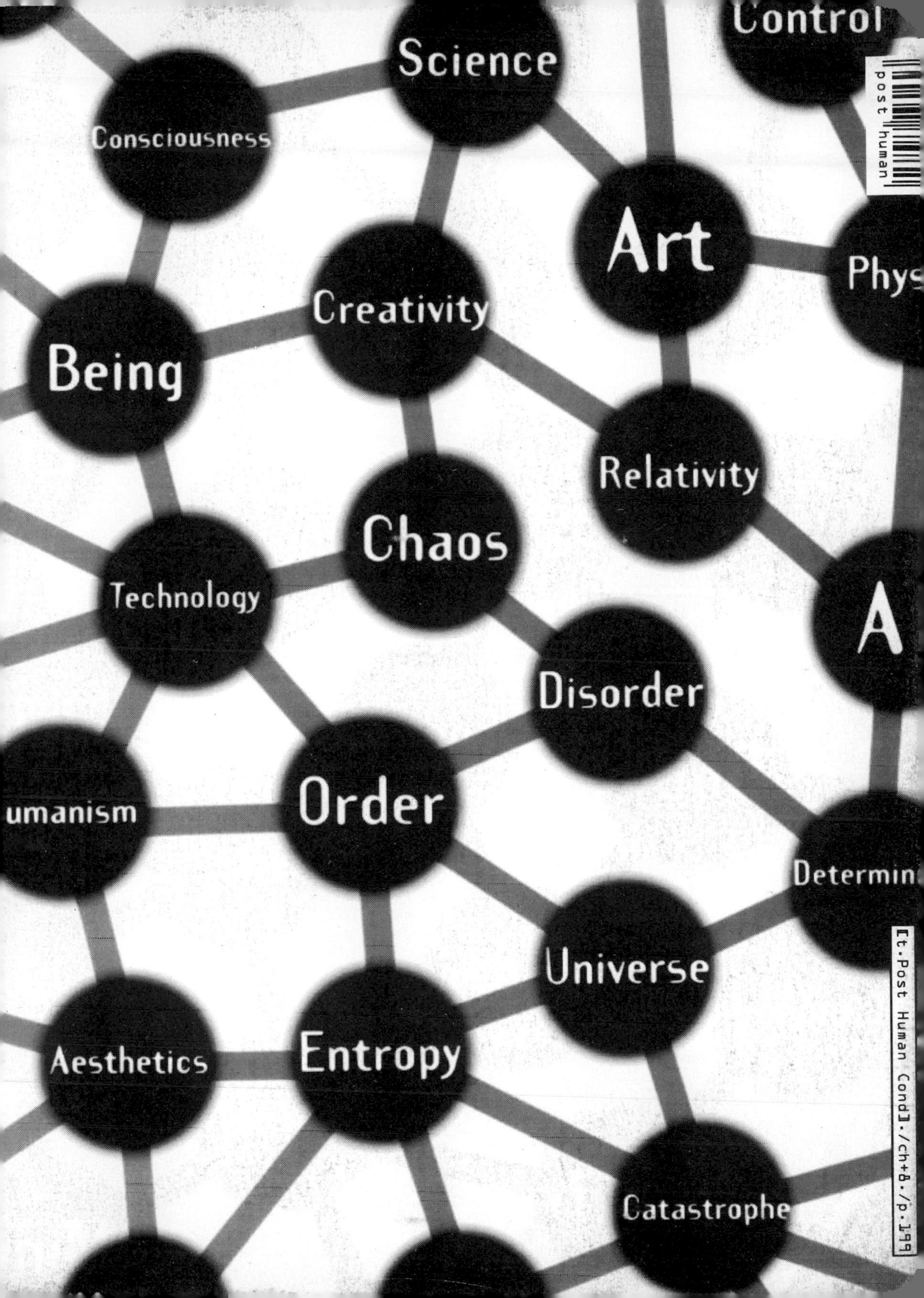
Control
Science
post human
Consciousness
Art
Phys
Creativity
Being
Relativity
Chaos
Technology
A
Disorder
umanism
Order
Determin
Universe
Aesthetics
Entropy
Catastrophe
[t.Post Human Cond]./ch+8./p.199

Bibliography and selected references

Introduction
Benjamin Woolley, *Virtual Worlds*, London: Penguin, 1993.
Harvey Rheingold, *Virtual Reality*, London: Secker, 1991.
K. Eric Drexler, *Engines of Creation*, Oxford: Oxford University Press, 1992.
Nanotechnology World Wide Web page,
'http://www.nas.nasa.gov/NAS/Education/nanotech/nanotech.html'
Richard Dawkins, *River Our of Eden*, London: Weidenfeld & Nicolson, 1995.
William Gibson, *Neuromancer*, London: Grafton, 1986.

Chapter 1
John D. Barrow and Frank J. Tipler, *The Anthropic Cosmological Principle*,
Oxford/New York: Oxford University Press, 1988.
John Searle, *Minds, Brains and Science*, London: Penguin, 1991.
Roland Barthes, *Mythologies*, Paris: Editions du Seuil, 1957.
Kevin Kelly, *Out of Control, The new biology of machines*, London: Fourth Estate,
1994.
Daniel Dennett, *Explaining Consciousness*, London: Penguin Books, 1991.
David Peat, *Einstein's Moon*, Chicago: Contemporary Books, 1990.
Roland Penrose, *The Emperor's New Mind*, London: Vintage, 1990 .
John Searle, *The Rediscovery of the Mind*, Cambridge: Massachusetts Institute of
Technology Press, 1992.
James Gleick, *Chaos, Making a new Science*, London: Heinemann, 1988.
Stephen Levy, *Artificial Life*, London: Cape, 1992.
Paul Davies and John Gribbin, *The Matter Myth*, London: Penguin, 1992.

Chapter 2
M. Mitchell Waldrop, *Complexity*, London: Viking, 1992.
Stephen Hawking, *A Brief History of Time*, London: Bantam Press, 1988.
John D. Barrow, *Theories of Everything*, London: Viking, 1988.
Steven Weinberg, *Dreams of a Final Theory*, London: Hutchinson, 1993.
Benoit B. Mandelbrot, *The Fractal Geometry of Nature*, New York: Freeman, 1983.
René Thom, *Structural Stability and Morphogenesis*, New York: Addison-Wesley,
1975.
David Bohm and F. David Peat, *Science, Order and Creativity*, London: Routledge,
1987.
William Broad and Nicholas Wade, *Betrayers of the Truth*, London: Century, 1983.
F. Cramer, *Chaos and Order, The Complex Structure of Living Systems*, Weinheim:
VCH, 1993.

Chapter 3

Ivar Ekeland, *Mathematics and the Unexpected*, Chicago: University of Chicago Press, 1988.
Ervin Laszlo, *The Creative Cosmos*, New York: Floris, 1993.
Mike Hales, *Science or Society?*, London: Free Association, 1982.
Heraclitus, *Fragments*, trans. Charles H. Kahn, Cambridge: Cambridge University Press, 1989.

Chapter 4

Anika Lemaire, *Jacques Lacan*, London: Routledge and Kegan Paul, 1977.
Ferdinand de Saussure, *Course in General Linguistics*, London: Duckworth, 1990.
Roland Barthes, *Elements of Semiology*, London: Cape, 1967.
Richard F. Thompson, *The Brain: A neurological primer*, New York: Freeman, 1993.
Lewis Carroll, *Jabberwocky, Alice Through the Looking Glass*,
Ludwig Wittgenstein, *Philosophical Investigations*, Oxford: Basil Blackwell, 1958.
Christopher Norris, *Derrida*, London: Fontana, 1987.
Erich Harth, *The Creative Loop*, London: Penguin, 1993.

Chapter 5

E. H. Gombrich, *The Sense of Order*, London: Phaidon, 1984.
André Breton, *What is Surrealism?* Collected writings, London: Pluto, 1978.
Denise Hooker, ed., *Art of the Western World*, London: Boxtree/Channel 4, 1989.

Chapter 6

Margaret Boden, *The Creative Mind*, London: Weidenfeld & Nicolson, 1990.
Marvin Minsky, *The Society of Mind*, Cambridge: Massachusetts Institute of Technology Press, 1994.
Douglas Hofstadter, *Gödel, Escher, Bach: An eternal golden braid*, London: Vintage, 1980.
Vladik Kreinovich and Ongard Sirisaengtaksin, *Analog Optical Computers Are Really Fast*, Texas: Department of Computer Science and Advanced Manufacturing Laboratory, Unversity of Texas, El Paso, 1995 (taken from the internet).
John Gribbin, *In Search of Schrödinger's Cat*, London: Black Swan, 1992.
Manuel de Landa, *War in the Age of the Intelligent Machine*, New York: Zone, 1991.

Chapter 7

Carol Karlsen, *The Devil in the Shape of a Woman*, New York, Norton, 1987.
Edward F. Fry, *Cubism*, Oxford: Oxford University Press, 1964.
E. H. Gombrich, *Art and Illusion*, London: Phaidon, 1960.
Max More, and information on *Extropians* and other Transhumans 'http://www.acm.usl.edu/~dca6381/c2_mirror/exi/extropy.html'
Newsgroup for *Extropians* 'alt.extropians'".

Further suggested reading

On science, quantum physics and scientific method:
David Bohm, *Wholeness and the Implicate Order*, London: Ark, 1983 (Bohm's compelling theory of an integrated reality).
Alexander Woodcock and Monte Davis, *Catastrophe Theory*, London: Penguin, 1980 (an accessible account of René Thom's work in morphogenesis).
J.C. Polkinghorne, *The Quantum World*, London: Penguin, 1986 (brief, but clear, account of the main concepts used in quantum physics).
Tony Hey and Patrick Walters, *The Quantum Universe*, Cambridge: Cambridge University Press, 1987 (well illustrated and documented history of the development of quantum physics).
Robert Anton Wilson, *Quantum Psychology*, Phoenix: Falcon Press, 1990 (persuasive argument against reductionist science and for a relativistic view of the universe).

On child development and psychoanalysis:
Margaret Donaldson, *Children's Minds*, London: Fontana, 1987 (clear, concise overview of current ideas in child development).
Jacques Lacan, *Écrits, A Selection*, London: Tavistock, 1980 (the standard collection of theoretical writings available in one abridged volume).

On art and science:
Leonard Shalin, *Art & Physics: parallel visions in space, time and light*, New York: Morrow, 1991 (comparisons of ideas in art and science including a discussion of the relationship between Cubism and relativity).

On deconstruction:
Jacques Derrida, *Writing and Difference*, London: Routledge and Kegan Paul, 1981 (a collection of essay regarded as having initiated the deconstructionist movement).

On evolution and computers:
Richard Dawkins, *The Selfish Gene*, Oxford University Press, 1989 and *The Blind Watchmaker*, London, Penguin, 1989.

On artificial intelligence:
Margaret Boden, *Artificial Intelligence and Natural Man*, Hassocks: Harvester Press, 1977 (for many the standard text on AI, an Open University set text, now quite dated but clear in setting out the main problems in this field).

On Post-Humanism:
Norbert Weiner, *The Human Use of Human Beings*, London: Free Association Press, 1989 (first published 1950, this is a classic text of cybernetics – the theory of man/machine integration).

Ed Regis, *Great Mambo Chicken and the Transhuman Condition*, London: Viking, 1991 (an interesting overview of developments in science and technology which suggest man and machine are co-evolving).

Bruce Mazlish, *The Fourth Discontinuity, the co-evolution of humans and machines*, New Haven: Yale University Press, 1993 (a book with similar aims to Great Mambo Chicken).

Michael Benedikt, ed., *Cyber Space, First Steps*, Cambridge: Massachusetts Institute of Technology Press, 1993 (collected essays discussing various theoretical aspects of virtual reality and digital communications).

Jeffrey Deitch, *Post Human*, Lausanne: FAE Musée d'Art Contemporain, 1992 (catalogue from the Post Human art exhibition).

Further World Wide Web resources and links

Complex (Adaptive) Systems Information
'http://www.seas.upenn.edu/~ale/cplxsys.html'

Welcome to the Principia Cybernetica Web
'http://pespmc1.vub.ac.be/'

HyperDOC: The Visible Human Project
'http://www.nlm.nih.gov/extramural_research.dir/visible_human.html'

Justin's Links from the Underground
'http://www.links.net/'

The Posthuman Body
'http://www.c2.org/~arkuat/post/Post.html'

Anders Main Page
'http://www.nada.kth.se/~nv91-asa/main.html'

The Post-Human Manifesto
'http://www.southern.com/PIPE/01phmfaq.html'

Further newsgroups of interest

alt.consciousness
alt.discordia
alt.postmodern
comp.ai
sci.philosophy.meta
sci.philosophy.tech
comp.ai.philosophy
rec.arts.sf.science

Index